Trauma, Gender and Ethics in the Works of E.L. Doctorow

This project approaches four of E.L. Doctorow's novels—*Welcome to Hard Times* (1960), *The Book of Daniel* (1971), *Ragtime* (1975) and *City of God* (2000)—from the perspectives of feminist criticism and trauma theory. The study springs from the assumption that Doctorow's literary project is eminently ethical and has an underlying social and political scope. This crops up through the novels' overriding concern with injustice and their engagement with the representation of human suffering in a variety of forms. The book puts forward the claim that E.L. Doctorow's literary project—through its representation of psychological trauma and its attitude toward gender—may be understood as a call to action against both each individual's indifference and the wider social and political structures and ideologies that justify and/or facilitate the injustices and oppression to which those who are situated at the margins of contemporary US society are subjected.

María Ferrández San Miguel is a lecturer at the Department of English and German Studies (University of Zaragoza). Her work has been published in journals such as *Atlantis, The Nordic Journal of English Studies* and *Orbis Litterarum*, and in volumes such as *Memory Frictions: Conflict, Negotiation, Politics* (Palgrave Macmillan).

Routledge Research in American Literature and Culture

Wallace and I
Cognition, Consciousness, and Dualism in David Foster Wallace's Fiction
Jamie Redgate

Articulations of Resistance
Transformative Practices in Arab-American Poetry
Sirène H. Harb

Poetic Encounters in the Americas
Remarkable Bridge
Peter Ramos

The Shape of Fantasy
Investigating the Structure of American Heroic Epic Fantasy
Charul Palmer-Patel

Transnational Politics in the Post-9/11 Novel
Joseph M. Conte

Spectres from the Past
Slavery and the Literary Imagination in West African and African-American Literature
Portia Owusu

Trauma, Gender and Ethics in the Works of E.L. Doctorow
María Ferrández San Miguel

Trauma, Gender and Ethics in the Works of E.L. Doctorow

María Ferrández San Miguel

NEW YORK AND LONDON

First published 2020
by Routledge
52 Vanderbilt Avenue, New York, NY 10017

and by Routledge
2 Park Square, Milton Park, Abingdon, Oxon, OX14 4RN

Routledge is an imprint of the Taylor & Francis Group, an informa business

© 2020 Taylor & Francis

The right of María Ferrández San Miguel to be identified as author of this work has been asserted by her in accordance with sections 77 and 78 of the Copyright, Designs and Patents Act 1988.

All rights reserved. No part of this book may be reprinted or reproduced or utilised in any form or by any electronic, mechanical, or other means, now known or hereafter invented, including photocopying and recording, or in any information storage or retrieval system, without permission in writing from the publishers.

Trademark notice: Product or corporate names may be trademarks or registered trademarks, and are used only for identification and explanation without intent to infringe.

Library of Congress Cataloging-in-Publication Data
Names: Ferrández San Miguel, María, author.
Title: Trauma, gender and ethics in the works of
E.L. Doctorow / María Ferrández San Miguel.
Description: New York, NY : Routledge, 2020. |
Series: Routledge research in american literature and culture | Includes bibliographical references and index. |
Summary: "This project approaches four of E. L. Doctorow's novels-Welcome to Hard Times (1960), The Book of Daniel (1971), Ragtime (1975), and City of God (2000) from the perspectives of feminist criticism and trauma theory"—Provided by publisher.
Identifiers: LCCN 2019058638 |
ISBN 9780367236274 (hardback) |
ISBN 9780429280870 (ebook)
Subjects: LCSH: Doctorow, E. L., 1931–2015—Criticism and interpretation. | Doctorow, E. L., 1931–2015—Ethics. | Doctorow, E. L., 1931–2015—Political and social views. | Psychic trauma in literature. | Sex role in literature. | Literature and morals. | Literature and society.
Classification: LCC PS3554.O3 Z64 2020 | DDC 813/.54—dc23
LC record available at https://lccn.loc.gov/2019058638

ISBN: 978-0-367-23627-4 (hbk)
ISBN: 978-0-429-28087-0 (ebk)

Typeset in Sabon
by codeMantra

Contents

	Acknowledgments	vii
	Introduction	1
1	*Welcome to Hard Times*: The Frontier Reconsidered	41
	Shame, Guilt, Violence and Trauma 42	
	In Search for a New Gender Order 54	
	Discussion and Conclusion 63	
2	*The Book of Daniel*: A Memoir Gone Awry	72
	The Trauma of a Grievous Past 73	
	Gender Oppression and/as Power 89	
	Discussion and Conclusion 97	
3	*Ragtime*: Remembering the Future	106
	Trauma and Resilience 107	
	The Politics of Gender 122	
	Discussion and Conclusion 130	
4	*City of God*: With Eyes Past All Grief	144
	Fictionalizing the Holocaust 145	
	Voicing Gender 162	
	Discussion and Conclusion 168	
5	Discussion: The Ethics and Politics of Literature	179
	Conclusion	198
	Index	201

Acknowledgments

I would like to express my sincere gratitude to the many people who in various ways have made the completion of this book possible. First and foremost, I am deeply indebted to Francisco Collado Rodríguez, who not only provided crucial critiques of the manuscript in its early stages that were essential to the final form of the book, but has also been a source of expert guidance and constant support over these years. Without his help and encouragement I could never have written this book. Also invaluable in this process has been Carmen Pérez-Llantada Auría, whose kindness and support have always been an inspiration. I furthermore extend my heartfelt gratitude to the members of the Contemporary Narratives in English Research Team at the University of Zaragoza for stimulating discussions on the topic, and in particular to Susana Onega Jaén, Mónica Calvo Pascual, Sonia Baelo Allué, Silvia Martínez-Falquina and Silvia Pellicer Ortín for their generous mentorship.

I am indebted as well to Gordon Henry, of Michigan State University, and Sonya Andermahr, of the University of Northampton, who kindly welcomed me in their institutions and offered generous feedback and engaging discussions in the early stages of this project. The anonymous readers for Taylor & Francis gave me insightful critiques and valuable suggestions, for which I am very grateful. I would like to thank the editorial staff at Taylor & Francis for their help and work on the different stages of the manuscript. Last but not least, thanks are due to the Spanish Ministry of Education for granting me a fellowship to begin the first version of this book, and to the Spanish Ministry of Science, Innovation and Technology and the Aragonese Government for financial support for research stays, permission costs and travel bursaries toward a number of conferences, for all of which I am truly grateful.

On a personal level, I want to express my heartfelt gratitude to my partner Ángel for his good humor, unconditional affection and continued encouragement through these years. I cannot even begin to thank you for never doubting that I can accomplish whatever I set out to do. Thanks also go to my parents, Inma and Manolo, who inspired in me an early passion for stories and taught me the value of hard work and resolve. Finally, I extend my gratitude and appreciation to Pablo, Nines,

Jose, Marina, Marco, Alfredo and Pili for their warm affection and generosity.

I also thank those who have given me permission to reprint excerpts from previously published material:

From *Welcome to Hard Times* by E.L. Doctorow. Copyright © 1960 by E.L. Doctorow. Used with permission of Random House, an imprint and division of Penguin Random House LLC, and of ICM Partners. All rights reserved.

From *The Book of Daniel* by E.L. Doctorow. Copyright © 1971 and renewed 1999 by E.L. Doctorow. Used with permission of Random House, an imprint and division of Penguin Random House LLC, and of ICM Partners. All rights reserved.

From *Ragtime* by E.L. Doctorow. Copyright © 1974, 1975 by E.L. Doctorow. Used with permission of Random House, an imprint and division of Penguin Random House LLC, and of ICM Partners. All rights reserved.

From *City of God: A Novel* by E.L. Doctorow. Copyright © 2000 by E.L. Doctorow. Used with permission of Random House, an imprint and division of Penguin Random House LLC, and of ICM Partners. All rights reserved.

Portions of the following chapters appeared in slightly different form in previously published essays and are printed here with permission. An earlier and shorter version of Chapter 3 originally appeared in *Orbis Litterarum* 73.2 (2018): 146–169, under the title "Towards a Theoretical Approach to the Literature of Resilience." An earlier and shorter version of Chapter 4 originally appeared in my chapter "'No Redress but Memory': Holocaust Representation and Memorialization in E.L. Doctorow's *City of God*," in *Memory Frictions in Contemporary Literature*, edited by María Jesús Martínez-Alfaro and Silvia Pellicer-Ortín (Palgrave Macmillan, 2017).

Introduction

Beginnings are usually hard, and when E.L. Doctorow began his career as a writer, back in the 1960s, not many critics could foresee that he would become one of the most relevant and widely acclaimed contemporary novelists of the United States. In fact, his first two novels tended to be praised by reviewers but were generally disregarded by academic critics (Williams 60). Things started to change with the astonishing critical and commercial success of *Ragtime* (1975), Doctorow's fourth novel. Its popularity and the subsequent interest that it elicited among critics and scholars led to a reexamination of his previous novels. From then on, Doctorow's fame as a writer only continued to grow. He is widely celebrated for the versatility, audacity and originality of his fiction, whose subversive power and stirring passion leave no one indifferent. An incorrigible fabulator, he loved playing games with his readers. His works are located in the unstable position of stories that frequently question their own truth while still affirming their possibility to teach readers valid ethical lessons for the times we live in. Indeed, if anything can be said of Doctorow is that he was, above all, a firm believer in the power of literature to influence culture and improve society.

A true fictionist from an early age, in a certain sense Doctorow started his literary career as a child: in a public seminar with Joseph Papaleo—chairman of the Department of English at Sarah Lawrence College—Doctorow explained that, as a junior at the Bronx High School of Science, he took a course on journalism where the students were given an assignment to do an interview. He submitted an interview with Carl, the stage doorman at Carnergie Hall, a lovable old man who had a broad knowledge of musical literature, wore worn-down shoes and was a refugee from the Nazi genocide with a strong accent whom all the artists knew and loved. The teacher was deeply touched and greatly impressed by young Edgar's work, and suggested taking a picture of the kind doorman and publishing the interview in the school newspaper. Running out of excuses why the doorman could not be photographed, Doctorow finally admitted that he had made the whole thing up, which earned him a trip to the principal's office and an early understanding of the power of fiction to touch people's lives and souls (Nieman Reports 16, Navasky 60).

2   *Introduction*

By the time of his death, fifty-five years after starting his career as a professional writer, he had published twelve novels, three short story collections, a play and four volumes of essays, leaving behind a literary legacy that has earned him a reputation as one of the most important American literary figures of the past half century. As the *Washington Post*'s literary critic David Segal put it, "Doctorow [...] occupies one of the narrowest subsets in American letters: the million-selling author who is taken seriously" (n.p.). He has been called the "epic poet of America's past" (S. Kaplan n.p.), and praised as "a visionary who seeks in time past occasions for poetry" (Updike 295), as a "[l]iterary time traveler [who] stirred past into fiction" and as "one of contemporary fiction's most restless experimenters" (Weber n.p.). Upon his death, President Barack Obama paid tribute to him as "one of America's greatest novelists" (bbc.com n.p.).

E.L. Doctorow: Life, Works and Criticism

Edgar Lawrence Doctorow was born on January 6, 1931 in the Bronx, the son of Rose and David Doctorow, second-generation Americans of Jewish-Russian origin. His father owned a music store in Manhattan and his mother was a pianist. He attended Kenyon College, where he majored in Philosophy and graduated with honors in 1952. Then, he completed a postgraduate course on English Drama at Columbia University, where he met his future wife, Helen Setzer. He served for two years with the US Army in Germany and, in 1954, married Helen. They had three children: Richard, Caroline and Jenny. After being discharged from the army, Doctorow found work as a reservations clerk at La Guardia Airport and subsequently as a script reader for CBS Television and Columbia Pictures in New York.

Doctorow began his literary career in 1960 with *Welcome to Hard Times*, a post-Western, while working as senior editor with the New American Library. This first novel was a response to the poor-quality scripts that he had reviewed as script reader for CBS Television and Columbia Pictures. He moved onto Dial Press in 1964, where he became editor-in-chief. In 1966 he published *Big as Life*, a science fiction novel that never satisfied readers, publisher or the author himself, who did not allow it to be reissued. While working on his third novel—*The Book of Daniel* (1971), a historical fiction inspired by the Rosenberg case— Doctorow was offered a post as writer in residence at the University of California, Irvine. This was the first of a number of teaching appointments that he achieved throughout his life, including positions at Sarah Lawrence College, Utah, Princeton and New York University, where he held the Loretta and Lewis Glucksman chair of English and American Letters until his death. *The Book of Daniel* granted Doctorow a reputation as a respected novelist. Yet, critical and commercial success did not come together until 1975 with the publication of *Ragtime*, a historical fiction set in New York during the Ragtime Era. In the following years, he wrote an experimental play—*Drinks before Dinner* (1979)—and began to articulate his innovative views on narrative in a number of essays, among them his most influential "False Documents" (1977). Four new works were published in the 1980s: the dazzling and eerie postmodern novel *Loon Lake* (1980), Doctorow's first short story collection *Lives of the Poets* (1984), *World's Fair* (1985)—considered by critics his most autobiographical text—and *Billy Bathgate* (1989), an unconventional gangster story that was runner-up for the 1990 Pulitzer Prize. *The Waterworks*, a Gothic-like detective story, followed in 1994. During the last fifteen years of his life, the writer published some of his most ambitious works. His end of the millennium novel, *City of God* (2000), has baffled critics with its sophisticated philosophical and spiritual concerns. His second collection, *Sweet Land Stories* (2004), together with *The March* (2005)—a historical fiction set in the last years of the American Civil War—and *Homer and Langley* (2009)—a rewriting of the life of the eccentric Collyer brothers—would follow, confirming Doctorow's position as one of America's most appreciated and widely read contemporary writers. The title of his last collection of short stories, *All the Time in the World* (2011), seemed to foresee a long list of books to come, but it would only be followed by *Andrew's Brain* (2014). Doctorow's last novel, considered by some to be the odd one out, continues to puzzle readers with its unconventional narration, which offers the possibility to peek inside the mind of a cognitive scientist.

Written over the course of five decades, Doctorow's fiction has garnered numerous prices and honors, such as three National Book Critics Awards (for *Ragtime*, *Billy Bathgate* and *The March*), the National Book Award (for *World's Fair*), two Pen/Faulkner Awards (for *Billy Bathgate* and *The March*), the National Humanities Medal, the PEN/Saul Bellow Award for Achievement in American Fiction, the Medal for Distinguished Contribution to American Letters, the American Academy of Arts and Letters Gold Medal for Fiction and the Library of Congress Prize for American Fiction, among others. His work has been translated into more than thirty languages. It has also been adapted into five films and a Broadway musical. Doctorow's readiness to experiment with different narrative genres and the intense social and historical concerns of his fiction draw the portrait of a very distinctive author from other writers of his period. He passed away on July 21, 2015, at the age of eighty-four, following complications from lung cancer.

E.L. Doctorow's *oeuvre* has been object of steady academic interest since the early 1980s. Several book-length critical analyses dealing with Doctorow's work have been published over the last two decades. First, we have a number of volumes which compile the most provocative scholarly articles written on Doctorow's fiction at the time of their publication

4 *Introduction*

(Trenner 1983, Friedl and Schulz 1988, Morris 1999, Siegel 2000, Bloom 2002). Second, several introductory books have been written which provide comprehensive academic introductions to Doctorow's oeuvre (Levine 1985, Harter and Thompson 1990, Parks 1991, Fowler 1992). These works follow a survey approach and offer summaries and critical readings of Doctorow's novels and short stories which consolidate and extend issues already explored in scholarly essay format. Finally, there are a number of monographs which have approached Doctorow's work from a specific framework of analysis (Morris 1991, Tokarczyk 2000, Walker Bergström 2010). To these book-length analyses, a number of academic articles published in international journals must be added, which have provided focused readings of Doctorow's fiction. Some of the issues that have recurrently captured the critics' attention have been Doctorow's conception and deployment of history, his political vision, his relationship with Jewish culture and his distinctly postmodern narrative style. His fiction has been approached from perspectives as varied as historiography, sociology, postmodernism, psychoanalysis, Marxist criticism and deconstruction, among others. Taken together, this body of criticism not only confirms Doctorow's firm position within the US literary canon; it also provides a solid foundation on which to build the present study.

Corpus of Analysis

Of Doctorow's extensive *oeuvre*, this project focuses on four of his novels: *Welcome to Hard Times* (1960), *The Book of Daniel* (1971), *Ragtime* (1975) and *City of God* (2000). The reasons for selecting these are varied and wide-ranging. While very dissimilar in narrative style, setting and plot, these books share a number of common key features. First, they deal with central episodes of the history of the United States—namely the colonization of the West, the social unrest of the Ragtime Era, the political crisis of post-war North America and the spiritual and ideological drift of the turn of the millennium. As such, the four novels map the progression of history from the years of the forging of the nation to the end of the twentieth century, while simultaneously undermining the humanist notion of endless historical progress and mocking our natural inclination toward nostalgia. Second, as we shall see shortly, the four novels are inspired by the postmodernist spirit of subversion and skepticism as well as owing much to postmodernist aesthetics, on account of their experimentalism, metafictional concerns, intertextuality and complex attitude toward history, reality and fiction, among other features. However, the novels simultaneously share a strong commitment to some sort of realism and stage a return to the position of the subject and its relation to the Other, thus avoiding the ultimate epistemological skepticism and pervasive relativism usually associated with the postmodern ethos.

Last but not least, the four novels collectively paint a vivid picture of the ills of North-American society, and they explore similar human dilemmas and experiences. Apart from their engagement with common concerns, their postmodernist allegiances and historical themes, the books have been selected on account of their versatility and openness to a wide variety of readings. As we shall see, *Welcome to Hard Times*, *The Book of Daniel*, *Ragtime* and *City of God* are among the most highly crafted and provocative novels that the US author produced, generating as they have lively debates and encouraging a myriad of literary interpretations. Finally, their interest also lies in the fact that they offer a deep insight into Doctorow's literary project, mapping the author's narratological and ideological evolution throughout his literary career.

Initial Hypothesis, Aims and Structure

This study springs from the assumption that Doctorow's literary project is eminently ethical. In other words, the initial hypothesis that lies behind this book is that *Welcome to Hard Times*, *The Book of Daniel*, *Ragtime* and *City of God* have an underlying social scope. This crops up through their overriding concern with injustice and their engagement with the representation of human suffering in a variety of shapes. In order to test such thesis, this study will concentrate on the novels' representation of psychological trauma on the one hand, and on their attitude toward gender on the other. With the help of narratology and close reading—which are the main methods of enquiry—my goal is to determine the specificities of the novels' commitment to these concerns, for which I will resort to the analytical tools provided by two key critical frameworks: trauma studies and feminist criticism. Ultimately, the aim will be to provide a new and better understanding of the ethical impulse in Doctorow's novels. With this purpose in mind, the collusion of the novels' ethical and postmodernist allegiances will also be explored. This pursuit will additionally seek to reveal Doctorow's attitude toward the social meanings of literature and its potential to promote ethical and empathic responses to the suffering of others on the part of the readers.

This book is divided into six chapters. Chapter 1 focuses on E.L. Doctorow's debut novel, *Welcome to Hard Times*, a historical fiction set in the Dakota Territory in the 1870s, following the discovery of gold. The chapter draws on some key Freudian concepts and notions from classical trauma theory as well as on recent theories about shame and guilt and their connection to trauma and violence to analyze the psychological condition of the main protagonists. The chapter also explores the limits between the trauma categories of victim, perpetrator and bystander. Another central focus of enquiry is the novel's representation of masculinity and femininity and its attitude toward power relations, oppression and gender dialogue. *Welcome to Hard Times*, I will argue, establishes a

6 *Introduction*

tight connection between the aftereffects of trauma and the subversion of hegemonic gender configurations, and provides critical commentary on some of the ills of postwar North America: its fierce individualism, its hegemonic gender configurations and its lack of empathy, emphasizing their impact not only on the individual but also on the community.

Chapter 2 concentrates on *The Book of Daniel*, a fictional rendering of the conviction and execution of a communist couple—inspired in the Rosenbergs—from the viewpoint of their surviving son. This chapter investigates the novel's thematic and formal exploration of the psychological aftereffects of childhood trauma, drawing on some key notions from classical and second-wave trauma theory. I also set out to examine the representation of traumatic memory and the novel's attitude toward the power of narrative as a healing mechanism. From the perspective of feminist criticism, this chapter analyzes the novel's articulation of female otherness and gender violence, as well as its degree of openness to the perspectives of women. A related focus of enquiry in this chapter is the book's undermining of the traditional character-logic and its encouragement of alternative forms of reader identification. The novel, it will be claimed, seeks to warn of the disastrous consequences of psychological trauma for the individual, who might eventually end up becoming a perpetrator. It further exposes a number of social, economic and political structures as mechanisms of oppression that have a strong traumatizing potential, and advocates readers' duty to bear witness to the suffering of the Other.

Chapter 3 analyzes *Ragtime*, a historical fiction set in New York which tells the story of the encounter of three families—one WASP, one Jewish immigrant and one African-American—who interact with a number of historical figures and participate in some of the most transcendental events in North-American history at the turn of the twentieth century. This chapter examines the novel's thematic and formal representation of psychological trauma and the psychosocial phenomenon of resilience, assessing the potential of traumatic experiences to act as a transformative force. It further draws on Freud's theorization of sublimation, Maria Root's notion of "insidious trauma" and some key postcolonial theorists' criticism of what they perceive as serious shortcomings of classical trauma theory. Another focus of enquiry is the novel's representation of gender identity and dialogue, and its emphasis on the intersecting nature of oppression. This chapter also explores the novel's explicit adherence to a number of second-wave feminist concerns. My claim is that *Ragtime*'s engagement with the traumatizing potential of racism, gender discrimination and injustice plays a crucial role in Doctorow's denunciation of how certain legal, social and economic structures may generate and perpetuate the victimization of the underprivileged and disenfranchised, while emphasizing resistance and drawing attention to the collective nature of oppression.

Chapter 4 focuses on *City of God*, a *sui generis* collection of skillfully interwoven plots and voices that create a kaleidoscopic universe of alternative ontological levels. Drawing on key theories for the analysis of Holocaust fiction, the main focus of this chapter is the novel's treatment and attitude toward the Holocaust with regard to issues of memory and representation. My analysis is further supported by Peter Novick's exploration of the "Americanization" of the Holocaust and Marianne Hirsch's notion of "postmemory," as well as by current notions about Jewishness and Jewish identity. The novel, I contend, approaches the Holocaust through a self-conscious discussion of the problems and limits of its representation, while emphasizing the problematics of ranking atrocities and denouncing human barbarity and capacity for evil. The chapter also explores the novel's representation of gender models and roles, and its attitude toward voice. It is argued that *City of God* carries out a quest for a form of spirituality that is appropriate for the twenty-first century and constitutes an outcry against injustice and a call to memory and ethics.

These chapters are followed by two closing ones. Chapter 5 discusses the wider implications of Doctorow's literary project on the basis of the results obtained in the analytical chapters. It first explores the collusion of the novels' ethical and postmodernist allegiances, for which Magali Cornier-Michael's concept of "impulse" will be taken up. Returning to the initial hypothesis from which this project sprang, Chapter 5 also considers whether literature is a suitable vehicle for ethics and whether it may have a political dimension. A discussion of readers' possible reactions to the novels' ethical and political invitations will follow, for which I will rely on a number of theories about reader response. Another focus of enquiry is the notion of narrative empathy. Finally, Emmanuel Levinas's theory of the infinite responsibility toward the inaccessible and radically different Other, and Jill Bennett's call for a conjunction of affect and critical awareness will be taken up to discuss the novels' potential to encourage critical awareness and intellectual distance while also inspiring powerful emotional and ethical responses. Chapter 5 is followed by a Conclusion chapter which outlines this study's main results.

Theoretical Framework

Trauma studies have acquired great relevance for cultural and literary studies in recent times, achieving the status of a solid theoretical framework for the analysis of literary texts. For obvious reasons, providing a fully detailed genealogy of trauma is well beyond the purposes and scope of this project, and has, furthermore, been more than adequately accomplished by other scholars.[1] Nevertheless, a few introductory comments might be in order here. In its broadest definition, trauma originates from a physical and/or psychological wound that leaves long-term mental scars on the survivor. It is an individual response to dramatic events whose intensity affects normal emotional or cognitive functioning and may result in temporary or long-lasting psychological disruption. Although at first trauma was mainly associated with physical and, then, psychological injuries and was, therefore, the exclusive concern of medical professionals and researchers, it has now become a critical paradigm that has deeply affected contemporary sociology, anthropology, history, literature, culture and critical theory.

Issues of trauma started to receive prominent critical attention in the 1990s, after the American Psychiatric Association officially acknowledged the phenomenon of psychological trauma and defined the effects of a new illness that would come to be known as Post-Traumatic Stress Disorder.[2] PTSD, first included in the third edition of the *Diagnostic and Statistical Manual of Mental Disorders*, encompassed the symptoms of what had previously been called "shell shock," combat stress, delayed stress syndrome and traumatic neurosis, and referred to delayed responses to an overwhelming, life-threatening event outside the range of human experience (American Psychiatric Association, DSM-III 236). This definition, however, soon began to be challenged by a number of medical professionals (see Herman 1992, Brown 1995), who argued that events such as rape, incest or child molestation are regrettably too frequent experiences so as to be considered outside the range of normal human experience, and yet have the uncontestable potential to be equally traumatizing. Psychologist Laura S. Brown warned against a narrow definition of trauma that is constructed within the experiences and realities of the dominant group, advocating that "*real* trauma is often only that form of trauma in which the dominant group can participate as a victim rather than as the perpetrator or etiologist of the trauma" (102; emphasis added). Thus, the realization that the first definition of PTSD was somewhat narrow led a number of voices to call for an understanding of the traumatic event as owing its traumatic quality not to its nature, but to the person's reaction to it. Consequently, the fourth edition to the *Diagnostic and Statistical Manual of Mental Disorders* (American Psychiatric Association, DSM-IV-TR 463–468) was modified to rely more on the person's subjective perceptions of fear, threat or helplessness, and on the effects of witnessing as much as suffering the traumatic event.

From the grounds of critical theory, scholars such as Cathy Caruth, Shoshana Felman and Geoffrey Hartman—prominent Yale literary scholars who were influenced by Derrida's philosophy of deconstruction—inaugurated the field of trauma theory by producing and editing groundbreaking studies of the effects of trauma on war survivors and victims of the Holocaust, natural catastrophes, rape and childhood traumatic experiences. Trauma theory emerged in the United States at a time when, as Roger Luckhurst explains, "various lines of inquiry converged to make trauma a privileged critical category" ("Mixing Memory" 497).

What he is referring to is the connection that scholars such as Caruth, Felman and Hartman perceived and famously drew between emerging medical notions of psychological trauma and deconstructionist discourse about reference and representation, and about the limits of language and knowledge. As Luckhurst further points out, Hartman and Felman "turned from work on the undecidability of interpretation in literature to publish work on Holocaust memory and witness [...]" while "Cathy Caruth signaled that trauma as the limit of knowledge was a continuation of the Yale project" ("Mixing Memory" 497).

Cathy Caruth's 1996 book, entitled *Unclaimed Experience*, is perhaps still today the most influential book of trauma studies, since it develops the key tenets of trauma theory as it emerged in the 1990s. It was preceded by the edited volume *Trauma: Explorations in Memory*, which began to articulate Caruth's theory of trauma and included essays by leading psychiatrists, psychologists and sociologists. Taken together, the two books set the basis for what is now considered "classical trauma theory" (Rothberg xiii).[3] Built upon the scientific theories of prominent psychologists and psychiatrists such as Judith Herman and Bessel van der Kolk,[4] and indebted to the enduring legacy of Freudian theories about the workings of the human mind,[5] Caruth articulated a view of trauma as amnesic, unspeakable, unrepresentable, and of belated effects. For Caruth, the traumatic experience is overwhelming in that it shatters the brain's normal processing mechanisms. Trauma is, in her theorization, "an event whose force is marked by its lack of registration" (*Explorations* 6), not "fully owned" because it is "not assimilated or experienced fully at the time, but only belatedly, in a repeated *possession* of the one who experiences it" (*Explorations* 4–5; emphasis in the original). Indeed, in Caruth's view, to be traumatized is to be "possessed by an image or event" (*Explorations* 5). This latent trauma,[6] which is temporarily absent from the survivor's mind, eventually returns and is reenacted through flashbacks, dreams or other symptoms. Thus, the images of trauma, although accurate and precise, are largely inaccessible to conscious control (*Explorations* 151). In addition, due to the failure of the mechanisms of memory and consciousness to naturally process the traumatic experience and also owing to its aporetic nature (in the Derridean sense of the term), it becomes unspeakable, unrepresentable (*Explorations* 152).

The failure of representation that, in this classical model, characterizes trauma was famously furthered in another foundational book of trauma theory: Shoshana Felman and Dori Laub's *Testimony: Crises of Witnessing in Literature, Psychoanalysis, and History* (1991). Like Caruth's, Felman's first contribution to the emerging field (with psychoanalyst Dori Laub) was also characterized by a combination of psychoanalytic and deconstructionist notions to explore the aporetic nature of some texts, of texts produced after the historical trauma of the Holocaust in particular. In their book, Felman and Laub speak of "the *radical historical crisis in witnessing* the Holocaust has opened up" (201; emphasis in the original). In other words, they identify the Holocaust as a turning point in human history because it radically exceeds our capacity to come to terms with it, to understand it in its stark horror and disquieting unspeakability.

Geoffrey Hartman, the other leading trauma theorist within this "first wave" of criticism (Pederson 334), also started his critical career as a deconstructionist. He wrote extensively on the difficulties and limitations, but the simultaneous importance, of representing the Holocaust in literature and other cultural texts, most famously in his book *The Longest Shadow: In the Aftermath of the Holocaust* (1996). This collection of Hartman's own scholarly and personal essays deals with the cultural aftermath of the Holocaust, epitomizing its alienating power and the irresolvable tension that resulted from it, between the need to speak and the imperative to remain silent, between the inadequacy of language and the unbearability of giving it up. In *The Longest Shadow*, Hartman also famously claims that "[t]he role of art remains mysterious [...], for art is testimony" (52), thus inaugurating a more or less optimistic discourse regarding the role of art in representing the unfathomable horror of the Holocaust and its implications. Hartman's work has also been largely responsible for the centrality of the Holocaust within trauma theory. Proof of that lies in the widespread insistence among trauma and Holocaust scholars on the inexplicability and unrepresentability of the Holocaust, features that have come to define all experiences of trauma as understood by classical theory.

Another central theorist in the establishment of the basic tenets of classical cultural trauma theory is the historian Dominick LaCapra. He has, like the scholars mentioned above, successfully applied psychological notions and psychoanalytical concepts to the study of Holocaust memory, while retaining a certain belief in language, reference and the possibility of representation. As Michael Roth aptly explains, "LaCapra has been adept at recognizing both the challenge of the concept of the traumatic for historical representation and the temptation of the concept for those eager to escape the constraints of some connection to the real" (xxiii). Indeed, perhaps his most useful contribution has been the drawing of a differentiation that the aforementioned critics might have failed to establish between what he terms "structural trauma" and "historical trauma."[7] In his influential essay "Trauma, Absence, Loss" (1999), LaCapra defines structural trauma as related to "transhistorical absence (absence of/at the origin) [which] appears in different ways in all societies and all lives" (721–722). Historical trauma, on the contrary, is construed as "specific [since] not everyone is subject to it or entitled to the subject-position associated with it" (723). In *Writing History, Writing Trauma* (2001), LaCapra further warns of two opposed errors:

To generalize structural trauma so that it absorbs or subordinates the significance of historical trauma, thereby rendering all references to the latter merely illustrative, homogeneous, allusive, and perhaps equivocal, or, on the contrary, to explain all post-traumatic, extreme, uncanny phenomena and responses as exclusively caused by particular events or contexts. (82)

He usefully elaborates on the distinction: "Everyone is subject to structural trauma. But, with respect to historical trauma and its representation, the distinction among victims, perpetrators, and bystanders is crucial" ("Trauma" 723). Indeed, LaCapra may be credited with inaugurating discussion on the different subject positions or categories associated with (historical) trauma and their specificities. He also famously introduced the possibility of the existence of a gray zone (*Writing History* 79)—borrowing Primo Levi's notion—and warns about the risk of over-identification with, and wrongful appropriation of, the status of victim through vicarious victimization ("Trauma" 725). Finally, classical trauma theory owes LaCapra the introduction into its interpretative texture of the notions of "acting-out" and "working-through," which he borrows from Freud in order to refer to "interrelated modes of responding to trauma" ("Trauma" 713): in post-traumatic acting out, "one is haunted or possessed by the past and performatively caught up in the compulsive repetition of traumatic scenes" (*Writing History* 21), whereas working through

> is an articulatory practice: to the extent one works through trauma [...], one is able to distinguish between past and present and to recall in memory that something happened to one (or one's people) back then while realizing that one is living here and now with openings to the future. (*Writing History* 22)

As this quotation reveals, despite LaCapra's undoubtedly outstanding contribution to the field of trauma theory and his early attempts to correct the problems that he already perceived in the work of Caruth and other 'deconstructive' trauma theorists, his own theory manifests certain shortcomings that later critics soon began to point out, namely the emphasis on trauma's exclusive nature as amnesic.

In more recent times, the field has continued evolving thanks to the impulse provided by some of the dissenting voices that have been raised in recent years and that are critical of what is perceived as the first wave of trauma theory's limited focus and scope. Some have called out the depoliticization implicit in trauma studies' excessive tendency to pathologize and psychologize socio-historical phenomena and their representation (Traverso and Broderick 9); others have attacked the classical model's lack of self-reflexivity and its elevation of the concept of trauma into the status of a new master narrative (Kansteiner and Weinböck 229); others resent the exclusively Western focus of the model in terms of both focus and critical methodologies, and warn of the risks of a simplistic transposition of the model to postcolonial and other non-Western contexts (Buelens and Craps 2; Craps, *Postcolonial Witnessing* 12; Radstone 24); many of these critics are also suspicious of classical trauma theory's exclusive focus on events (rather than systems) (Root 240; Craps "Beyond Eurocentrism" 49; Erikson 185). Other critics have questioned the emphasis on victims' widespread pyscho-physical incapability to remember the traumatic events and talk about them (Pederson 336); Others point to the role played by other determining circumstances, such as the affects of shame and guilt to explain survivors' reluctance to talk about their trauma (Escudero 224; Roth xxii); others have called for the need to "de-provincializ[e] trauma" (i.e. by combining trauma studies with other fields and methodologies of inquiry) (Rothberg, xiv); while others have argued against its ubiquitous emphasis on the negative (i.e. pathological) consequences of trauma (Rousseau and Measham 278; Root 248) and its overshadowing of the psychobiological phenomenon of resilience (Konner 300). The work of these critics—and of many others who cannot be duly addressed due to space limitations—has contributed to shifting the emphasis away from the individual (usually Western) mind and its problems to work through trauma toward an interest in the problematic nature of extreme human suffering and its social and political implications. As Buelens et al. note (via Luckhurst, *Trauma Question* 14–15) in the Introduction to their volume *The Future of Trauma Theory* (2014), today "issues of trauma theory are characterized by a 'knot' tying together representation, the past, the self, the political and suffering" (4).

The development of trauma theory has taken place hand in hand with the rise of memory studies, a field that has also increased its size and influence exponentially in the last few years. Reflecting a broader cultural interest in memory as a phenomenon that is at once neurological, psychological, cultural and socio-political, the academic study of memory has engaged scholars from diverse disciplines who attempt to understand a subject that, as Antonio Traverso and Mick Broderick explain, seems to escape traditional disciplinary boundaries (5). Memory scholars share a common central focus on the multiple ways in which memory comes to be known and represented and, more broadly, on how the personal, social and cultural realms come to be constituted and articulated through memory.

As a result of such combined efforts, trauma studies have acquired paradigmatic relevance for theory and criticism, reaching the status of a solid theoretical framework for the study of literature. A number of literary scholars have applied the main tenets of trauma theory to the analysis of creative literature, producing groundbreaking studies of the so-called "trauma novel" (Granofsky 5). It is worth adding that most key theorists of trauma share a belief in the privileged role of literature where it comes to giving voice to trauma.[8] Perhaps owing to the tight relationship that is perceived to exist between the language of trauma and the language of literature, the last few decades have seen an outstanding proliferation of novels (and other cultural products) dealing with trauma and traumatic memories. The first to notice was Ronald Granofsky, who coined the term "trauma novel" in his book *The Trauma Novel: Contemporary Symbolic Depictions of Collective Disaster* (1995) to refer to "a distinct sub-genre of contemporary fiction" (5) that had begun to emerge in the Western world after the Second Wold War. He identifies as these novels' basic origin "the shock at the destructive potential in human depravity given free rein by modern technology" (11). He further claims that they "explor[e] through the agency of literary symbolism [...] the individual experience of collective trauma, either actual events of the past, alarming tendencies of the present, or imagined horrors of the future" (5). In his study, Granofsky explains that psychological trauma in the trauma novel may be defined as "*a painful experience which defies assimilation and demands accommodation*" (8–9; emphasis in the original). He, then, lists and explores a number of features that symbolically represent collective disaster in trauma novels, such as the abandonment of traditional categories of understanding (time, space, causality and number), a symbolic rendering of the four elements and a portrayal of the quest for identity, which is often depicted through the structure of trauma response (fragmentation, regression and reunification) (16–19). Finally, he may be credited with reminding literary critics that "we are dealing here [...] with the fictional depiction of imagined trauma" (7).

Another seminal contribution to the theorization of how contemporary literature deals with trauma is Laurie Vickroy's *Trauma and Survival in Contemporary Fiction* (2002). Vickroy's main contention is that contemporary trauma narratives are individual responses to Western culture's emerging awareness of the catastrophic effects on the individual psyche of traumatic events such as wars, poverty, colonization and domestic abuse. According to her, "trauma narratives go beyond presenting trauma as subject matter or character study. They internalize the rhythms, processes, and uncertainties of traumatic experience within their underlying sensibilities and structures," which in her view is best achieved through experimental narrative (3). In order to prove that, she surveys the main features of trauma as described by Caruth, Felman and Laub, and Hartman and ascribes them to specific stylistic experimental techniques, such as voice shifts, repetition, aporias (textual gaps) and breaks in linear time. Interestingly, the book also discusses the effect of these stylistic devices on the reader, who becomes "witness to these kinds of stories through the unconventional narrative translations of traumatic experience and memory that give them a different kind of access to the past than conventional frameworks" (20).

A similar spirit of uncovering the main features of contemporary trauma fiction—although perhaps performed in a somewhat less prescriptive and more cautious manner—guides Anne Whitehead's influential book *Trauma Fiction* (2004). In it, Whitehead explores the ways in which some key contemporary novelists incorporate the theme of trauma. She further examines the effects of trauma on narrative, identifying some of the main stylistic features associated with it, namely "intertextuality, repetition and a dispersed or fragmented narrative voice" (84). One of the book's key notions is precisely that "the impact of trauma can only be adequately represented by mimicking its forms and symptoms, so that temporality and chronology collapse, and narratives are characterized by repetition and indirection" (3). Such an aesthetic model for trauma fiction as Whitehead maps in effect constitutes an act of translating into narratological features the main tenets of the classical trauma paradigm.

These critics coincide in their attempt to think through the relation between literature and trauma by means of a combination of analyses of individual texts and wider generic considerations. Together, they map the development of a model of trauma fiction that favors a fragmented, aporetic, modernist aesthetics. The enduring influence of these critics owes to the fact that they paved the way that numerous trauma scholars have covered in more recent years. Some have focused on the figure of the (traumatized) author, seeking to explore the effects of his/her condition on the narrative. Others have thought it better to avoid leaning too much on biographical details and have instead tracked narrative features and themes that can be ascribed to trauma in the plot, characters and formal elements, discussing as well the widespread influence of notions of trauma on contemporary authors. As Roger Luckhurst notes, trauma "has been turned into a repertoire of compelling stories about the enigmas of identity, memory and selfhood that have saturated Western cultural life" (*Trauma Question* 80).

Drawing on these theories and analytical notions, the following chapters will explore Doctorow's reliance on thematic and formal tools for the representation of trauma in his fiction. A central focus of enquiry will be the books' attitude toward the trauma categories of victim, perpetrator and bystander. The concept of insidious trauma also proves essential for an analysis of the novels' denunciation of pervasive victimization resulting from some of the characters' condition as members of gender, racial and class minorities, relying also on notions of the intersectional nature of oppression. The representation of the affects of shame and guilt and their close connection to violence and trauma will also be considered. In a more positive note, the novels' attitude toward healing and the human capacity for resilience in the face of traumatic victimization are addressed as well. Finally, Doctorow's position toward Holocaust representation and memorialization will be analyzed.

Moving on to our second framework of interpretation, it is impossible to overstate the impact of feminism on society over the past four decades. Accounting for all the areas of social, political, cultural and academic life that it has shaped worldwide in a detailed and comprehensive manner seems hardly feasible, being as it is one of the most far-reaching—while also openly contested from within and without—socio-political movements of recent history. Suffice it to say, *Google* yields thirty-four million results when one enters the word 'feminism' and over fifty-four for 'feminist.' Feminism starts from the premise that women are treated inequitably on the mere basis of their gendered socialization within patriarchal societies. In its most recent manifestations, feminism has sought to expose how different levels of discrimination and inequality intersect, in order to understand and denounce how systemic injustice and oppression occur within society.

From the perspective of literary criticism, feminism has dramatically transformed the way we read literary texts, both by contesting the traditional (exclusively male) literary canon and by setting up a new agenda for the academic analysis of literature. Proof of this lies in the fact that, despite the backlash of the nineties and the threat posed by postfeminism, English departments and literature programs all over the world continue to be the stronghold of feminism. This might be because, as Lisa M. Hogeland contends, feminism is "a kind of literacy, a way of reading both texts and everyday life from a particular stance" (1). Indeed, it is to feminism that we owe the now widespread awareness of the sexual politics of language and style. Nevertheless, it is key to acknowledge that the founding notion of feminism that "the personal is political" has contributed to blurring the limits between literature, life writing, theory, politics, the academy and activism. Indeed, a number of feminist activists, especially in its origins, were also theorists, literary critics and often also creative writers themselves, and many drew on their personal experiences for their (feminist) writing. Yet, as Gill Plain and Susan Sellers helpfully explain, the difference for literary criticism lies "in the dimension of textuality" (2), so this is what the analyses to be carried out in the following chapters will stick to.

The origins of feminist criticism lie in the aftermath of the second wave of feminism that took place in Britain and the United States in the 1960s. Yet, as Maggie Humm aptly puts it, "[t]he growth of the feminist movement itself is inseparable from feminist criticism. Women become feminists by becoming conscious of, and criticizing, the power of symbolic misrepresentations of women" (3). Feminist criticism has been generally considered to be based on three main assumptions. The first is that gender is constructed through language and is visible through style; style, therefore, represents in some way the articulation of ideologies of gender. The second, and one of the most contested ones, is that there are sex-related writing strategies—although they may be used by authors of either gender non-exclusively. And the last assumption is that the tradition of literary criticism has tended to use masculine norms to exclude or undervalue women's writing and scholarship (Humm 4–5). These assumptions have been discussed, problematized, contested or endorsed by most feminist critics since the late 1960s. What most seem to agree upon, as Rita Felski points out, is that all of literature is about gender in the minimal sense that it deals with characters who are usually shown to be either men or women, and a great deal of literature is about gender in a much more deliberate and self-conscious sense (11).

Ever since its 'birth,' the ever-expanding and self-critical field of feminist criticism has been constantly reshaped and redefined by a number of thinkers whose work has allowed for the formulation of new critical and theoretical approaches to the study of literature informed by feminism. These go from the groundbreaking work of the founding critics like Kate Millett and Mary Ellmann, to Anglo-American second-wave scholars like Elaine Showalter, Judith Fetterley, Sandra Gilbert and Susan Gubar, and their African-American and/or Lesbian detractors, namely Barbara Smith, Deborah McDowell, bell hooks, Audre Lorde, Bonnie Zimmerman and Adrienne Rich, among others, through the "writing the body" perspective put forward by French feminist theory and the influence of poststructuralism, deconstruction and psychoanalysis on gender studies, and up to contemporary feminist criticism informed by postcolonial studies, queer theory and cybernetics, among others. As a result of such combined efforts, spanning five decades of increasingly more sophisticated and theoretically informed scholarship, feminist criticism has acquired paradigmatic relevance for literary criticism, altering our vision of literature *as* literature.

Although the history of feminist criticism proper begins alongside the emergence of second-wave feminism in England and the United States, it is important to acknowledge that the process has a preface. As Gill Plain makes clear, the history of women's engagement with literature and textuality "far exceeds the parameters of second-wave feminism, and this history is integral to contemporary understandings of feminist practice" (6). Protofeminists like Mary Wollstonecraft, Virginia Woolf and Simone de Beauvoir began to articulate feminist ideas and critical positions before such categories existed, inspiring feminist critics and thinkers from Mary Ellman to Judith Butler (Plain 10).

The rise of feminist criticism is associated with the groundbreaking work of Mary Ellmann (1968), Kate Millett (1969), Germaine Greer (1970) and Eva Figes (1970). Their works, referred to as "the 'totalizing' studies of the oppression of women" (Eagleton 105), exposed and attacked the patriarchal belittlement of women, androcentrism and cultural misogyny, according literature a central role in their dissemination. Indeed, as Mary Eagleton usefully explains, these critics "saw literature as a key location for the creation, expression and maintenance of a sexual politics that oppressed women" (106). Consequently, they made literary analysis a central element of their methodology, which resulted in an understanding of literary criticism as playing an essential role toward women's liberation. With *Sexual Politics* (1969), Kate Millett was the first to call attention to the political dimension of gender. In her book, she clearly identifies patriarchy as the belief system responsible for the oppression of women, defining it as an "ancient and universal scheme for the domination of one birth group by another—the scheme that prevails in the area of sex" (24). Millett provides an inflammatory analysis of the patriarchal bias and phallocentrism that underlay male-authored literature, focusing particularly on the stereotypical representation of women in the literary works of Henry Miller, D.H. Lawrence and Norman Mailer. As Helen Carr explains, the publication of the book led to a storm of controversy and debates on both sides of the Atlantic; it was extensively attacked for its polemic content and style, and later for what was perceived as a lack of sophistication and a limited scope (121).[9]

Published a year earlier, Mary Ellmann's *Thinking about Women*, although perhaps less influential at the time, had already addressed the common stereotypes of the female that she identified in male-authored literature and criticism: formlessness, passivity, instability, confinement, piety, materiality, spirituality, irrationality, compliancy (55). She also identified "two incorrigible figures: the shrew and the witch" (55). With its witty and biting style, the book offers an exemplary review of the politics of gendered representation in the works of authors such as Matthew Arnold, James Joyce, Sigmund Freud and Norman Mailer. She also draws attention to the misogyny of what she terms "phallic criticism," whereby some female and male writers were despised among (male) critics for their "femininity" and some women writers were both appreciated and distrusted for their ability to reach a "supra-feminine condition" (40). Furthermore, in her critique of stereotypical representations of women, she discussed also works by some female authors, such as Willa Cather and Jane Austen, reprehending them for reproducing the same stereotypes and compliantly promoting biased representations of their own gender.

The revolutionary inquiries of these critics set the basis for what Elaine Showalter would term "feminist critique" ("Feminist Poetic" 128). This practice, also famously called the "images of women" approach to literature by Toril Moi (42), was defined as a "historically grounded inquiry which probes the ideological assumptions of literary phenomena" and which is "essentially political and polemical" (Showalter, "Feminist Poetic" 128–129). Indeed, as Mary Eagleton aptly explains, these critics' polemic style, at odds with the formalism that had become the norm in literary criticism at the time, served the aim of proving that their analyses were "a legitimate form of criticism that asked fundamental questions about literary history and literary production" (107). The main problem of 'feminist critique,' as Showalter was quick to point out, is that it was to a large extent male-oriented. This led a number of feminist critics to increasingly turn their attention to women's texts.

Nevertheless, feminist critics have never stopped exploring the representation of the female in male-authored texts. A particularly influential early example is Judith Fetterley's *The Resisting Reader: A Feminist Approach to American Fiction* (1978). Her main thesis was that the American canon is largely unreadable for women since so many texts rely on patriarchal power dynamics of female submission and subjection, while the narrative strategies of these texts oblige the woman reader to identify as male: "The female reader is co-opted into participation in an experience from which she is explicitly excluded; she is [...] required to identify against herself" (xii). Her approach, however, is not without its limitations: like the work of Millett and Ellmann, it articulates a form of reading that resists aesthetic pleasure at all costs and cuts female readers off from the possibility of ever being affected, inspired or touched by men's texts, and assuming an equally biased critical position that gives the text no chance to prove the resisting reader's assumptions wrong.

Rather, the key for contemporary feminist criticism of male-authored texts has been to find a middle point that balances the aesthetic merit of literary texts with a socio-political analysis that resists naïve readings which justify everything in the name of art. Feminist critics have continued addressing the works of male writers from Chaucer and Shakespeare right up to contemporary authors, providing more nuanced readings informed by feminism and other contemporary theories that take issue with complex notions of gender and subjectivity, assessing also how these intersect with race, sexuality and class. Without abandoning a concern for the representation of gender stereotypes and roles, feminist critics of men's texts have focused on issues such as gender-power relations, the use of stylistic resources compatible with the aims of feminism at a structural level and the existence of gender dialogue. It is also worth adding that, as Calvin Thomas explains, despite its shortcomings, the critical pursuit inaugurated by these early "images of women" critics has also had the effect of encouraging male critics to assess stereotypical representations of men and masculinity, leading to the emergence of masculinity studies (198). Indeed, feminist critics' concern with questions of female subjectivity and representation has made it possible to interrogate how men have come to inhabit and replicate the destructive patterns of patriarchal masculinity, helping to illuminate the social construction of masculinity and the reproduction of patterns that are harmful not only to women but also to men.

In the late seventies a new feminist literary project started to emerge that sought to recover forgotten or undervalued female authors from history. The aim was to unearth a "female subculture" (Showalter,

"Feminist Poetic" 131) that would yield alternative representations of women. Books like Patricia Meyer Spacks's *The Female Imagination* (1975), Ellen Moers' *Literary Women* (1976), Elaine Showalter's *A Literature of Their Own: British Women Writers from Charlotte Brontë to Doris Lessing* (1977), and Sandra Gilbert and Susan Gubar's *The Madwoman in the Attic: The Woman Writer and the Nineteenth-Century Literary Imagination* (1979) inaugurated a form of literary criticism that, for the first time, answered the question that many had been asking themselves: 'where were the women writers (other than Jane Austen, Emily and Charlotte Brontë, and George Elliot)?'

Nevertheless, gynocriticism and its emphasis on establishing a female tradition also entailed certain risks or limitations, which Mary Eagleton brilliantly brings to the fore:

> [b]y naming a literary tradition as 'female' she [Showalter] exposes the exclusivity of the dominant tradition and raises questions about the construction of literary history and the aesthetic values that have always seemed to find women's writing lacking. But the phrase also suggests that there is a specificity and a commonality about women's writing and this proved difficult to establish without drifting into stereotypes about feminine sensibilities and values. (109)

Thus, although for Showalter a female tradition seemed to rely not so much on innate dispositions common to all female writers of all ages, but rather on certain self-awareness (Eagleton 109), the notion of female tradition could never completely avoid certain essentialist overtones, certain assumptions about women as a whole. This would indeed be a source of criticism, especially among later feminist scholars who identified with the anti-essentialist possibilities that the notion of *écriture féminine* put forward by French feminist theory opened. Another important shortcoming of the critical practice that those early gynocritics undertook was that, although it was critical with the biased nature of literary history and doubted traditional aesthetic values, it ended up constituting an equally restrictive canon: a canon that in effect excluded black, lesbian and experimental (i.e. modernist) women writers, and established a white and essentially upper-middle-class tradition. Indeed, far from being a monolithic entity, feminist criticism was from its very origins internally diverse, divergent and self-critical, being as it was a movement devised—at least in theory—to address the needs and expose the inequalities to which no less than half of the human race was subjected. It soon became obvious, as the 1980s approached, that the oppression that white, middle-class women faced could not be so unproblematically equated with that to which women belonging to racial and sexual minorities were exposed, which gave rise to what came to be known as "black feminist criticism" and "lesbian feminist criticism."[10]

In 1977, Barbara Smith, in an essay entitled "Towards a Black Feminist Criticism," complained about white feminists' concern with rediscovering "dozens of truly obscure white women writers" while refusing to take the work of black women writers seriously (172). One of her main theses was that "thematically, stylistically, aesthetically, and conceptually Black women writers manifest common approaches to the act of creating literature as a direct result of the specific political, social, and economic experience they have been obliged to share" (174). Barbara Christian's *Black Women Novelists: The Development of a Tradition* (1980) became the first critical work of many to unearth, map and analyze a literary tradition of African-American women writers (in Keizer 157). Her steps would be followed by critics as influential as Alice Walker, bell hooks and Audre Lorde who, along with many others, contributed to shaping the field of black feminist criticism as the interplay between recovery of ignored texts and analysis of literary representations of black female experience (Keizer 158, 164). A further extension of the range of interest and interpretation of women's creative work came from feminist lesbian critics, such as Bonnie Zimmerman, Audre Lorde and Gloria Anzaldúa, who resented and attacked the heterosexism of the 'mainstream' (i.e. white, heterosexual) feminist critics of the 1970s. Much of early lesbian feminist criticism was concerned with identifying literary lesbians and lesbianism: lesbian authors, lesbian texts, lesbian characters or lesbian images (Gonda 171). Indeed, Zimmerman's widely anthologized essay, titled "What Has Never Been: An Overview of Lesbian Feminist Criticism" (1981), exposes the equally oppressive nature of mainstream feminist criticism and traditional literary studies in their denial of lesbian artistic and aesthetic expression and the suppression of lesbian literary history (Humm 227–228).[11]

What the black and/or lesbian theorists rehearsed in this subsection made obvious was that the category of "woman" could not be easily and unproblematically maintained without incurring in acts of either naïve essentialism or oppressive marginalization. Their work stirred a spirit of dissent within feminist criticism as the new decade advanced and the impact of psychoanalysis and poststructuralism started to be strongly felt. While the pursuits inaugurated by the critical positions discussed so far continued to yield interesting results, feminist criticism from the 1980s onward became increasingly more complex, diverse and wide-ranging. As Maggie Humm explains, "[o]ne of the great achievements of Anglo-American feminist criticism in the 1980s was its ability to identify and conduct a very diverse gendered literary criticism" (15). However, it was also increasingly more divided, progressively evolving into a complex set of discourses that problematized most of the assumptions on which Anglo-American feminist critics had relied up to then—mainly a universal category of "woman" and the assumed tight connection between women's writing and their personal experience. As the decade advanced, feminist criticism started to move toward analyses informed by theories of Marxism, poststructuralism and psychoanalysis.

A special case in point is that of Marxist/socialist feminist critics, whose work increasingly showed a combination of political commitment and theoretical sophistication. Critics like Tillie Olsen, Juliet Mitchell, Michèle Barrett and Cora Kaplan, influenced by socialist ideas, incorporated into their analyses considerations about the historical contexts and the material conditions of cultural products and practices. Their criticism was tightly associated with polemic and advocacy. These critics interrogated the representation of women's experience in literature in terms of social determinations, supporting their criticism on the understanding that the forms and contents of literature have a direct relationship with the ideological world in which they are produced. As such, they took issue with the notion that gender and oppression could no longer be considered in isolation from their intersection with race and especially class. Many of these critics were also interested in the theories of post-Freudian psychoanalysis. Juliet Mitchell's *Psychoanalysis and Feminism* (1974) was the first feminist text to engage with the theories of Freud, Lacan and feminism in order to explain women's experience. Others, such as Mary Jacobus and Shoshana Felman, would follow Mitchell's lead. Psychoanalytic theories of femininity have provided feminist critics with the tools to describe the relation between female sexuality, woman's unconscious, and their representation in discourse and literature, offering them a reading of the female that is rooted not entirely in the social construction of femininity, nor entirely in biology, but through language and subjectivity.

Another revolution for feminist criticism was brought about by the impact of poststructuralism. As a result of the influence of French poststructuralist thought on the Anglo-American academy, feminist critics have increasingly adopted alternative, theoretically informed textual approaches to the analysis of literary texts. One of the most important contributions of poststructuralism to feminist criticism is to have forced reflection on the existence or absence of race, sexuality, class and gender relations in literature. Poststructuralism also ridicules the idea that texts simply carry the messages of authors or that they can only be understood in terms of the authors' biography or intention. Furthermore, some feminist critics turned to deconstruction because of its criticism of binary thinking and its cultural construction, its potential to uncover the ideological patterns that shape all acts of interpretation and its recognition of phallocentrism in language. Yet, as Mary Poovey explains, deconstruction and its antihumanist premises had to undergo a feminist rewriting so as to incorporate its strategies into a political and critical literary project (51). One of the earliest and most influential texts of feminist deconstruction was Toril Moi's *Sexual/Textual Politics* (1985).

As the title of her book already suggests, Moi was one of the first to articulate a divide between the pragmatic but naïve and essentialist humanism of much early Anglo-American criticism and the subtle, if apolitical and idealistic, sophistication of the French feminist theory of thinkers such as Hélène Cixous, Julia Kristeva and Luce Irigaray. Moi's fundamental critique of second-wave feminist critics was based on the notion that they had failed to challenge basic patriarchal presumptions of categorical thinking that distinctly separate the sexes into a binary relation in which one side of the dichotomy—the white, male, heterosexual one—would have been privileged. Indeed, her book also successfully made the point that French feminist theory is profoundly important for feminist criticism because it opened the possibility for a linguistic space where gender divisions might disappear.

The questions raised by the outburst of theory in the 1980s led to further diversification of critical discourse, to the extent that it is impossible, given the character and format of this section as a concise and modest introduction to the critical framework, to analyze in depth the myriad of ideologies, methodologies and perspectives into which feminist criticism has expanded since the 1990s. Suffice it, then, to say that the influence of the theories described so far on the rise of gender, queer, postcolonial and posthuman studies cannot be overstated, inspiring the work of later theorists such as Judith Butler, Gayatri Spivak, Gloria Anzaldúa, Eve Kosofsky Sedgwick and Donna Haraway in a plurality of feminist discourses. As Plain and Sellers explain, the willingness that feminist criticism shows to interrogate questions of increasing ontological and epistemological complexity made it open and receptive to work being undertaken in related disciplines (104). Indeed, as the 1990s progressed, the insights emerging from gender studies, postcolonial studies, queer theory and cyberfeminism began to be embraced by feminist critics, who have sought new ways of articulating the problems of human subjectivity as represented in literature.

Starting from the premise that literature conveys more than simple information—since it also encodes indirect, intuitive and nonverbal understandings that may only be uncovered when the texts are read against the grain—the focus in the following chapters will be on issues of oppression, objectification, gender difference, power struggle and gender dialogue. The following questions will be asked of Doctorow's novels: how is the relationship between the genders portrayed? What sort of power relationships emerge between male and female characters? How are male and female roles defined? What constitutes the masculine and the feminine and how are these represented or undermined? What do the books reveal about the (economic, political, social and psychological) operations of patriarchy? Do the texts put forward any forms of resistance to it? Is there gender dialogue in the texts? What is the gender of the voices and focalizations that hold narrative control?

The surveys carried out above underscore the specificities and particular focus of enquiry of trauma studies and feminist criticism. Yet, they also reveal the underlying similarities of the questions that each framework sets out to ask of literary texts and of the variety of motives that stand behind the critical pursuit informed by each. Both critical perspectives are similarly constructed as narratives through which a new world-view is presented that opens alternative ways to ethically and aesthetically encounter the Other in literature, with politically significant effects. In other words, both frameworks of interpretation share a belief in a strong connection between art and life. That is, they share a rejection of the understanding that ethical and political judgments of literary texts have nothing to do with the realm of the aesthetic.[12] This is precisely the key point at which trauma theory and feminist criticism intersect: the ethics, aesthetics and politics of representation. Indeed, in these forms of literary criticism, the ethical, the political and the aesthetic are inextricably linked. After all, trauma theory and feminist criticism are both, at root, attempts to trace and denounce the inexhaustible shape of human suffering and injustice. As such, both frameworks are closely linked to the "ethical turn" that took place in the 1980s and 1990s in the fields of literary criticism and philosophy. On the one hand, both the resurgence of ethical criticism and the interest in psychological trauma respond to a sense of outrage at the aggressive relativism of poststructuralist and postmodernist thought. Furthermore, the rise of trauma theory unmistakably took place in the wake of the turn to ethics in criticism and cannot be understood outside of this context. On the other hand, the concerns that feminist scholars placed on the contemporary critical agenda are widely acknowledged to have paved the way for a return to an understanding of literature as saturated with social meanings and of literary forms as aesthetic, ethical and political.

The "turn to ethics" is basically a critical label that is widely employed to refer to the shift that started to take place in the late 1980s toward a renewed critical interest in the ethics of reading and in the ethical potential of literature. As Bárbara Arizti and Silvia Martínez-Falquina aptly explain, it has been partly motivated by "the excessive radicalism and relativism dictated by some forms of Theory" (x). This is certainly the view that most advocates of ethical criticism hold (see for example Booth 25, Bertens 301), who share the belief that postmodernism as a critical framework "did more than merely discredit ethical criticism of the arts; [it] tended to discredit ethics as a general human enterprise" (Gregory 274). In the last few decades, as the influence of rhetorical deconstruction receded and as this framework was integrated into more mimetic approaches, Daniel Schwarz explains, hermeneutical questions have again come to the fore (3). However, in most cases the ethical turn is not a return to an ethics of universalizing moral truths; it has been influenced by postmodernist and poststructuralist theory, to the extent that the simplistic, uncomplicated prescription of external ethical forces regarding so many different literatures and cultures is no longer possible (Davis and Womack ix–x). As Tammie Amiel-Houser and Adia Mendelson-Maoz claim—with others such as Andrew Gibson (11)—far from eradicating it, "postmodern thinking has actually played, and continues to play, an important role in the renewed interest in the field of ethics" (200). Indeed, as they argue, "this approach has unsettled the established doctrines of modern ethical thinking" (200). Not even the fiercest defendants of the ethical value of literature, such as Wayne Booth, Daniel Schwarz or Martha Nussbaum, seem to be able to believe in an unproblematic return to the dogmatically prescriptive or doctrinaire form of reading of liberal humanism.

The shape that the revival of interest in ethics after Theory (in the double meaning of "after" as "following" and "extending") has often taken is an increased attention to philosopher Emmanuel Levinas's 'ethics of alterity.' His postmodern conceptualization of the infinite responsibility toward the "face of the Other" has provided a new theoretical perspective for reconsidering the complexities of ethical response after the demise of humanism, given its failure in the face of two world wars, the threat of nuclear weapons and the horror of genocide. For Levinas, ethics is tied to the utter particularity of the Other and the Self in their engagement with one another; in his philosophy, our obligation to the Other always takes priority and is extreme, in the sense that there are no limits to it. In Levinas's view, thus, we are responsible for all others, all the time, in every way. The analyses to come in the following chapters, informed by key notions of feminist criticism and trauma theory, will be firmly anchored in the awareness of both frameworks' tight connection to ethics. Keeping in mind the impact of Theory, the upcoming study will pay homage to the belief that ethics is not only a legitimate human enterprise, but a necessary one and that, to borrow Doctorow's own phrase, "writing matters" ("The Beliefs of Writers" 618).

The relevance of these frameworks in today's critical grounds, together with the contemporary emphasis on, and interest in hybrid approaches for the study of fiction, opens a door for a multidimensional analysis that may bring about innovative readings of literary texts. This possibility seems particularly appropriate for a novelist like E.L. Doctorow for several reasons. His Jewish heritage, as well as his own condition as leftist writer in a country where the Left never seems to have been very welcome, may call for a revision of his works from the perspective of trauma studies. Furthermore, it is worth keeping in mind what Maria Root explains about the socio-political climate of the 1960s and 1970s, in which Doctorow took his first steps as a writer: "It was an era marked by a generation's search for meaning and justice" (231) which led to a renewed interest in understanding trauma and memory. She further claims that,

[m]uch of the upheaval and rebellion associated with the 1960s and '70s might be characterized as a 'generational posttraumatic stress response' to the experience of profound betrayal by authority figures (the 'establishment') of a generation of young people crossing the threshold of adulthood. The world for which this generation hoped did not exist. Oppression was rampant and affected major portions of the population. The civil rights were being violated daily […]. Anger and confusion were catalysts for the activism and power of this generation, who spoke about the realities and atrocities of their lives and those of previous generations. (231)

This era, marked by the Vietnam War, international conflict, gay liberation and the second reconstruction of the civil rights movement, was also characterized by the revolution brought about by the Women's Rights Movement. Yet, against the dramatic cultural impact of second-wave feminism, Doctorow has been accused by some critics of assigning a very limited role to women in his literary depiction of the United States, and of failing to open his texts to the voices of women (see Gentry 132). As a counterpoint, asked in an interview about his position toward the movement, Doctorow said that he favored feminism, since he considered it "an indisputable important advance in human apprehension of what life is," even though he claimed that he had not written from an explicitly feminist point of view (in Morris, *Conversations* 110). Furthermore, after being questioned in another interview about his concern with sexual interaction in his novels, Doctorow stated that gender issues were important to him as a form of politics: "I think more likely it is a preoccupation having to do with sex as power, either perhaps using sex as a metaphor for political relations, or helplessly annotating what passes for sex in a society that suffers paternalistic distortions" (in Morris, *Conversations* 121).

Preliminary Analysis: Postmodernism and Beyond

Despite the above, it is worth keeping in mind that, with a few notable exceptions, Doctorow's critics have recurrently classified him as a postmodernist writer. Many of his early critics emphasize the fact that a wide number of thematic and stylistic features of the author's fiction emanate from the postmodern context in which he took his first steps as a writer. We might also add that some of the most widely acclaimed scholars of postmodernist literary theory have referred to E.L. Doctorow's novels in their seminal contributions to the field (see Waugh 1984, Hutcheon 1988, Jameson 1991). Thus, John Williams is probably right when he claims that any critical attempt to approach Doctorow's fiction must start from and take into consideration its indebtedness to the impact of postmodernism and poststructuralism (6).

E.L. Doctorow's formal and thematic affinities with postmodernist fiction are, indeed, undeniable. *Welcome to Hard Times*, *The Book of Daniel*, *Ragtime* and *City of God* arguably incorporate key themes of postmodernism. First of all, they seem to give expression to the poststructuralist understanding of the indeterminacy of meaning and the impossibility of truthful representation that resulted from the influence of the theories of Derrida and Foucault, among others. And so, although in his essays Doctorow generally advocates the authority and superiority of fiction, he ultimately recognizes the indeterminacy of not only writing, but also human experience. This may be seen in the structural indefiniteness of his early and middle novels. Further, the books depict individual responses to the overwhelming sense of uncertainty that characterizes contemporary existence. This is particularly obvious in the case of *Welcome to Hard Times*, *The Book of Daniel* and *City of God*, where the protagonists—who respectively stand for the figure of the writer—grapple with their untimely realization that whatever their efforts to capture reality, meaning seems to slip away from their hands, leaving them with serious doubts as to the possibility of ever representing truth. And so, for instance, Blue claims in *Welcome to Hard Times*: "I scorn myself for a fool for all the bookkeeping I've done; as if notations on a ledger can fix life, as if some marks in a book can control things" (184). Pem, in *City of God*, similarly warns Everett: "You write well enough [...] but no writer can reproduce the actual texture of living life" (53).

Doctorow's early-middle novels also carry out a critical interrogation and revision of the universalizing metanarratives of science, religion, myth, politics and reason. They reflect the postmodernist decentering of culture characterized by mistrust of grand narratives and an all-encompassing sense of plurality as theorized by Lyotard. As John G. Parks has noticed, "Doctorow's fiction shows a willingness to take risks, to counter the tendency of a culture to monopolize the compositions of truth" ("The Politics of Polyphony" 462). The contestation of totalizing narrative traditions based on the allegedly objective communication of facts is one of the key issues dealt with by Doctorow in his seminal essay "False Documents" (1977). There, he coins the terms "regime language" and "language of freedom" to refer to precisely this division between the power of language residing in verifiability and the superior power of ideal imagined language that is unverifiable and derives its strength from "what we threaten to become" (152-153). The decentering of metanarratives becomes a central project in *Welcome to Hard Times*, *The Book of Daniel*, *Ragtime* and *City of God*, where the grand narratives of myth, politics, history and religion are respectively undermined. These novels seem to fulfill the general aim of deconstructing assumed official versions of history by opposing them to minority perspectives on historical events. Indeed, the use of Lyotardian "petites histoires" that supersede "grand narratives" of official history is a recurrent tendency in Doctorow's works. And so, for instance, *The Book of Daniel* becomes the protagonist's attempt to rewrite the history of the North-American Left through the narration of his own family's engagement with it. The same effect is achieved in *City of God*, where readers are confronted with Yehoshua's account of his life in a ghetto in Nazi Europe.

Doctorow's affinities with postmodernism become manifest in the novels' attitude toward history, reality and fiction. In them, the confusion of the fact with its model evokes the Baudrillardian notion that the real and the copy are no longer distinguishable (175). The novels' main thematic concerns are historical events. This confirms Doctorow's predilection for historical plots, since they become an ideal subject matter to reflect on "the 'fictiveness' of all discourse about reality and history" (Bevilacqua, "Narration and History" 94). In fact, the constant intermingling of what is generally considered verifiable historical fact and the author's fictive imagination allows Doctorow to redefine the historicized past and open it to new and multiple interpretations. This is particularly obvious in *The Book of Daniel* and *Ragtime*, where the categories of history, reality and fiction become helplessly blurred in a postmodernist celebration of uncertainty and plurality of meanings. In *Ragtime*, for instance, the multiplication of characters and the blurring of historical and fictional records are not aimed at testing the readers' capacity to discriminate between authorial identities and ontologies; rather, it seeks to bring to the fore the uselessness of trying to differentiate, in this case, between fictional and historical events and personages, thus leveling history and fiction to the same category of human discourse. As Doctorow concludes in his aforementioned essay, "there is no fiction or non-fiction as we commonly understand the distinction: there is only narrative" (163).

In his early and middle novels, Doctorow's postmodernist subversive drive is also revealed in stylistic terms. In a well-known article published in 1967, John Barth first draws attention to what he terms "the literature of exhaustion." His essay constitutes Barth's first attempt to document the exhaustion of the aesthetics of modernism and the emergence of what would be later called postmodernist fiction, articulating the sentiment that "the novel's time as major art form is up" (71). However, far from showing pessimism about the future of fiction, Barth explains that "one way to handle such a feeling might be to write a novel about it" (72). Thus, his influential article heralds the rise of a highly self-reflexive mode of writing that is characterized by narrative experimentalism, the decentering of subjectivity, parodic revision of traditional forms and intertextual playfulness. Drinking as he did from these theoretical waters, Doctorow's aesthetic affinities with postmodernism may be seen, first of all, in the paradoxical rejection of objectivity and simultaneous decentering of subjectivity that his early and middle novels deploy. In an interview to Herwig Friedl and Dieter Schulz, Doctorow seems to advocate a dismissal of the central authority of the writer, who is instead replaced by a "multiplicity of witnesses": "since history can be composed, you see, then you want to have as many people active in the composition as possible. A kind of democracy of perception. Thousands of eyes, not just one" (in "Multiplicity" 113). According to the writer, then, the plurality of perspectives that literature generates can provide a better understanding of different models of reality. Such an aspiration manifests itself in the novels mainly in terms of experimentation with the narrating subject. In the case of *Welcome to Hard Times* and *The Book of Daniel*, this takes the shape of a conflict between narratorial reliability and unreliability, and specifically in the latter through voice shifts. As for *Ragtime*, the voice of the narrator is ultimately unplaceable, since it remains impossible to establish whether the narrative voice is merely that of the mock historian or the Little Boy in the family: "Our knowledge of this clandestine history comes to us [...]" (205). In *City of God*, Doctorow's commitment to the representation of "thousands of eyes" becomes a motto, the novel's *raison d'être*.

The postmodernist revision of metanarratives that the writer's early novels thematically represent also materializes formally in the blurring and reassessment of the traditional conventions of literary genres. This is mainly achieved through the use of parody. In *Welcome to Hard Times*, *The Book of Daniel* and *Ragtime*, the genres of the Western, life writing and the historical chronicle respectively are parodically appropriated, destabilizing and playing against traditional frameworks of generic interpretation. And so, for instance, asked in an interview about his motivation for recuperating the Western, Doctorow explains that he "liked the idea of using disreputable genre materials and doing something serious with them" (in Trenner 36). *City of God* goes even further in that it utterly and completely escapes generic classification, becoming a kaleidoscopic combination of plots and storylines that exposes readers to a myriad of literary genres, from the war memoir to the horror story. Similarly, Doctorow's favoring of postmodernist aesthetics can be observed in the parodic intertextual references that pervade his novels. Discussing Jorge Luis Borges's experiments with fiction as an example, Barth already points to the continuous importance of intertextuality for the emerging postmodern novel in his 1967 essay (73). As Linda Hutcheon eloquently elaborates in her seminal book on postmodernist poetics, intertextual parody "offers a sense of the presence of the past, but a past that can be known only from its texts, its traces—be they literary or historical" (125). In this sense, it is worth highlighting that the titles of the four novels underscore their intertextual nature through their parodic connections to literary intertexts—namely Dickens's *Hard Times*, *The Bible* and Augustine's *The City of God*—and historical ones—the Ragtime Era. More specifically, in the case of *The Book of Daniel* and *City of God*, intertextuality plays a paramount role not merely in their engagement with historical events, but also in their ironic reworking of the textual literary past, which deeply affects issues of characterization and symbolism.

Finally, Doctorow's indebtedness to postmodernist aesthetics can be seen in his early and middle novels' metafictional self-reflexivity. According to Patricia Waugh's definition, a metafictional text is one that self-consciously draws attention to its own status as an artifact (*Metafiction* 2). This is something that Doctorow's novels actively seek; in the four books, the narrators and fictive authors constantly reflect on the process of their own textual composition, which is presented to us as the text that we are reading. And so, Daniel begins his narration as follows: "This is a Thinline felt tip marker, black. This is Composition Notebook 79C made in USA. by Long Island Paper Products, Inc. This is Daniel trying one of the dark coves of the Browsing Room" (3). In the same vein, the Little Boy in *Ragtime* feels compelled to reveal his sources: "Our knowledge of this clandestine history comes to us [...]" (205). *City of God*, for its part, may be claimed to be a novel about the act of writing a (Holocaust) novel. The books' self-reflexivity is also enhanced by constant references to the reader. Blue, in *Welcome to Hard Times*, asks: "Do you think, mister, with all that settlement around you that you're freer than me to make your fate?" (184). Daniel similarly claims: "I know there is a you. There has always been a you. YOU: I will show you that I can do the electrocution" (359).

All things considered, it seems reasonable to agree with Hutcheon's analysis of E.L. Doctorow's early and middle novels as paradigmatic examples of the postmodernist mode of writing, and, more specifically, of what she has termed "historiographic metafiction" (ix). This label encompasses "those well-known and popular novels which are both intensely self-reflexive and yet paradoxically also lay claim to historical events and personages," incorporating "theoretical self-awareness of history and fiction as human constructs" (5). Summing up, when considered collectively and in the light of Doctorow's declarations of sentiments in his essays and interviews, the four novels thematically and stylistically epitomize the strong spirit of subversion, sense of skepticism and experimentalism that typically characterizes postmodernist fiction.

Yet, while Doctorow's thematic and aesthetic affinities with postmodernism and his indebtedness to the postmodern cultural context are unquestionable, there is a strong sense of contradiction inherent both to his fiction and non-fiction. Doctorow's novels engage with social, political and historical realities in an extremely meaningful way. This suggests a movement beyond postmodernism and toward the recuperation of faith in meaning and the possibility of truthful textual representation. Also worth considering, when asked about the specific postmodern features of his novels, Doctorow has repeatedly assured critics of his realist allegiances: "I used certain postmodern devices. However, I did that, I think, for very traditional novelistic purposes. [...] My final intention, or faith, is in the traditional novel, or the traditional function of the novelist" (in Bevilacqua, "Interview" 134). Certainly, some of Doctorow's critics agree with the tenet that despite sharing some of the most common features traditionally associated with a postmodernist poetics, Doctorow's fiction also implicitly rejects the postmodernist contempt for the outside world. In fact, as this study will attempt to show, *Welcome to Hard Times*, *The Book of Daniel*, *Ragtime* and *City of God* stage a return to the idea that art can provide a sense of reality. This reinforces the novelist's own claim that his novels endorse a "poetics of engagement" with the ills of contemporary North-American society (in Trenner 48).

Some considerations about the collusion of postmodernism, feminist criticism and trauma theory seem in order at this point, given its complexity and wide-ranging nature. On the one hand, critics like Rita Felski (70), Patricia Waugh (*Feminine Fictions* 6–10) and Molly Hite (1–2) have famously claimed that feminism and postmodernism are incompatible. For one thing, postmodernism is traditionally premised on the undermining of individual subjectivity, reason and truth, as argued above. Feminism, however, in its many variants, has adamantly retained a belief in the primacy of individual agency and the actuality and historicity of women's oppression and subordination. As Magali Cornier-Michael has put it,

> [p]ostmodern fiction's tendency to reduce individual agency to corporate agency and sociopolitical forces to chance and patterns of coincidences has understandably drawn sharp criticism from feminist literary critics and, unfortunately, has also led many to a wholesale rejection of postmodernism. (3–4)

Indeed, many feminist critics have assumed a fairly standardized version of postmodernism as ahistorical, apolitical and relativistic that shatters the subject and excludes the possibility of individual agency. Yet, this may have been the result of the rather limited understanding of postmodernist fiction that (mostly white male) critics have developed due to their almost exclusive focus on the experimental avantgardist canonical texts written by white male writers. Furthermore, it is undeniable that poststructuralist theory supports itself on a list of almost exclusively male proper names that have been credited with establishing the foundations of contemporary cultural theory, many of whom have been mentioned above.

Against this perspective, critics such as Magali Cornier-Michael (1996) and Susan Hekman (1992) have argued that, when seen as plural and dynamic rather than as homogeneous and static, and as encompassing a wide range of subversive tendencies, feminism and postmodernism not only are *not* mutually exclusive but also have similar aims.[13] In keeping with that argument, Linda Singer claims that feminism and postmodernism have in common "an explicit discursive strategy of challenging the terms, conventions, and symbols of hegemonic authority in ways that foreground the explicitly transgressive character of this enterprise" (469). Similarly, the sociologist Janet Wolff argues that "the radical task of postmodernism is to deconstruct apparent truths, dismantle dominant ideas and cultural forms, and to engage in the guerrilla tactics of undermining closed and hegemonic systems of thought," which she characterizes as "the promise of postmodernism for feminist politics" (87). Cornier-Michael is right when she claims that "as an active oppositional politics, feminism transforms or translates the strategies it co-opts so as to satisfy its political aims" (6). Indeed, some formal strategies that radically subvert Western metaphysics and are commonly associated with postmodern aesthetics are also prevalent in fiction with feminist impulses since the 1960s. Among these, some of the most common ones have to do with the disruption of traditional and essentialist notions of subjectivity, character development, representation, language, narrative, history and binary logic in general, the pastiche of various types of texts or discourses, the dislocation of traditional spatial-temporal contexts, the self-conscious refusal to grant narrative authority or closure, and the appropriation and reworking of popular forms (see Cornier-Michael 5). Furthermore, it should not be forgotten that postmodernism, as a cultural movement, shares with feminism its subversive drive precisely in that it has led to the decentering of dichotomies and the inscription into history of previously silenced groups that have traditionally occupied the margins of society due to their gender, race, sexual orientation, ethnicity, religion or class. This is certainly also a key aim of intersectional feminism. As Hutcheon has noted, the 1970s and 1980s saw an increasingly fast inscription of those she calls "ex-centrics" into theoretical discourse and artistic practice, in effect challenging the traditional "centrisms" of our culture (61).

As for the relationship between postmodernism and trauma theory, their projects appear equally difficult to reconcile at first sight, given the latter's tight connection to ethics, its traditional reliance on a stable understanding of subjectivity, and its concern with the representation of traumatic reality and post-traumatic culture.[14] This is precisely the point that Ronald Granofsky is seeking to make when he explicitly claims that, in terms of genre and ideology, "the trauma novel and the postmodern novel must be seen in certain fundamental ways as antithetical" (11). He speaks of a "bifurcation of post-war English fiction into two distinct sub-genres that emerge out of literary modernism: the modernist trauma novel and the postmodern novel" (11). Despite some similitudes that result from a common historical context, the main and irreconcilable difference between the two, in Granofsky's view, would be that "in postmodernism the perceiving subject is no longer assumed to be a coherent, meaning-generating entity" (12); that is, the differences between the postmodern novel and the trauma novel, according to Granofsky, center on the issue of human identity and on the vehicle which allows postmodern fiction to call human identity into question: language itself (155). Thus, he contends that a clash between trauma literature and postmodernism results from the opposing tendency toward humanism in the former and relativism in the latter (13), arguing that "while the latter is based on a reading of history, the former prefers a sceptical historiography" (155).

Against this perspective, Anne Whitehead usefully emphasizes the connections between the two frameworks, arguing that "trauma fiction overlaps with and borrows from both postmodern and postcolonial fiction in its self-conscious deployment of stylistic devices as modes of reflection or critiques" (3). Formal features are precisely the clearest point of collusion between postmodernist and trauma fiction for Whitehead, who further claims that "trauma fiction emerges out of postmodernist fiction and shares its tendency to bring conventional narrative techniques to their limit" (82). Extending Whitehead's analysis, Laurie Vickroy discusses the similarities between the two in terms of values and properties. Among these, she emphasizes their common effort to bear witness to social and personal fragmentation, their criticism of the uses of power and its attendant discourses, their rejection of simplistic narratives of closure and of traditional ideologies, and their similar reliance on a sense of fracture and fragmentation (*Trauma Narratives* 4–6). In short, it seems apt to claim that far from undermining the ethical motivations behind Doctorow's literary project as manifested in *Welcome to Hard Times*, *The Book of Daniel*, *Ragtime* and *City of God*, the postmodernist features that they show have, at the very least, the potential to extend their ethical concerns. Whether this is indeed the case will be discussed in Chapter 5.

By way of conclusion to this Introduction, I would like to add that a theoretical approach to Doctorow's fiction that brings together trauma studies, feminist criticism, narratology and ethical considerations can create a nuanced, critical discussion of the four books that make up this study's corpus of analysis. This may hopefully also bring to the fore the role of literary criticism as the nexus where fiction and the world meet, where literary texts are revealed for their investments within culture and society.

Notes

1 For a comprehensive genealogy of the term "trauma," see Luckhurst (*Trauma Question* 19–62). This critic usefully maps the development of the concept from its physical origins inextricably linked to the expansion of the railways

Introduction 33

in the 1860s, through its psychological drift thanks to the neurological and then psychoanalytic research carried out by Charcot, Janet and Freud on neurosis, dissociation and hysteria, to the notion of 'shell shock' and its different psychological models, culminating in the arrival of PTSD in the 1980s, which would eventually bind together the psychological conditions of Vietnam veterans, Hiroshima survivors, victims of the Nazi regime, targets of segregation and racism, and incest and rape victims. Medical health professionals working in these areas, Roger Luckhurst explains, "mutually reinforced each other; what emerged was a general category of 'the survivor' that strongly linked trauma to identity politics" (*Trauma Question* 61–62). Another particularly illuminating genealogy of trauma and PTSD is the one carried out by Leys (2000).

2 Geoffrey Hartman links the rise and rapid growth of interest in trauma to a specific socio-cultural tension: "[A]n awareness of the persistence of violence in a culture that no longer condones the martial virtues of war" ("Limits" 269).

3 Also variously termed "the trauma paradigm" (Luckhurst, "Beyond Trauma" 12), "first wave trauma theory" (Pederson 334), "deconstructive trauma studies" (Kansteiner and Weilnböck 229), "Caruthian-PTSD critical perspective" (Gibbs 3) and "conventional trauma theory" (Traverso and Broderick 9).

4 For a capacious, comprehensive and multidisciplinary approach to trauma as a medical ailment that combines neurobiological, clinical and cultural (i.e. anthropological and sociological) insights into the phenomenon, see Kirmayer, Lemelson and Barad's edited volume (2007).

5 The most comprehensive analysis of Freud's legacy for trauma studies might be the one carried out by Leys (18–40). In her book, Ruth Leys maps the development of Freud's ideas about hysteria and assesses the importance of his writings about traumatic neurosis for the field in contemporary times. In her final chapter, Leys turns to Cathy Caruth, providing an insightful and well-researched study of her re-interpretation of, and indebtedness to Freud (266–297). See also Radstone (2007), who maps trauma theory in its inception by Caruth back to what she calls "the US-based 'postmodernization' of Freud" (13).

6 Caruth borrows the Freudian term "latency" to designate the "period during which the effects of the [traumatic] experience are not apparent" (*Explorations* 7).

7 Indeed, LaCapra (2001), with Leys (2000) and Roth (in E.A. Kaplan 34) among others, was among the first to call attention to the shortcomings that they identify in Caruth's and the other Yale school trauma critics' approach to trauma, which they ascribe to their training in deconstruction (both Caruth and Felman were indeed students of de Man). Roth would later add: "In critical theory the traumatic has been framed as a window onto more general issues of representation. The inability to properly represent some events is said to show the inadequacy of representation of any and all events" (xix).

8 See LaCapra (*Writing History* 190), Hartman ("Limits" 259) and Caruth (*Unclaimed Experience* 9).

9 Nevertheless, Millet may be credited with coining the term "sexual politics" which has become indispensable in feminist discussions and debates within most areas of contemporary life.

10 For detailed introductions to black feminist criticism and lesbian feminist criticism, see Keizer (2007) and Gonda (2007) respectively.

11 Some recent anthologies have sought to return to a search for lesbians in literature and the literature of lesbianism. However, lesbian feminism has

ended up to a large extent giving way to the less historical and less textual concerns of queer theory (Gonda 169, 180).
12 A view shared by New Critics and formalist analysts who, generally speaking, focused exclusively on the inherent features of a text, denying the importance of the text's historical, biographical and cultural context, as well as the social dimension of literature.
13 The theories of Judith Butler and of the French feminists from the 1970s onward suggest that bridging the gap between poststructuralist theory and feminism is not only possible but also productive. Yet, that strand of feminism, by focusing on the constructed nature of the category of gender in language and on issues of difference, has proved too theoretical to contribute to the actual oppositional project of contesting patriarchal oppression and hegemonic power structures for some.
14 It is important to keep in mind that trauma theory emerged when the most radical and relativistic features of postmodernism had started to lose their primacy in the context of the ethical turn in literature. Therefore, it comes as no surprise that fewer critics have concerned themselves with the potential collusion or collision of trauma theory and postmodernism.

References

American Psychiatric Association. *Diagnostic and Statistical Manual of Mental Disorders* (3rd ed.), 1980.

———. *Diagnostic and Statistical Manual of Mental Disorders* (4th ed., text rev.), 2000.

Amiel-Houser, Tammie and Adia Mendelson-Maoz. "Against Empathy: Levinas and Ethical Criticism in the 21st Century." *Journal of Literary Theory* 8.1 (2014): 199–218.

Arizti, Bárbara and Silvia Martínez-Falquina, eds. Introduction. *On the Turn: The Ethics of Fiction in Contemporary Narrative in English*. Newcastle: Cambridge Scholars Publishing, 2007. ix–xxiii.

Barth, John. "The Literature of Exhaustion." 1967. *The Friday Book: Essays and Other Non-Fiction*. Ed. John Barth. New York: The Johns Hopkins UP, 1984. 62–76.

Baudrillard, Jean. "Simulation and Simulacra." *Jean Baudrillard: Selected Writings. Jean Baudrillard: Selected Writings*. Ed. Mark Poster. Stanford: Stanford UP, 1988. 166–184.

BBC News. "US Novelist EL Doctorow Dies at 84." *BBC News* July 22, 2015. Web. 31 May, 2016. <www.bbc.com/news/entertainment-arts-33618570>

Bennett, Jill. *Empathic Vision: Affect, Trauma, and Contemporary Art*. Stanford: Stanford UP, 2005.

Bertens, Hans. "Postmodern Humanism." *Canadian Review of Comparative Literature/Revue Canadienne de Littérature Comparée* 39.3 (2012): 299–316.

Bevilacqua, Winifred F. "Narration and History in E.L. Doctorow's *Welcome to Hard Times, The Book of Daniel* and *Ragtime*." *American Studies in Scandinavia* 22 (1990): 94–106.

———. "An Interview with E.L. Doctorow." *Conversations with E. L. Doctorow*. Ed. Christopher Morris. Jackson: Mississippi UP, 1999. 129–143.

Bloom, Harold, ed. *Modern Critical Views: E.L. Doctorow*. Philadelphia: Chelsea House, 2002.

Booth, Wayne C. *The Company We Keep: An Ethics of Fiction*. Berkeley: University of California Press, 1988.
Brown, Laura S. "Not Outside the Range: One Feminist Perspective on Psychic Trauma (1991)." *Trauma: Explorations in Memory*. Ed. Cathy Caruth. Baltimore: Johns Hopkins UP, 1995. 100–112.
Buelens, Gert and Stef Craps. "Introduction: Postcolonial Trauma Novels. Postcolonial Trauma Novels." Spec. issue of *Studies in the Novel*. Eds. Stef Craps and Gert Buelens 40.1/2 (2008): 1–12.
Buelens, Gert, Sam Durrant, and Robert Eaglestone, eds. Introduction. *The Future of Trauma Theory*. London and New York: Routledge, 2014. 1–8.
Carr, Helen. "A History of Women's Writing." *A History of Feminist Literary Criticism*. Eds. Gill Plain and Gill and Susan Sellers. Cambridge, New York: Cambridge UP, 2007. 120–137.
Caruth, Cathy, ed. Introduction to Part I. *Trauma: Explorations in Memory*. Baltimore: Johns Hopkins UP, 1995. 3–12.
———. Introduction to Part II. *Trauma: Explorations in Memory*. Baltimore: Johns Hopkins UP, 1995. 151–157.
———. *Unclaimed Experience*. Baltimore: Johns Hopkins UP, 1996.
Cornier Michael, Magali. *Feminism and the Postmodern Impulse: Post World War II Fiction*. Albany: State University of New York Press, 1996.
Craps, Stef. *Postcolonial Witnessing: Trauma Out of Bounds*. New York: Palgrave Macmillan, 2013.
———. "Beyond Eurocentrism: Trauma Theory in the Global Age." *The Future of Trauma Theory*. Eds. Gert Buelens, Sam Durrant, and Robert Eaglestone. London and New York: Routledge, 2014. 45–62.
Christian, Barbara. *Black Women Novelists: The Development of a Tradition*. 1980. Westport and London: Greenwood, 1985.
Davis, Todd F. and Kenneth Womack, eds. Preface. *Mapping the Ethical Turn: A Reader in Ethics, Culture, and Literary Theory*. Charlottesville and London: University of Virginia Press, 2001. ix–xiv.
Doctorow, E.L. *Welcome to Hard Times*. 1960. New York: Random House Trade Paperback, 2007.
———. *The Book of Daniel*. 1971. London: Penguin, 2006.
———. *Ragtime*. 1974. London: Penguin, 2006.
———. *Drinks before Dinner*. 1976. New York: Theatre Communications Group, 1996.
———. "False Documents." 1977. *Jack London, Hemingway, and the Constitution: Selected Essays 1977–1992*. Ed. E.L. Doctorow. New York: Random House, 1993. 149–164.
———. *Loon Lake*. 1980. New York: Random House Trade Paperbacks, 2007.
———. *Lives of the Poets: Six Stories and a Novella*. 1984. New York: Plume, 1997.
———. "The Beliefs of Writers." *Michigan Quarterly Review* 24 (Fall 1985): 609–619.
———. *World's Fair*. 1985. New York: Random House Trade Paperbacks, 2007.
———. *Billy Bathgate*. 1989. New York: Random House Trade Paperbacks, 2010.
———. *The Waterworks*. 1994. New York: Random House, 2010.
———. *City of God*. 2000. London: Abacus, 2006.

———. *Sweet Land Stories*. 2004. London: Abacus, 2007.
———. *The March*. 2005. London: Abacus, 2008.
———. *Homer and Langley*. 2009. London: Abacus, 2011.
———. *All the Time in the World*. London: Little Brown, 2011.
———. *Andrew's Brain*. London: Abacus, 2014.
Eagleton, Mary. "Literary Representations of Women." *A History of Feminist Literary Criticism*. Eds. Gill Plain and Susan Sellers. Cambridge, New York: Cambridge UP, 2007. 105–119.
Ellmann, Mary. *Thinking about Women*. New York: Harcourt, 1968.
Erikson, Kai. "Notes on Trauma and Community." *Trauma: Explorations in Memory*. Ed. Cathy Caruth. Baltimore: Johns Hopkins UP, 1995. 183–199.
Escudero, Maite. "The Burden of Shame in Sarah Waters' *The Night Watch*." *Trauma in Contemporary Literature: Narrative and Representation*. Eds. Marita Nadal and Mónica Calvo. New York and London: Routledge, 2014. 223–236.
Felman, Shoshana and Dori Laub. *Testimony: Crises of Witnessing in Literature, Psychoanalysis, and History*. New York: Routledge, 1991.
Felski, Rita. *Literature after Feminism*. Chicago: University of Chicago Press, 2003.
Fetterley, Judith. *The Resisting Reader: A Feminist Approach to American Fiction*. 1978. Bloomington: Indiana UP, 1981.
Figes, Eva. *Patriarchal Attitudes*. 1970. New York: Persea Books, 1987.
Fowler, Douglas. *Understanding E.L. Doctorow*. Columbia: South Carolina UP, 1992.
Friedl, Herwig and Dieter Schulz, eds. *E.L. Doctorow. A Democracy of Perception: A Symposium with and on E. L. Doctorow*. Essen: Verlag Die Blaue Eule, 1988.
———. "A Multiplicity of Witness." *Conversations with E. L. Doctorow*. Ed. Christopher Morris. Jackson: Mississippi UP, 1999. 112–128.
Gentry, Marshall B. "'Ventriloquists' Conversations: The Struggle for Gender Dialogue in E.L. Doctorow and Philip Roth." 1993. *Modern Critical Views: E.L. Doctorow*. Ed. Harold Bloom. Philadelphia: Chelsea House, 2002. 113–132.
Gibbs, Alan. *Contemporary American Trauma Novels*. Edinburgh: Edinburgh UP, 2014.
Gibson, Andrew. *Postmodernity, Ethics, and the Novel*. London and New York: Routledge, 1999.
Gilbert, Sandra and Susan Gubar. *The Madwoman in the Attic: The Woman Writer and the Nineteenth-century Literary Imagination*. 1979. New Haven: Yale UP, 2000.
Gonda, Caroline. "Lesbian Feminist Criticism." *A History of Feminist Literary Criticism*. Eds. Gill Plain and Susan Sellers. Cambridge, New York: Cambridge UP, 2007. 169–186.
Granofsky, Ronald. *The Trauma Novel: Contemporary Symbolic Depictions of Collective Disaster*. New York: Peter Lang, 1995.
Greer, Germaine. *The Female Eunuch* (1970). New York and Toronto: Harper Collins, 2008.
Gregory, Marshall W. "Redefining Ethical Criticism. The Old vs. the New." *Journal of Literary Theory* 4.2 (2010): 273–301.

Harter, Carol C. and James R. Thompson. *E. L. Doctorow*. Boston: Twayne, 1990.
Hartman, Geoffrey. *The Longest Shadow: In the Aftermath of the Holocaust*. Bloomington: Indiana UP, 1996.
——. "Trauma within the Limits of Literature." *European Journal of English Studies* 7.3 (2003): 257–274.
Hekman, Susan J. *Gender and Knowledge: Elements of a Postmodern Feminism*. Boston: Northeastern UP, 1992.
Herman, Judith L. *Trauma and Recovery: The Aftermath of Violence – From Domestic Abuse to Political Terror*. New York: Basic Books, 1992.
Hirsch, Marianne. "Past Lives: Postmemories in Exile." *Poetics Today* 17.4 (1996): 659–686.
Hite, Molly. *The Other Side of the Story: Structures and Strategies of Contemporary Feminist Narrative*. Ithaca: Cornell UP, 1989.
Hogeland, Lisa Maria. *Feminism and Its Fictions: The Consciousness-Raising Novel and the Women's Liberation Movement*. Philadelphia: University of Pennsylvania Press, 1998.
Humm, Maggie. *A Reader's Guide to Contemporary Feminist Literary Criticism*. New York and London: Harvester Wheatsheaf, 1994.
Hutcheon, Linda. *A Poetics of Postmodernism: History, Theory and Fiction*. New York: Routledge, 1988.
Jameson, Fredric. *Postmodernism, Or the Cultural Logic of Late Capitalism*. Durham: Duke UP, 1991.
Kansteiner, Wulf and Harald Weilnböck. "Against the Concept of Cultural Trauma." *Cultural and Memory Studies: An International and Interdisciplinary Handbook*. Eds. Astrid Erll and Ansgar Nünning. Berlin and New York: de Gruyter, 2008. 229–240.
Kaplan, E. Ann. *Trauma Culture: The Politics of Terror and Loss in Media and Literature*. New Brunswick, NJ, and London: Rutgers UP, 2005.
Kaplan, Sarah. "E.L. Doctorow, 'Epic Poet' of America's Past, dies at 84." *The Washington Post* July 22, 2015. Web. 30 May 2016. <www.washingtonpost.com/news/morning-mix/wp/2015/07/22/e-l-doctorow-epic-poet-of-americas-past-dies-at-84/>
Keizer, Arlene R. "Black Feminist Criticism." *A History of Feminist Literary Criticism*. Eds. Gill Plain and Susan Sellers. Cambridge, New York: Cambridge UP, 2007. 154–168.
Kirmayer, Laurence J., Robert Lemelson, and Mark Barad, eds. *Understanding Trauma: Integrating Biological, Clinical and Cultural Perspectives*. Cambridge and New York: Cambridge UP, 2007.
Konner, Melvin. "Trauma, Adaptation, and Resilience: A Cross-Cultural and Evolutionary Perspective." *Understanding Trauma: Integrating Biological, Clinical and Cultural Perspectives*. Eds. Laurence J. Kirmayer, Robert Lemelson, and Mark Barad. Cambridge and New York: Cambridge UP, 2007. 300–338.
LaCapra, Dominick. "Trauma, Absence, Loss." *Critical Inquiry* 25.4 (Summer 1999): 696–727.
——. *Writing History, Writing Trauma*. Baltimore: Johns Hopkins UP, 2001.
Levinas, Emmanuel. *Totality and Infinity: An Essay on Exteriority*. 1961. Trans. by Alphonso Lingis. The Hague: Martinus Nijhoff Publishers, 1979.

Levine, Paul. *E.L. Doctorow: An Introduction*. New York: Methuen, 1985.
Leys, Ruth. *Trauma: A Genealogy*. Chicago and London: The University of Chicago Press, 2000.
Luckhurst, Roger. "Mixing Memory and Desire: Psychoanalysis, Psychology, and Trauma Theory." *Literary Theory and Criticism: An Oxford Guide*. Ed. Patricia Waugh. New York: Oxford UP, 2006. 497–506.
———. *The Trauma Question*. London and New York: Routledge, 2008.
———. "Beyond Trauma: Torturous Times." Beyond Trauma: The Uses of the Past in Twenty-First Century Europe. Spec. issue of *European Journal of English Studies* 14.1 (2010): 11–21.
Meyer Spacks, Patricia. *The Female Imagination*. New York: Knopf, 1975.
Millett, Kate. *Sexual Politics*. 1969. Urbana and Chicago: University of Illinois Press, 2000.
Mitchell, Juliet. *Psychoanalysis and Feminism*. 1974. New York: Basic Books, 2007.
Moers, Ellen. *Literary Women*. Garden City, New York: Doubleday, 1976.
Moi, Toril. *Sexual/Textual Politics: Feminist Literary Theory*. London and New York: Routledge, 1985.
Morris, Christopher D. *Models of Misrepresentation: on the Fiction of E.L. Doctorow*. Jackson: Mississippi UP, 1991.
———. ed. *Conversations with E. L. Doctorow*. Jackson: Mississippi UP, 1999.
Navasky, Victor. "E.L. Doctorow: I Saw a Sign." *Conversations with E.L. Doctorow*. Ed. Christopher Morris. Jackson: Mississippi UP, 1999. 59–63.
Nieman Reports. "Ragtime Revisited: A Seminar with E.L. Doctorow and Joseph Papaleo." *Conversations with E.L. Doctorow*. Ed. Christopher Morris. Jackson: Mississippi UP, 1999. 14–34.
Novick, Peter. *The Holocaust in American Life*. Boston: Houghton Mifflin, 1999.
Parks, John G. *E. L. Doctorow*. New York: Continuum, 1991.
———. "The Politics of Polyphony: The Fiction of E.L. Doctorow." *Twentieth Century Literature* 37.4 (Winter 1991): 454–463.
Pederson, Joshua. "Speak, Trauma: Toward a Revised Understanding of Literary Trauma Theory." *Narrative* 22.3 (Oct. 2014): 333–353.
Plain, Gill and Susan Sellers, eds. Introduction. *A History of Feminist Literary Criticism*. Cambridge, New York: Cambridge UP, 2007. 1–3.
Plain, Gill. Introduction to Part I. *A History of Feminist Literary Criticism*. Eds. Gill Plain and Susan Sellers. Cambridge, New York: Cambridge UP, 2007. 6–10.
Poovey, Mary. "Feminism and Deconstruction." *Feminist Studies* 14.1 (Spring 1988): 51–65.
Radstone, Susannah. "Trauma Theory: Contexts, Politics, Ethics." *Paragraph: A Journal of Modern Critical Theory* 30.1 (2007): 9–29.
Root, Maria. "Reconstructing the Impact of Trauma on Personality." *Personality and Psychopathology: Feminist Reappraisals*. Eds. Laura S. Brown and Mary Ballou. New York: Guilford, 1992. 229–265.
Roth, Michael S. *Memory, Trauma and History: Essays on Living with the Past*. New York: Columbia UP, 2012.
Rothberg, Michael. Preface: Beyond Tancred and Clorinda—Trauma Studies for Implicated Subjects. *The Future of Trauma Theory*. Eds. Gert Buelens,

Sam Durrant, and Robert Eaglestone. London and New York: Routledge, 2014. xi–xviii.

Rousseau, Cécile and Toby Measham. "Posttraumatic Suffering as a Source of Transformation: A Clinical Perspective." *Understanding Trauma: Integrating Biological, Clinical and Cultural Perspectives*. Eds. Laurence J. Kirmayer, Robert Lemelson, and Mark Barad. Cambridge and New York: Cambridge UP, 2007. 275–293.

Schwarz, Daniel R. "A Humanistic Ethics of Reading." *Mapping the Ethical Turn: A Reader in Ethics, Culture, and Literary Theory*. Eds. Todd F. Davis and Kenneth Womack. Charlottesville and London: University of Virginia Press, 2001. 3–15.

Segal, David. "The Time Travels of E.L. Doctorow." *Washington Post* Oct. 1, 2005. Web. 31 May, 2016. <www.washingtonpost.com/wp-dyn/content/article/2005/09/30/AR2005093001847.html>

Siegel, Ben, ed. *Critical Essays on E.L. Doctorow*. New York: G. K. Hall, 2000.

Singer, Linda. "Feminism and Postmodernism." *Feminists Theorize the Political*. Eds. Judith Butler and Joan W. Scott. New York: Routledge, 1992. 464–475.

Showalter, Elaine. *A Literature of Their Own: British Women Writers from Charlotte Brontë to Doris Lessing*. 1977. London: Virago, 2014.

———. "Toward a Feminist Poetic." *The New Feminist Criticism: Essays on Women, Literature & Theory*. Ed. Elaine Showalter. New York: Pantheon Books, 1985. 125–143.

Smith, Barbara. "Towards a Black Feminist Criticism." 1977. *The New Feminist Criticism: Essays on Women, Literature & Theory*. Ed. Elaine Showalter. New York: Pantheon Books, 1985. 168–185.

Thomas, Calvin. "Men and Feminist Criticism." *A History of Feminist Literary Criticism*. Eds. Gill Plain and Susan Sellers. Cambridge, New York: Cambridge UP, 2007. 187–208.

Tokarczyk, Michelle M. *E. L. Doctorow's Skeptical Commitment*. New York: Peter Lang, 2000.

Traverso, Antonio and Mick Broderick. "Interrogating Trauma: Towards a Critical Trauma Studies." *Interrogating Trauma: Collective Suffering in Global Arts and Media*. Eds. Mick Broderick and Antonio Traverso. London and New York: Routledge, 2011. 3–16.

Trenner, Richard, ed. *E.L. Doctorow: Essays and Conversations*. Princeton: Ontario Review, 1983.

Updike, John. "A Cloud of Dust." *Due Considerations: Essays and Criticism*. New York: Alfred A. Knopf, 2007. 293–299.

Vickroy, Laurie. *Trauma and Survival in Contemporary Fiction*. Virginia: Virginia UP, 2002.

———. *Reading Trauma Narratives: The Contemporary Novel and the Psychology of Oppression*. Charlottesville: University of Virginia Press, 2015.

Walker Bergström, Catharine. *Intuition of an Infinite Obligation: Narrative Ethics and Postmodern Gnostics in the Fiction of E. L. Doctorow*. Frankfurt: Peter Lang, 2010.

Waugh, Patricia. *Metafiction: the Theory and Practice of Self-conscious Fiction*. London and New York: Routledge, 1984.

40 Introduction

———. *Feminine Fictions: Revisiting the Postmodern*. London and New York: Routledge, 2012.
Weber, Bruce. "E.L. Doctorow Dies at 84; Literary Time Traveler Stirred Past Into Fiction." *The New York Times* 21 July, 2015. Web. 31 May, 2016. <www.nytimes.com/2015/07/22/books/el-doctorow-author-of-historical-fiction-dies-at-84.html?_r=0>
Whitehead, Anne. *Trauma Fiction*. Edinburgh: Edinburgh UP, 2004.
Williams, John. *Fiction as False Document: The Reception of E. L. Doctorow in the Postmodern Age*. Columbia: Camden House, 1996.
Wolff, Janet. *Feminine Sentences: Essays on Women and Culture*. Cambridge: Polity Press, 1990.
Zimmerman, Bonnie. "What Has Never Been: An Overview of Lesbian Feminist Criticism." 1981. *Making a Difference: Feminist Literary Criticism*. Eds. Gayle Green and Coppélia Kahn. London: Routledge, 2002. 178–210.

1 *Welcome to Hard Times*
The Frontier Reconsidered

Published in 1960, *Welcome to Hard Times* is E.L. Doctorow's debut novel. It has been called a minor work by some of Doctorow's critics, probably dazzled by the bright success of later works. Indeed, its reception upon publication was rather cold. It received a number of positive reviews, such as by Wirt Williams, who found the novel "taut and dramatic, exciting and successfully symbolic" (7). But steady critical attention did not turn toward the book until after the publication of *Ragtime*, whose commercial and critical success led to what John Williams has termed the "canonization" of the novel (60). Kevin Starr, for instance, writing for the *New Republic*, called the novel "a superb piece of fiction" when it was reissued in 1975 (25). Yet, criticism of the novel has remained rather scarce, especially when compared to Doctorow's later novels.

At its simplest, *Welcome to Hard Times* is a historical fiction set in the Dakota Territory in the 1870s, right after the discovery of gold. It deals with the destruction, rebirth and final eradication of a small Frontier settlement during the colonization of the West. However, in spite of its setting, characters and action, the novel is a highly crafted and socially committed novel masquerading as a Western that may be claimed to have inaugurated what has been termed the 'new Western' or 'post-Western.'[1] Asked in an interview about his reasons for writing a Western when such type of fiction was diametrically opposed to the kind of books that most serious writers had been producing at the time, Doctorow explained that he "liked the idea of using disreputable genre materials and doing something serious with them" (in Morris 77). His efforts are coherent with the postmodernist trend that was emerging at the time in opposition to modernist high-brow poetics which sought to replenish fiction through the assimilation of marginal, non-canonical genres—such as science fiction, the detective story or the Western—into mainstream literature. In addition, the popular Western plausibly attracted Doctorow's attention because, in the socio-political climate of the time, the mythical vision of the West that the genre had been projecting offered interesting possibilities for ironic reformulation. That vision had depicted the extension of the Frontier as an essential factor in the myth of American exceptionalism by allowing for constant personal and national regeneration.

In spite of its apparent simplicity and short length, *Welcome to Hard Times* succeeds in engaging the reader through its intense tales of suffering and pain. It narrates the ruination of a prostitute who endures rape and severe injury at the hands of a ruthless outlaw. It relates the struggle of an old man to rebuild his community, who finally sees all his hopes wrecked and faces death alone, surrounded by post-apocalyptic ruin. It recounts the moral corruption of a young boy at the hands of a mad woman and her insatiable thirst for revenge. And it depicts the physical and moral destruction of a small frontier settlement. Most interestingly, the novel manages to convey all these stories in a well-crafted narrative that both updates and subverts the thematic and narratological conventions of the classical Western and, in so doing, it sends an important message about the ills of contemporary US society.

Shame, Guilt, Violence and Trauma

Welcome to Hard Times opens *in medias res*, with an extremely violent scene. By the end of the first chapter half of the inhabitants of Hard Times—the fictional frontier settlement in which the events take place—will have been killed, the other half will have hastily packed up their things and left, and the town will have burned to the ground. Only a badly injured prostitute, a newly orphaned boy, the old and broken Mayor and a detached Native-American healer remain in the place to fend for themselves. From then on, *Welcome to Hard Times* becomes Mayor Blue's account of this new surrogate family's physical and psychological plight to survive and rebuild the town, up to their death and the whole place's inexorable final destruction. As I will attempt to prove, the articulation of the novel's two main characters—Molly Riordan and the homodiegetic narrator and fictive author Mayor Blue[2]—throws *Welcome to Hard Times* into a fictional exploration of the imagined psychological aftereffects of traumatic experiences, namely rape, extreme physical injury and loss.[3]

Post-Traumatic Stress and the Death Drive

As the short plot survey above suggests, the novel provides a fictional rendition of the female protagonist's post-traumatic condition. Molly is a prostitute in the settlement's old saloon who is savagely raped and burned almost to death by Clay Turner, dubbed the Bad Man from Bodie. This extremely traumatic encounter causes her to sustain long-lasting physical and psychological scars, locking her into an inescapable spiral of pain, fear, hate and thirst for revenge. Reminiscent of classical (Freudian) theory of trauma, Molly's obsessive re-experiencing of the traumatic moment is depicted, and may be read, as a process of post-traumatic 'acting out' (LaCapra 21). Thus, for instance, when the orphan boy Jimmy falls ill and the Native-American healer John Bear spreads a healing paste on his body, she holds him tightly against her chest, whispering: "Let it burn, let it burn deep!" (Doctorow, *Hard Times* 95).[4] As this quotation suggests, Jimmy's burning pain and his feeble attempts to free himself from it force Molly to relive the experience that traumatized her, caught in a sort of transfixed nightmare. Such description echoes Cathy Caruth's theorization that "to be traumatized is precisely to be possessed by an image or event" (4–5).

Molly's possession by the past also seems to involve a fixation with the idea that the Bad Man will return: "'I can't forget him. I see him in my sleep.' [...] 'I keep hearing his voice: 'I'll be back', he says. It's what he said to me'" (132). Indeed, to Blue's warning that Turner is not the only Bad Man riding the land, she replies: "Oh Christ there are hundreds, yes I know, Thousands. And they're going to get me—they're all coming for me!" (148). Such response recalls Donald Winnicott's theorization of traumatic reenactment: "In traumatic wounding, in terms of memory and expectation, the anxiety that occurs is driven by an implicit certainty that what has already happened is going to happen" (in Kauffman 7). In other words, when the traumatic event occurs, the self does not experience it in the present but, rather, the anxiety that he or she feels results from anticipating the event. Molly's behavior also recalls Maurice Blanchot's view that when the trauma is re-enacted through its post-traumatic effects, the self anticipates again "what has already happened but not been experienced" (in Kauffman 7). Furthermore, Molly's condition is not only fixed in her mind; it is not merely psychological, but also physical. The pain stays with her for months until the blisters on her back heal, but then the scars remain. The traumatic event, it follows, has been inscribed into her body, carved into the skin of her back. It is worth pointing out that, as Anne Whitehead explains, although the body has been central to Western conceptions of memory, it has tended to be subordinated to consciousness and thereby overlooked (11). Anticipating the importance of body memories for recent trauma theory, Molly's body charts a graphic cartography of pain through the physical marks that remain in her back, which mirror the scars that mar her psyche.

Molly's psychological condition is also characterized by an obsessive need to remember, to the extent that it appears as if she consciously or unconsciously wanted to commemorate the past traumatic encounter. This may be seen in her symbolic monumentalization of the stiletto: "She found the stiletto she had dropped the day of the fire and came back to nail it, teary-eyed, above our door" (85). This knife is the weapon that Blue gives her as he pushes her through the saloon doors at the beginning of the novel, hoping that she will kill the Bad Man and rid the whole town of the problem. But upon seeing her friend Florence's dead body, naked and bent over the stairs railing, the stiletto slips out of Molly's hand. Thus, the dropped stiletto that Molly feels compelled to nail outside her house for everyone else to see symbolically stands for her helplessness. Helplessness, let it be said, has been widely acknowledged to be vital to making an extremely negative experience traumatic (see van der Kolk and van der Hart 175). Molly's sense of helplessness results from society's failure or unwillingness to protect her, from the deficiency of the Western community as a social body that guarantees the survival and well-being of its members. From the very beginning, it seems obvious that the only tie connecting the first inhabitants of Hard Times is economic (self-)interest, to the extent that it is hardly surprising that the arrival of the Bad Man could cause the whole community to disintegrate. This seconds a point also made by David Gross, who claims that Doctorow's central concern is "the terrible helplessness in a world where humans are connected only by profit" (135). And so, when the threat of destruction materializes in the figure of the Bad Man, those who have not been murdered swiftly pack up and leave, not bothering themselves with the dreadful screams that are coming from the saloon. Such behavior underscores a general lack of sense of belonging to the community, no attachment to the land and little interest in the fate of neighboring human beings. As Blue aptly puts it on the second page of the novel, "[i]n this country a man's pride is not to pay attention" (4).

Furthermore, the protagonist's need to remember her traumatic experience has important connotations. For one thing, it hints at the conflict that has got hold of her, which might be the key to understanding the character. As the novel progresses, it becomes obvious that Molly is deeply torn by the battle that is being waged inside her between the pull of the past and the drive toward the future. Such conflict brings to mind Freud's latter model of trauma, and its opposition between *Eros* and *Thanatos*. Taking two concepts that were inseparable in earlier Greek thought, Freud articulates his theory of the 'death drive'—opposed to his previously theorized 'pleasure principle'—as an effort to understand the cause of the repetition of past traumatic events. In *Beyond the Pleasure Principle*, Freud observes that there is a tendency to repeat or re-enact traumatic experiences, a phenomenon that he terms "compulsion to repeat" (19) and which is related to a human impulse toward self-destruction. Thus, with his rearticulation of *Eros* and *Thanatos*, Freud described a conflict within human nature between a drive toward death and a push to perpetuate life through self-preservation.

Echoing Freudian theory, the novel articulates Molly's condition as a fictionalized conflict between the instinctive need to put herself out of harm's way and the urge to risk her life in order to take revenge. At first, Molly repeatedly begs Blue to take her away from Hard Times, obsessed with the idea that Turner is going to return to get her: "Molly broke down crying and said: 'Blue, for God's sake let's leave this place'" (148). In her attempt to leave the past behind, Molly even seeks to rebuild her life with Blue and Jimmy, building a sort of surrogate family amid all the destruction. Thus, she becomes Blue's common-law wife and, for a while, bonds with him at a psychological and physical level:

> And as I sat with Molly another evening under the sky, with a new moon making us shadows to each other, I talked so easy I almost didn't know myself; and she talked with me and it was as if we were two new people sprung from our old pain. (131)

As for Jimmy, Molly adopts him as her child and clumsily mothers him through his illness: "Molly tended to him each minute of the time and didn't ask any help from me" (99). In short, after a dreadful winter during which her burns have slowly healed, a big change seems to have been operated on Molly: "The frown was gone from her forehead, a measure of joy in her eyes" (115). Yet, the promise of happiness and the hope for a better future that the spring seems to represent do not last long, and Molly soon "giv[es in] to the devil that grinned at her" (150). It becomes obvious that Molly's psychological wounds are too deep, and have remained open all the while. For Freud, as for Doctorow, the drive toward death seems to be stronger than the push toward life. And so, as the reader eventually finds out, Molly's traumatic embitterment wins out, triggered by her panicked reaction every time the rest of the inhabitants welcome new settlers into the town: "It was as if each person coming to town was taking away a little more of her air to breathe" (157). After a period in which her trauma has been lying dormant, Molly progressively turns into a cruel and violent creature, and her main survival strategy becomes the projection of her pain onto others, as we will see presently.

Another remarkable way in which Molly is shown to have been changed by her traumatic experience is in her newly found Christian faith. And so, for instance, when she is found by the new prostitutes at John Bear's shack, she suffers a fit:

> She was crying and beating her fists on the ground: 'For Godsake I'll die if they touch me, oh God, keep them away...' But what was worse, she suddenly left off and crawled around the dirt until she found her little cross. She clutched it in her hands and began to mumble to herself, her lips moved fast and her eyes began to roll upwards. (42)

Throughout the narrative, she is described as always carrying that cross hanging from her neck, the very cross that she clutched when the blisters in her back were at their most painful. However, the religion that she embraces is not one inspired by forgiveness, but one based on a belief in God's punishing nature and in retribution. Indeed, Molly's sole obsession is to take revenge on the man who caused her those tremendous physical and psychological scars, regardless of what harm this may bring to herself or others. She is so fixated on the idea of taking revenge that the purpose of her life becomes to wait for the Bad Man's return: "[…] this was what she wanted, for the Bad Man to return! She'd been waiting for him, a proper faithful wife. Nothing mattered to her, not me, not Jimmy, just herself and her Man from Bodie" (197). Furthermore, Molly is willing to do anything to achieve retribution: she trains Jimmy to obey her every command and has him learn how to shoot. Then, when the Bad Man finally returns, she tries to convince the deadshot Jenks to kill him, and offers herself in exchange for his services, causing him to be killed by Turner: "Her voice was as soft and natural as a sane woman's. […] 'Just *him*' Molly gripped his shirt again, 'just him, just that Bad Man from Bodie, you know what he did to me, you have any idea?'" (198; emphasis in the original).

It seems evident, therefore, that Molly has been dramatically transformed by her traumatic encounter with the Bad Man, to the point of acknowledging that "[t]he woman in John Bear's shack was no longer Molly. What had happened in Avery's saloon could never be undone" (36). Molly carries the Bad Man's presence in her mind and body as a permanent inscription that haunts her. Trapped in a Freudian spiral of repetition compulsion and finally submitting to the death drive, she dies locked in a deadly embrace with the Bad Man, their blood mixing, both killed by Jimmy. In short, it seems adequate to claim that in Molly's fictional journey after facing an overwhelming traumatic event, there is no working through; no healing is possible.

Shame and Guilt

Mayor Blue is similarly shown to suffer post-traumatic stress right after the apocalypse brought about by the Bad Man. Although he has sustained no physical injuries, he is deeply affected by the destruction of the town that he helped build in the middle of the wilderness. As he puts it, he cannot get over "the shock of seeing air where the town had been" (32) before the fire:

> It was no pain I felt but a steady ache, like some hand was gently squeezing my heart. It never left me. I would look out to the graves in the flats or look up to the rocks or over at the scar of the old street and always I saw the face of the Man from Bodie. (72)

After the town's destruction, death permeates life in Hard Times in the form of a wound that cannot be fully healed. As Blue bitterly puts it, "[y]ou could step out the door and the scar of the old town was blocked from your sight, but the scar was still there" (149). What affects Blue the most, however, is witnessing Molly's ongoing suffering and having to live with the knowledge that he did nothing to avoid it. In that sense,

Blue's initial post-traumatic response to the traumatic events progressively gives way to a complex condition that is mainly characterized by strong feelings of guilt and shame.

At this point a brief reflection on the cultural meanings of both concepts might be in order. In the 1950s, Silvan Tomkins put forward his revolutionary theory of affects as a response to what he perceived as Freud's trivialization of the affect system in favor of a theory based on drives (Kosofsky Sedgwick and Frank 7, 34).[5] In his seminal study of affects, Tomkins defined shame as "the affect of indignity, of defeat, of transgression and of alienation" (in Kosofsky Sedgwick and Frank 133). He further explained that "shame strikes deepest into the heart of man" and that "[it] is felt as an inner torment, a sickness of the soul" (133). However, he argued that shame and guilt cannot be distinguished from each other at the level of affect, claiming that shame is the affect that underlies guilt: "[S]hame at a failure to cope successfully with a challenge and guilt for an immorality are the same experience" (143). Contrarily, Timothy Bewes believes that "[s]hame should not be talked about alongside guilt. [...] The difference between guilt and shame is a difference between the narrative viability of the individual as an ethical category, including the possibility of its expression and/or redemption" (28). The contrast between shame and guilt might, thus, be found at the intersection between oneself and the other, between the omission to act and the failure to act ethically. In other words, shame arises from the discontinuity between a person's sense of self and his/her reflection in the eyes of the other, from the shock of looking from the position of the other and finding someone that one is not. Guilt, however, has to do with the subconscious feeling that one has done something morally wrong (Kauffman 4). Maite Escudero further points to a clear difference between the two in that "whereas guilt attaches to what one does, therefore signaling a specific experience, shame attaches to and sharpens the sense of what one is [...]" (225).

In keeping with this understanding, Blue's guilt might be said to stem from his active role in Molly's suffering, from his decision to push her through the saloon doors rather than help her escape or hide. In other words, Blue's role as accomplice of sorts collides with his own moral code as can be inferred from his behavior throughout the narrative, arousing in him strong feelings of guilt. Blue's shame, however, originates from two different sources. On the one hand, it is directly connected to his failure to confront the Bad Man, which causes Blue to appear like a coward in everyone's eyes, including Turner's. In a society in which a man's worth is measured by his bravery, as we will see, Blue is deeply ashamed of the paralysis that seized him before the Bad Man, making him comply with his demands: "Right then my hand began to move and I meant it to go for my gun. But it went instead for the glass on the bar" (18). As Jeffrey Kauffman has noted, "traumatic grief shame occurs in fragmentations or dissociations, defilements and humiliations, helplessness, and other overwhelming grief anxieties" (8). Similarly, Victoria Burrows associates shame with feelings of powerlessness, degradation, deficiency and misery. Such is the shame that Blue feels that the scene keeps intruding into his imagination: "The Bad Man's grinning face came back to me and I felt my shy hand choosing the glass he offered [...]. the same rage rose in my throat for something that was too strong for me, something I could not cope with" (27).

On the other hand, Blue's shame also responds to Molly's contempt for him. Blue realizes that Molly is unable to forgive him, projecting on him all her spite and resentment: "[...] when she had a mind to she could make anything in the world seem like a taint on me" (72). Both through Blue's narrative perspective and her own words, it becomes obvious that Molly's shattered mind cannot reconcile his original impassivity with his later vows to protect her, once the damage has been done: "I suppose you'll protect me! I suppose you'll take care of me, just like the last time. Good old Mayor, fast with the gun he is, no worries with Mayor Blue marching behind your skirts. No worries at all!" (149). Furthering research on the affect, it should be added that Victoria Burrows defines shame as

> toxic, as destructively disorientating, as a moment of heightened and tormenting self-consciousness in which the self is confronted by the self at its most despicable. [...] It is an acute, painful, inarticulate experience, which leaves its subjects feeling exposed, silenced, impotent. (126–127)

Echoing this theorization, Blue is shown to be still tormented by his sense of disgrace and his feelings of inferiority with respect to Molly: "Her chin was always in the air and the chain and cross was always plain to see around her neck. So that whenever I looked at her I was looking at rebuke" (71).[6] The weight of Blue's self-contempt is such that he considers leaving the town and abandoning Molly and the orphan boy Jimmy to their fate, but he is "locked" by Molly's "terrible green gaze" (30); that is, he is paralyzed by the shame that he feels at perceiving such contempt in her eyes. Levinas speaks of the effects of shame in such terms: "Its deepest manifestations are an eminently personal matter [...] the necessity of fleeing, in order to hide oneself, is put in check by the impossibility of fleeing oneself" (64).

At other times, Blue admits to have been moved to violence: "[...] great anger rose in me [...] I damned her for the grip she had on my life, this unrelenting whore" (93). Indeed, a central feature of the affects of shame and guilt is that they have been documented to often co-occur with violent behavior. A key study in this respect is James Gilligan's groundbreaking prison research (2003). Gilligan finds that shame and guilt can potentially lead to violence (toward the self and/or toward others) in cases of overwhelming humiliation and mortification, as a result of what he calls "the death of the self" (1153). By this he refers to a "feeling of deadness and numbness more intolerable than anything" (1152), "more tormenting than the death of the body could possibly be" (1153). This feeling of extreme humiliation, Gilligan suggests, is the basic psychological motive of violent behavior, since it may lead either to the "wish to ward off or eliminate the feeling of shame [...] and replace it with its opposite, the feeling of pride" through hurting others (1154), or to the need for self-punishment—the wish to harm oneself—after experiencing the impulse to injure others (1168). As a result, Gilligan explains, after extreme humiliation, if a person does not perceive him- or herself as having nonviolent means for restoring their pride (their self-love) "the activity and aggressiveness stimulated by shame can manifest itself in violent, sadistic, even homicidal behavior" (1168). Guilt feelings, on the contrary, "motivate [people] to introject the anger instead, directing it against themselves, as a result of which they experience a need for punishment, which may manifest itself in masochistic or even suicidal behavior" (1168).

Returning to Doctorow's novel, it soon becomes obvious that what Mayor Blue desperately needs is for Molly to forgive him. And when the spring comes and they start a brief lapse of peaceful cohabitation, his condition briefly improves: "If I can be alright in your eyes I'll be alright in my own" (132), which Molly seems to do as she concedes—"We've both suffered" (132). Thus, against Molly's scars as constant reminder of what happened and the inescapable sight of the burnt ruins of the old town, Blue strives to leave the past behind and move on. In other words, his desperate need to reconcile himself with his share of blame for Molly's psychological devastation as well as with his inability to confront the Bad Man is directly connected to his subsequent obsession with rebuilding Hard Times, feeling that "anyone new helped bury the past" (123). He longs to recover a sense of community to which they can all belong in order to ease his conscience. Ever the optimist, he takes it upon himself to rebuild Hard Times and convince new settlers to stay—"more fools for [his] town," as Molly calls them (118). Blue has firm confidence in the idea of community as the only means to resist evil: "[...] I doubt it but if it's so, if he [the Bad Man] does come back then we'll be ready for him. We'll all be ready" (132). He seems to be convinced, or rather needs to believe, that it is possible to build a peaceful community in the wilderness, grounded on ties of respect, empathy and cooperation that will guarantee the social health of the town as well as the well-being of its inhabitants. Indeed, as Hard Times starts to grow again, Blue's optimism makes him see good signs everywhere: "A person cannot live without looking for good signs, you just cannot do it, and I thought these signs were good" (89). However, Molly's fear that Turner will return finally turns her against Blue, rekindling that "almost forgotten pain" (149) and burying him in the depths of shame with her renewed contempt.

The Bad Man does eventually come back, literally bringing the past traumatic experience back into the present for Molly and Blue. The novel's articulation of Turner's second coming may be seen as a fictionalized representation of the Freudian 'return of the repressed' as it plays out in the context of trauma—what Cathy Caruth has described as "the literal return of the event against the will of the one it inhabits" (5). After a period of "latency" (Freud, *Moses and Monotheism* 66) in which the prosperity of the town and the need to hold on to good signs have kept at bay Blue's memories of the traumatic event and his own sense of the shamefulness of his behavior, the repressed memories are belatedly repeated in a more than literal manner: upon his return, Turner sees Mae, one of the new prostitutes in town and calls, "Hey honey" (195); Blue explains that "[i]n that moment I could feel my heart tipping, spilling out its shame, its nausea. I had to run from the Trick, I couldn't tolerate it, what other name is there for the mockery that puts us back in our own steps?" (195). As this quotation suggests, Blue does not merely re-experience the events, triggered by the return of the Bad Man; they unfold again right in front of his eyes, giving him an odd second chance to redeem himself in his own eyes and Molly's.

Blue does seize the opportunity and indeed, this time, he manages to knock down the Bad Man. Yet, in order to do so his mind dissociates to spare him the suffering of literally reliving the traumatic source of his shame: "The voice in my throat someone else's, some stranger's voice doing my work while I watched quietly [...]" (205). Such description echoes Sandra Bloom's theorization of dissociation as an evolutionary survival strategy that guarantees our nervous system's protection from extreme stress: "Dissociation is a primary response to traumatic experience [... that] allows us to [...] tolerate irreconcilable conflicts" but "the result is diminished integration and therefore impaired performance" of vital mental functions (201–212). Indeed, it is worth pointing out that, at this point, Blue's narration starts to become delusional and furiously paced, mirroring his own mental breakdown:

> She stood against the wall as far as she could and watched me drop him on the table. [...] And I wish now I could not have seen what happened, or if I had to see it that my mind could split me from the memory. I would like to die on some green somewhere in the coolness of a tree's shadow, when did I last sit with my back against a tree? The wish is so strong in me, like a thirst, I believe I must perish from it. (208)

Furthermore, as the end of the story approaches, there are constant references to the present time of the narration as well as intrusive prolepses, which anticipate the long-hinted-at outcome of events and offer a glimpse of Blue's tormented mind: "In all that noise I can't be sure what I saw, there was moonlight hot as the sun, bright as noon, but it was like the light of pain shining from the blackness. 'Jenks!' I remember Molly screamed [...]" (185). Toward the end of the novel, the narration also acquires a much more filmic quality, to the extent that the reader may become ensnared by the haunting apocalyptic images of destruction: "In the great silence between that saloon door and me there was no movement. But all around there was riot" (206). This is particularly true of Blue's final description of Hard Times the morning after the second arrival of the Bad Man, when he recounts the dead; one can even imagine the eye of the camera slowly moving from one cadaver to the next under a burning-red sun, as Blue's voice-over admits that "[he] can forgive anyone but [him]self" (210).

Blue's traumatic self-blame and his deeply rooted feelings of guilt and shame are brought back to their highest pitch by Molly's death at the hands of the orphaned boy Jimmy, an event caused by Blue's deranged decision to drag the unconscious Turner back to Molly's kitchen table, and by the spectacle of the buzzards feasting on the dead:

> When I think Ezra Maple might have put him [Jimmy] up on his mule and ridden him off to learn the storekeep's trade [...] before Molly ever put her hooks into him, a carpenter's son, just a hollow-eye orphan—a groan pushes through my lips like my ghost already in its Hell before I am dead. (208)

The circumstances of the terrible event compel Blue to write about what happened. Interestingly, Jennifer Biddle has described the ambivalent duality of the psychic structure of shame as follows:

> As much as shame seeks to avert itself—there is no feeling more painful—shame seeks to confess. To be heard, to be borne by another, to find a witness—shame seeks to be allowed the very condition denied it in its rupture —recognition by another. For shame arises from a failure to be recognized. (227)

Echoing such theorization, the narrator's desperate wish to be acknowledged as different from Molly's perception of him may be what motivates Blue to start writing the story of Hard Times, in the middle of its post-apocalyptic ruin and numbed by the pain of Jimmy's shot:

> I am writing this and maybe it will be recovered and read; and I'll say now how I picture some reader, a gentleman in a stuffed chair with a rug under him [...]. Do you think, mister, with all that settlement around you that you're freer than me to make your fate? Do you *click your tongue* at my story? (184; emphasis added)[7]

As this quote suggests, Mayor Blue is caught between the need to confess his guilt and shame and thus atone, and the fear to be judged for it. His narration seeks catharsis; he has tried to enact a textual burial of the dead through the act of storytelling. Narrative has been identified by trauma theorists as a therapeutic device because of its ability to transmit, as LaCapra has put it, "a plausible 'feel' for experience" (13). Blue's attempt to write his ghosts off, to heal through the act of writing, echoes Suzette Henke's concept of 'scriptotherapy,' which offers the possibility of "reinventing the self and reconstructing the subject ideologically" and "encourages the author/narrator to reassess the past" (xv). Such understanding also recalls Sandra Bloom's conclusion that "artistic performance is the bridge across the black hole of trauma, the evolved individual and group response to the tragic nature of human existence" (210).

However, the process of working through is not accomplished, for Blue is still deeply buried under his shame and guilt: "What more could I have done—if I hadn't believed, they'd be alive today. Oh Molly, oh my boy [...] no matter what I've done it has failed" (212). As Jeffrey Kauffman has argued, "[s]hame is the *concealment power* and *enforcer* of repression and dissociation. The shame of the repressed and dissociated returning compels their repetition" (8; emphasis in the original). In other words, shame is perceived as blocking the process of working through. This view seems to be echoed at the level of textual implications in *Welcome to Hard Times*, since it becomes obvious that the act of writing has not allowed Blue to find a long-sought peace of mind as he faces his own death: "And in the miserable waste of our three lives I want to declare only for my own guilt" (197).

Beyond Binarism: The Victim-Bystander-Perpetrator Figure

The question arises whether the implied author coincides with the homodiegetic narrator in his distribution of the blame. Dominick LaCapra has claimed that "with respect to historical trauma and its representation, the distinction between victims, perpetrators, and bystanders is crucial" (79). From this, it follows that the status of any participant in the experience of trauma should be ascribable, and yet that does not seem to be an easy task in the case of *Welcome to Hard Times*. The novel's textual implications seem to favor a non-judgmental, anti-categorical narration in which Blue, Molly and Jimmy occupy a liminal position in the continuum that trauma theory establishes between the categories of victim, bystander and perpetrator.

In the case of Blue, the analysis carried out so far reveals that, strictly speaking, he can be considered neither a perpetrator, nor an innocent bystander: he is not a rapist or a murderer but, at the same time, he has *not* merely failed to act to help Molly; for one thing, he does push her through the saloon doors even though she has dropped the stiletto, ignoring her pleas for help. Following Hannah Arendt's famous distinction between guilt and responsibility (146), while Blue is not guilty of hurting Molly, he is at least presented as responsible for her traumatic condition in that he complies with the Bad Man's violent demands. To complicate things further, Blue is indeed another victim of the Bad Man, since he has faced a near-death experience at his hands, he is deprived of a normal life and, as we have seen, he develops a number of symptoms that may be qualified as post-traumatic stress. Yet, his own guilt and shame, as well as his role as facilitator of Turner's violence, problematize an understanding of Blue as a victim. This may owe to the widespread tendency among some trauma commentators to associate the state of victimhood with that of moral superiority, as argued before. Thus, it is possible to claim that Blue has the mutual status of victim, perpetrator and bystander, for which the novel grants him neither full sympathy nor absolute disapproval.[8]

The problematization of trauma categories that the novel conducts is further substantiated by the articulation of Molly and Jimmy. In the case of the latter, he is orphaned by Turner's violence. The loss of his father does not appear to particularly affect him at a first stage, since the pain of seeing his father die in his arms seems not to have been registered by his brain. It is only belatedly that he reacts to his loss, when he sees the buzzards circling around his father's grave: "The boy was huddled on top of the mound with his hands over his head, he was crying and screaming although he had hardly whimpered when Fee died [...]. 'They're gonna get my Pa, the birds are gonna get my Pa'" (25–26). From the very beginning, Blue endeavors to take care of Jimmy, providing for him as best as he can in terms of food and shelter, but he fails terribly as a prosthetic father, for which he also blames himself: "I wished I had said something to make him feel better, or maybe tousled his head" (63). As a result of Blue's failure, Jimmy is left at the mercy of Molly's deranged bitterness: "Jimmy listened to everything she said like it was gospel [...] he would drink up her words like they were mother's milk" (151). The narrator's choice of words is particularly interesting, because Molly has become Jimmy's surrogate mother, and the nourishing milk that she has metaphorically given him throughout the story is poisoned with her spite and resent. Toward the end of the novel, it becomes obvious that Molly has turned Jimmy into her accomplice in her orchestrated revenge against Blue and the Bad Man, "a proper mount for her own ride to Hell" (160). Furthermore, he ends up killing both Molly and Turner, shocked by the sight of the entranced Molly as she stabs the Bad Man, "almost dancing with the grace of retribution" (209). Right afterward, he leaves Hard Times transformed, we learn, into another Bad Man. The ambiguity of these three characters with regard to the three trauma categories or subject positions brings to mind Primo Levi's 'gray zone.' As such, the novel raises the question of the existence of problematic cases which would contest classical trauma theory's reliance on clear-cut distinctions. In short, writing long before the basic trauma paradigm was configured, E.L. Doctorow debunks in *Welcome to Hard Times* the rule of the either/or that certain strands of trauma theory have tended to establish, as LaCapra's words quoted above suggest. The novel supports instead a rejection of binary thinking by stressing the notion that limits can easily become fuzzy in the context of trauma.

Concluding Remarks

As the analysis above has attempted to show, *Welcome to Hard Times* narrates events of extreme violence and suffering, representing the main characters' traumatic condition and emphasizing the complexity of their symptoms in a narrative that refuses to sentimentalize trauma. Furthermore, Doctorow's novel explores the disastrous consequences of guilt and shame, assessing the possibility of overcoming them through the act of writing. Finally, *Welcome to Hard Times* problematizes the relationship among the categories of victim, perpetrator and bystander, highlighting the extremely thin line that separates them in the context of psychological trauma. These concerns evidence a preoccupation on Doctorow's part with human suffering, with our capacity for evil and with the human drive toward self-destruction. The most crucial link between *Welcome to Hard Times* and trauma is precisely the haunting legacy of suffering and death, which has been described as "a universal/essential element of human experience that cannot be fully confronted but can be symbolized" (Vickroy 224).

In Search for a New Gender Order

Perhaps one of the features most widely associated with the Western by the popular imagination is the representation of the male protagonist as a violent, rugged individual hero. His female counterpart is, in turn, frequently articulated as a refined, virtuous and determined defendant of love, peace and community, whose vulnerability nevertheless requires and justifies the use of violence by the manly hero to guarantee her protection and the continuation of life in the Frontier (see Bevilacqua, "Revision" 81, 85). Weary of what he probably perceived as naïve oversimplification, it is my contention that E.L. Doctorow took it upon himself to subvert traditional gender configurations as portrayed in the classical Western. Indeed, the discussion of gender models becomes a key element in Doctorow's reworking of the conventions of the genre.[9] As I will attempt to prove, *Welcome to Hard Times* features alternative and transgressive models and attitudes toward the masculine and the feminine, and it engages in a complex exploration of gender violence and oppression.

Subversion of Gender Roles

To begin with, it is readily apparent that conflicting and often contradictory references to masculinity pervade *Welcome to Hard Times*.[10] A few comments about the notion of the masculine seem in order. As Raewyn Connell explains in her seminal study, "masculinities are configurations of practice structured by gender relations. They are inherently historical; and their making and remaking is a political process affecting the balance of interests in society and the direction of social change" (44). She further defines masculinity as "simultaneously a place in gender relations, the practices through which men and women engage that place in gender, and the effects of these practices in bodily experience, personality and culture" (71). Freud was the first to disrupt the "apparently natural object of masculinity" and made an enquiry into its composition "both possible and, in a sense, necessary" (Connell 8). Later on, in the 1970s and 1980s, it became a central focus of research thanks to the impulse provided by second-wave feminism and its examination of the concept of gender and its intimate connection to social relations and power structures. Interestingly, Connell explains, a key area of enquiry since the 'birth' of masculinity studies has been the cultural imagery of masculinity (31). Indeed, in mass culture "[t]rue masculinity is almost always thought to proceed from men's bodies—to be inherent in a male body or to express something about a male body" (Connell 45). Echoing this theorization, in the world of *Welcome to Hard Times*, masculinity is measured by most of the male inhabitants of the settlement by a man's ability to make himself respected through the use of force, hold his liquor and perform sexually. And so, for instance, hearing Florence's screams while she is being savagely raped, the men who are gathered in the saloon can only marvel at the Bad Man's sexual prowess: mistaking her wails for orgasm they jealously wonder "what kind of man it was who could make her scream" (4). As this quote suggests, such views of masculinity effectively place the saloon and its prostitutes at the center of male life in the Frontier.

A similar attitude seems to be held by Molly herself. Indeed, she represents the most overtly polarized attitude toward the masculine in the novel. For her, bravery and the skillful use of weapons are the only features that qualify a man as such. It is worth pointing out that, in her understanding of gender identity, maleness—male biological sex—and masculinity equal what has traditionally been termed "manliness"— possessing qualities considered appropriate to, or typical of, a man, such as courage or vigor. And so, when the barman Avery forces Molly to go to the saloon to get rid of the Bad Man, she complains to Blue in such terms: "He's some man, isn't he Blue?" (9). Paradoxically, for Molly the only real men in town seem to be the Bad Man—"Christ that Bad Man's the only man in town!" (16)—and later on the shooter Jenks, whose arrival in Hard Times becomes the perfect excuse to humiliate Blue for what she perceives as his previous cowardice: "'I thank you, Mr. Jenks', Molly said looking my way, 'It's good to find a man in these parts. I wish the Lord my husband knew the gun the way you do!'" (74).

The phallic symbolism of the gun, which has traditionally been perceived as an extension of the penis and, thus, as a mark of manliness, could not have escaped Doctorow through his early knowledge of Freudian psychology. Such association also brings to mind Lacan's idea of the masculine "parade" of virility—the male equivalent of the feminine masquerade (see endnote 12)—through which men attempt to approximate the phallic function, and how such display may force them into an overidentification with the male function, with the image of their sexuality (Dean 83). As Connell explains, "the constitution of masculinity through bodily performance means that gender is vulnerable when the performance cannot be sustained" (54). Echoing such understandings, Molly's attack on Blue for his inability to use the gun is, in fact, an assault on his masculinity as much as his manliness. It is precisely through demeaning comments like those that Molly exerts her revenge against Blue for his failure or unwillingness to save her from the Bad Man, as argued in the previous section. Interestingly, however, she perceives it as Blue's duty to protect her not because of a bond based on their shared humanity, but due to his gender. Thus, throughout the narrative, Blue dutifully reports Molly's constant references to his supposed cowardice, blaming his failure to act not on a defect in his ability to empathize, but on his defective masculinity: "Using a lady, for Godsake, marching brave behind a lady's skirts" (16). In short, there is a clear case to argue that the attitude toward masculinity that the inhabitants of Hard Times manifest corresponds to a very traditional view of gender models. This view was certainly the dominant one at the time in which the story is set and remained so at the time of the novel's publication.

Interestingly, the characterization of the novel's narrator and protagonist actively rejects such hegemonic understanding of masculinity. This seconds a point also made by Winifred Bevilacqua, who notes that in a classical Western Mayor Blue would naturally stand for the novel's hero and main representative of Good. As such, he would ultimately be forced to fight Evil as embodied by the story's villain, the Bad Man from Bodie, in order to defend the main female protagonist, Molly, and assure the supremacy of civilization on the Frontier ("Revision" 81). But that is certainly not the case in *Welcome to Hard Times*. When confronted with the crucial frontier crisis—civilization threatened by the wilderness and Good threatened by Evil, a crisis here represented by the arrival of the Bad Man—Blue is unable or unwilling to respond according to the traditional ethos of violent heroism. In opposition to such portrayal, he represents a more ambiguous, problematic or, why not, enlightened attitude toward gender models of behavior. Indeed, he actively confronts

Molly's and the rest of the town's views on hegemonic masculinity: "'Were you any good with a gun Mayor maybe you could teach the boy some manliness'. 'That's not Manliness'" (153). Blue's repudiation of weapons and the violence they stand for may be interpreted as a symbol of progressive masculinity. Major Blue is a pacifist and, as argued in the previous section, he manifests a firm belief in the power of a cooperative and peaceful community.

Blue's rejection of violence goes hand in hand with the pride that he takes in his ease with words, in his ability to influence or even manipulate people through "powerful talking" (82). And so, he manages to coax several people into staying and helping him rebuild the town, such as the pimp Zar, thanks also to his natural gift to interpret people's innermost desires and ambitions. Blue also succeeds in appeasing Molly, who had frequently asked him to take her away from there before the Bad Man would return and whom he coaxes with empty promises of safety until she eventually gives up: "'Oh lord' she wailed, 'Oh Jesus God, spare me from this man, this talker—'" (150). It comes as no surprise, then, that as surrogate father of Jimmy, Blue tries to educate the orphaned boy into his own pacifist values: "'[P]robably your Pa did only one shameful thing in his life and that was to rush in after Turner'. [...] 'That was the one time he was no example to you. He went in there to get himself killed'" (165). Jimmy, however, in spite of his young age, has already internalized the dominant model of masculinity and, under Molly's influence, makes the manly deadshot Jenks his role model. Blue's anti-essentialist views of gender will die with him at the end of the novel, having failed to instill them in the town's only child and symbol of the future. The alternative view of masculinity that Blue strives to defend is, nevertheless, neither stable nor unproblematic. It becomes obvious as the narrative progresses that Blue is tormented by having behaved before the Bad Man in a way that is generally understood as cowardly. As he puts it, "now the saying is common that Sam Colt made men equal [...] Colt gave every man a gun, but you have to squeeze the trigger for yourself" (32). Even with his gun drawn, he is perceived as harmless by the inhabitants of Hard Times, which vexes him deeply. After all, it is only lunatics and visionaries that succeed in going against the pervasive ideology of their society. In short, *Welcome to Hard Times* is extremely critical of the ways in which patriarchy teaches men to pursue unhealthy, hegemonic expectations of masculinity that are harmful not merely to women, as we will see shortly, but also to men in perhaps less obvious ways.

Gender Oppression and Violence

Another way in which traditional gender configurations shape the world of *Welcome to Hard Times* is through the representation of gender oppression and violence in the Frontier. The very first glimpse that the

58   Welcome to Hard Times

reader has of Hard Times is a scene of sexual harassment against the saloon girl Florence, which before long will result in her violent death:

> The man from Bodie drank down a half bottle of the Silver Sun's best; that cleared the dust from his throat and then when Florence, who was a redhead, moved along the bar to him, he turned and grinned down at her. [...] Before she could say a word, he reached out and stuck his hand in the collar of her dress and ripped it down to her waist so that her breasts bounded out bare under the yellow light. (3)

As the analysis so far has made clear, Molly too is subjected to extreme violence at the hands of the Bad Man, barely surviving brutal rape and severe burns all over her body. Finally, toward the end of the novel Mae, one of the new prostitutes, will have become Turner's new victim, and the reader will once again be confronted with a scene of extreme violence: Mae's body "lying across the table, her dress pulled up around her neck. Her skull is broken and her teeth scattered on the table and on the floor" (211). However, it is not merely at the hands of Turner—the novel's symbolic representative of evil—that the female characters suffer violence. Many of the male inhabitants of Hard Times soon reveal themselves to be agents of female oppression and violence. Indeed, it is Molly's 'employer' Avery that forces her to go back to the saloon, knowing that she is most likely going to get "ripped open" (9): "We heard Avery yelling with a laugh in his voice. 'Molly! Moll-y-y! [...] Molly where are you, gentleman here wants to see you'" (15). To convince her, Avery does not hesitate to use violence, slapping her hard across the face.

The character of Zar, whose only interest is profit, shows a similar disregard for the female sex. Zar is a Russian pimp who has been riding the Great Plains looking for a town to establish his business. Experience has taught him that the most profitable goods in the West are alcohol and women, to whom he disparagingly refers as "beef":

> Frand... I come West to farm... but soon I learn, I see... farmers starve... only people who sell farmers their land, their fence, their seed, their tools... only these people are rich. And is that way with everything...not miners have gold but salesmen of burros and picks and pans... not cowboys have money but saloons who sell to them their drinks [...] So I sell my farm... and I think... what need is there more than seed, more even than whiskey or cards is need for Women. (63–64)

As this quotation makes clear, Zar holds an attitude toward the female body as a commodity that may be bought and sold.[11] He becomes a *de facto* owner of the prostitutes he 'employs,' since he holds the money that they make, ensuring their dependence. In the case of the Chinese girl, this is literally so, since the narrative reveals that Zar bought her from a man who pretended to be her father, and later allows one of the miners to marry her for the sum of $300 and a compromise to find another woman as a replacement in the saloon. Therefore, it is no wonder that he refers to his prostitutes as his "prize herd" (40) and is consequently disappointed when Blue refuses to accept sexual intercourse with them in exchange for the use of well water. After all, "the ladies were his stock in trade" (40). This is precisely the kind of agreement that he reaches with the deadshot Jenks, exchanging the animal flesh that he hunts for the human body of his prostitutes. In addition, Zar's women are subjected to a humiliating treatment that reinforces their submission and powerlessness. And so, the reader is admitted to spy into the saloon on a Saturday night, while the Chinese girl offers drinks to the miners on her knees. On top of that, Zar does not hesitate to use violence to subdue the prostitutes: "'I say what we do, no one else!' Zar was shouting. And to make his point he was kicking Mae as she tried to get up" (57). In fact, references to violence toward them pervade the novel:

> The Russian was drinking up his own stock and it made him mean. He knocked a tooth out of the tall girl Jessie's mouth and on one occasion Miss Adah had to put him to sleep with a stick, he was going at the Chinagirl so. (108)

It is worth pointing out that the prostitutes do not submit without fighting; but their attempts to have their opinions considered and their rights respected inevitably end up in physical violence against them, thus assuring their passivity. Women are, therefore, presented as having no other choice than to comply. This seems to be the case of Mrs. Clemens, the "sad grey-haired woman, full of sags" (135) that is brought to replace the Chinese girl. Mrs. Clemens is presumably an old widow, who finding no other means to support herself in the inhospitable West is forced to find the "protection" of a pimp and become a prostitute in exchange for food and shelter. In short, *Welcome to Hard Times* paints an extremely bleak picture of the model of production and consumption in the Frontier, where the physical exploitation of women is the primary and most profitable economic activity. The novel presents a model of gender interaction that is characterized by unlimited male control over, and disregard for, female liberty and well-being, to the extent that there seems to be a refusal to extend the recognition of shared humanity to women.

Ethical Grounding?

The question now is whether there is sufficient evidence to support the claim that the novel's depiction of gender oppression and violence has an ethical grounding or, said differently, whether it is possible to argue that *Welcome to Hard Times* seeks to denounce such model of gender domination and does not merely depict it for the sake of dramatic power—that is, as a further element in the recreation of the atmosphere of a classical Western. After all, there is no denying that violence is a central element of the genre, even a defining characteristic of it. This task is somewhat more complex to accomplish than demonstrating how the novel debunks hegemonic views of masculinity, as argued above, because none of the characters engage in open criticism of gender violence and commodification of the female body, as arguably is the case with Blue's explicit questioning of traditional attitudes toward masculinity. However, there is a clear case to argue that the model of gender subordination and violence depicted in the novel does not go unchallenged; and it is precisely through the character of Molly that such criticism is achieved.

Granted that just as Molly participates in the perpetuation of hegemonic views of masculinity, she paradoxically becomes a key collaborator in the oppressive gender system of which she is a victim. This may be best perceived in her willing endorsement of her position as Blue's wife. After the first coming of the Bad Man, she becomes Blue's common-law wife and is accepted as such by the new settlers. This change of social status places Molly in a completely different position from that of the newly arrived prostitutes. These, upon learning that she is Blue's wife, quickly go from calling her names like "Madam Bitch" and "Lady Bacon Ass" to sympathizing with her suffering: "Poor woman, gettin' burned that way it's no wonder she ain't herself" (62). As Blue ponders, "[…] there is nothing that a whore will respect more than a married woman" (60–61). Molly, on the contrary, scorns the new prostitutes and treats them deplorably, mirroring male oppression. She is clearly oblivious to her own previous status, and indifferent to their shared condition as women in a deeply patriarchal society. After symbolically achieving the status of a married woman, Molly's behavior reflects her own hegemonic understanding of gender roles. This manifests itself in a number of attitudes, such as the assimilation of "ladylike" manners:

> She held up her hand, very ladylike, and smiled and shook her head. She had drunk her share in the old days […] but it gave her more pleasure to refuse, it set her apart from the ladies although she knew them better than they thought she did. (103)

Furthermore, Molly's desperate obsession with securing the protection of a manly man that will save her from the Bad Man in effect constitutes a reaffirmation of the traditional understanding of women as 'the weaker sex' and a reinforcement of the dichotomies masculinity/femininity and strength/weakness that pervade the cultural imagination of this fictional town. Her fixation must certainly be understood in the context of her traumatic condition, but it is also coherent with the character's attitude toward gender configurations.

Nevertheless, and this is the key issue, the character of Molly at the same time constitutes the novel's most important tool to challenge and subvert the hegemonic model of gender domination. This is achieved in three different ways. First of all, it is through Molly's change of status from prostitute to wife, through her self-delusion, that the text highlights the intrinsic similarities between both roles, particularly in terms of power. Molly's sense of empowerment is nothing short of chimerical, since as a wife she has not really achieved independence—economic or otherwise—and cannot even decide her own future, despite wanting to leave Hard Times as soon as she recovers. What Molly fails to understand, and the novel emphasizes at the level of textual implications, is that her willing progression from the position of prostitute to that of wife does not necessarily constitute an act of empowerment; she has merely moved to the other possible slot allotted to women in her society, thus remaining trapped in the patriarchal system of production and consumption that supports itself on the submission of women and that has been imported into the Frontier by the settlers. The tight connection between the two positions is, in fact, hinted at by Blue's comment that "she turned, little by little, so compliant, that I felt I was some duplicate Bad Man taking his pleasure" (158). In short, in such understanding of gender relations in the West, the novel suggests that there would have been fewer differences between the ways in which a client, a rapist and a husband *use* the female body than one might assume.

Second, Molly's artificial adoption of the manners and attitudes that, she understands, befit a married woman—that is, her artificial performance of femininity—suggests a far from innocent representation of sexual identity in the novel as mimicry, as a masquerade.[12] Such depiction points to Doctorow's precocious understanding of gender models as culturally shaped rather than biologically determined, thus anticipating later developments in gender theory that would expose femininity as a social construct. Finally, in spite of Molly's apparent conservative attitude toward gender and her willing submission to the capitalistic model of sexual domination, it is paradoxically undeniable that she shows a defiant and resolute attitude toward men. This is particularly evident in her relationship with Blue after the town starts to grow again, as well as through her skillful manipulation of Jenks and Jimmy, as argued above. Indeed, Jenks is presented as nothing short of a puppet, ready to risk a sure death at the hands of Turner over Molly's sexual promises: "Jenks, get him for me, you've got to get him, you have a hankerin' don't you Jenks, I've seen it, a woman can tell. Get him and I'll go with you anywhere, I'll be your natural wife, anything you please, I swear—" (186). As this quote suggests, Molly uses her sexuality as a tool to achieve her aims, which paradoxically may be seen as a reversal of the traditional model of sexual domination.[13] Similarly, Molly's training of Jimmy for when the Bad Man comes remarkably involves coaxing Blue to her bed and then shouting for Jimmy to come and defend her: "'You want to come over here, you want to come to your Molly? Alright. Alright. [...] Come here Blue. Come give me a hug [...]' I put my feet over the side of the bunk and she cried, 'JIMMY!'" (158–159).

Molly's inner strength and her power over these men endow her voice with a prominence that deserves further examination, because it raises relevant questions about the role of the female voice in the novel. In this respect, I follow the lead of Marshall B. Gentry, who in his article "Ventriloquists' Conversations" (1993) explores Doctorow's degree of success in relaxing male control over his novels and opening them up to the voices of women; in the only critical attempt to approach issues of gender in *Welcome to Hard Times*, Gentry concludes that Doctorow overcomes ventriloquism to give expression to a powerful, believable female voice that succeeds in telling her own story over the male narrator's own voice (132). Taking up the argument where Gentry drops it, it is my contention that Molly's voice is central to the narrative from a structural perspective. First of all, as one reads the novel it becomes obvious that what Molly says, does and is supposed to be thinking engage most of Blue's efforts to render the story of Hard Times. In that sense, it is possible to claim that Molly's voice plays a key role in advancing the narrative process. In fact, toward the end of the narrative her voice even seems to take over that of Blue at some points, almost usurping the position of central consciousness behind the novel's narration.

Second, Molly's voice frequently challenges Blue's narrative authority, providing commentary for his actions and motives, and paradoxically fulfilling the role of a sort of mediator or interpreter between narrator and reader. Thus, for example, she sees Blue's obsession with coaxing new settlers to stay for what it is: "You'll rope in every damn fool you can just to make up a herd. There's surety in numbers, ain't that what you think?" (84). Thus, as this quote exemplifies, Molly's voice succeeds in escaping Blue's (male) narrative control. Blue, however, is not unaware of Molly's power over what is supposed to be his own narration. At the beginning of the third ledger, he even bitterly voices his recognition of Molly's control over the course of events:

> I think Molly, Molly, Molly and she is the time, turning in her phases like the moon [...] Molly, could you really know what was coming? Or did it come because you knew it? Were you smarter than the life, or did the life depend on you? (147)

Finally, Molly's general understanding of events and of the nature of evil proves to be more accurate than Blue's, whose optimism and lingering hope for a better future are finally exposed as foolishness and self-delusion at the end of the novel. Thus, her voice acts as the novel's most reliable source of information with regard to the outcome of events, while Blue's hopefulness and need to "go with the [good] signs" (129) remain an impossible utopia. Molly's female voice[14] is allowed to resonate so clearly and powerfully that it almost appears to come through unmediated by the narrator's own consciousness. In that sense, it may be claimed that *Welcome to Hard Times* becomes a site of gender dialogue in a Bakhtinian sense of the term, since it too presents "a plurality of independent and unmerged voices and consciousnesses, a genuine polyphony of fully valid voices" (Bakhtin, *Problems* 6). The novel may be, therefore, understood as a gender-conscious heteroglossic text in two different ways. On the one hand, in spite of featuring a male narratorial voice, the story actually leaves sufficient room for the cohabitation and interaction of a female voice that at times challenges the narrator's discursive authority. On the other hand, the novel reveals itself to be a polyphonic—i.e. multi-voiced—text at a structural level, in that it facilitates a dialogic, disharmonized reading that disrupts and subverts patriarchal configurations.[15] Molly's powerful, believable voice and the strength and determination of her will allow *Welcome to Hard Times* to act as a feminist statement in spite of the main female character herself. The analysis suggests that the novel incorporates not only themes but also narrative forms compatible with feminism. Thus, Molly at once becomes a key collaborator in the patriarchal model of female subordination and the novel's main tool to denounce and subvert it at a structural level.

Concluding Remarks

As I hope the analysis has shown, *Welcome to Hard Times* inaugurates Doctorow's complex engagement with a number of feminist concerns. The novel succeeds in disrupting and subverting long-time fixed images of the masculine and the feminine, defending an alternative understanding of gender identity. In addition, it denounces the prevailing model of gender domination and violence. Its pages undermine the model of society that supports itself on patriarchal gender configurations of production and consumption. And Doctorow resorts to the conventions of the Western, the quintessentially manly genre, to subvert and debunk such views, anticipating himself to much later socio-political movements.

Discussion and Conclusion

Discussion

The analyses conducted in the two previous sections have attempted to show that in spite of its apparent thematic simplicity—life in the Frontier during the colonization of the West—*Welcome to Hard Times* is a socially committed novel that puts forward a newly critical and much bleaker version of the myth of the West. In it, as we have seen, social and gender relations are based on hegemonic gender and power structures, violence and oppression, which in turn cause the characters to sustain complex long-lasting psychological conditions. Before concluding this chapter, however, it seems pertinent to explore a number of issues that emerge when the results obtained through readings from the perspectives of trauma studies and feminist criticism are reconsidered alongside each other.

First of all, as we have seen, Molly's traumatic encounter with Turner leaves indelible physical and psychological scars. Interestingly, it is precisely the post-traumatic symptoms that she develops afterward that in effect empower her, paradoxically providing her with the necessary strength and determination to stand up for herself. In the manner of the protagonist of Gilman's "The Yellow Wallpaper," Molly's psychological ailment endows her with a new prominent voice that challenges Blue's narrative authority. This is an attempt neither to argue that psychological trauma is presented as liberating in the novel nor to extend certain feminist critics' idealization of madness as liberation.[16] Molly's traumatic condition is not liberating, it destroys her and drives her to her grave. At the same time, however, as happens to Gilman's protagonist, Molly's psychological deterioration provides her with a new power that she would not have had otherwise in the patriarchal society of Hard Times. Furthermore, it is to a great extent Blue's traumatic shame and guilt for his despicable role in Molly's suffering that obsesses him and compels him to convey Molly's voice in such a clear and unmediated manner.

Following this line of argumentation, the novel's emphasis on the main protagonists' traumatic condition constitutes an indispensable tool for its subversion of the gender conventions of the classical Western. First of all, as the analysis above has made clear, the character of Molly clearly diverges from the virtuous heroine that would be frequently found in the classical Western. The main female character, Bevilacqua notes, would traditionally be a sophisticated easterner or a spirited rancher's daughter who would exemplify the virtuous morals of the community. Adopting a discourse of love and forgiveness, she would speak out against violence and against the idea that human conflicts can only be solved by the use of force. She would also be the representative of communal solidarity, and of peaceful life in the Frontier ("Revision" 85). The same holds true in the case of Blue, who, as argued above, diverges markedly from the rugged, hyper-masculine, violent individualist hero of the classical Western, who would not hesitate to fight evil to protect the female heroine and guarantee the continuation of life in the Frontier (Bevilacqua, "Revision" 81).

Taking the argument where Bevilacqua drops it, Molly's traumatic encounter with the Bad Man and her bitterness at Blue's passivity transform her into a cruel and manipulative woman who is obsessed with revenge, indifferent to the harm that her desperate need for retribution may bring onto others. Indeed, far from representing the values of community, her traumatic experience also impairs her capacity to relate to those around her, rendering her incapable of ever establishing normal affective communal bonds. Similarly, it is precisely Blue's shame for his paralysis before the Bad Man and his guilt over his responsibility for Molly's suffering that moves him to go against the ethos of the West according to which "a man's pride is not to pay attention" (4). In other words, his traumatic experience and the complex condition that he develops afterward convince him of the importance of building a strong community that is based on ties of empathy and selfless cooperation. In short, Doctorow has replaced the hard-boiled, brave cowboy with a wounded but consequently enlightened anti-hero whose illustrated masculinity would make him a moral superior in any other context.

Indeed, a reading of *Welcome to Hard Times* from the combined perspectives of trauma studies and feminist criticism usefully foregrounds the important role that the idea of a well-functioning community plays in the novel's revisionist swing. As we have seen, despite Blue's traumatic need to rebuild the community after the town's destruction, the new settlers show neither a sense of collective purpose or destiny, nor empathy. And so, to provide an example, they only help Jenks build a stable on condition that he put their horses up without charge, but since "Isaac Maple [...] had no horse of his own [...] [he] saw no reason to join in" (85). Similarly, when Swede and Helga arrive, Isaac greets them with open arms and takes care of them as if they were members of his family, which Zar explains as follows: "Wal, [...] is no meestery. The man has wagon" (122). It seems clear, then, that all acts of cooperation or solidarity in Hard Times answer to nothing other than self-interest. Furthermore, just like the old settlers showed a disparaging, oppressive and openly violent attitude toward the women in the novel, the new inhabitants of Hard Times seem to refuse to extend recognition of shared humanity to women. In spite of the opportunity for personal and social regeneration that the extension of the Frontier was supposed to represent, women remain second-class citizens in this new Western community. Said differently, living up to the evocations of its name, the town remains an inhospitable society based on a patriarchal model of production and consumption in which women occupy the lowest possible level and whose bodies continue to be the most important commodity. In addition, the lack of empathy that the settlers show renders the community of Hard Times incapable of protecting its female inhabitants from traditionally gender-specific outside or inside threats. And so, Blue is ultimately defeated also because the society of Hard Times has not managed to move past traditional gender configurations.

Blue's attempts to cope with his shame through the reconstruction of life in the wilderness fail, but he finally, at the brink of death, reaches illumination: "[The town] had no earthly reason for being there, it made no sense to exist. People naturally come together but is that enough? Just as naturally we think of ourselves alone" (192). Thus, selfishness, lack of empathy and individualism once again bring about the town's destruction at the end of the novel. The inhabitants in Hard Times have not learned from past mistakes. Blue's dream of rebuilding the community has failed just as the Western community collapses. His despair, his renewed shame at having been defeated as he regards the dead bodies that are scattered on the ground, compel him to write the story of Hard Times. Interestingly, Gabriele Schwab has claimed that "storytelling itself requires a form of translation [...], that is, a psychic processing of cultural narratives and conversion into an individual story" (115). In *Welcome to Hard Times*, we witness the reversal of this statement, since there is a psychic processing of individual narrative—that of Blue—and a conversion of it into a cultural story: the allegoric and cautionary tale of the failure of the Western community, which is wiped off of the face of the earth by its own moral corruption.

Conclusion

As the analysis above has attempted to prove, *Welcome to Hard Times* inaugurates Doctorow's complex engagement with the themes of human suffering and oppression. The novel narrates events of extreme violence, representing the main characters' resulting psychological conditions, their causes and their consequences. Its pages also problematize the relationship among the trauma categories of victim, perpetrator and bystander, highlighting the extremely thin line that separates them. *Welcome to Hard Times* further succeeds in disrupting and subverting long-time fixed images of masculinity and femininity. In addition, the novel denounces the prevailing structures of gender domination and violence, seeking to undermine the model of society that supports itself on patriarchal gender configurations of production and consumption. This is achieved through the creation of a polyphonic text that not only incorporates themes but also forms compatible with feminism. Finally, the novel depicts the failure of the Western community, which is brought about by the town's inability to function according to the ethical dictates of empathy and selfless cooperation. Ultimately, the book deals with the social and individual impact of power relations, which can be shaped in very complex ways by issues of traumatic victimization that derive from a diminished sense of community.

Welcome to Hard Times 67

The novel's commitment to these themes may be seen as an ethical statement on Doctorow's part. With *Welcome to Hard Times*, the author paints a grim picture of human nature and social and gender relations in the Frontier, which in the novel functions as a metaphor for contemporary Western society. The novel draws relevant parallelisms between the historical period in which it is set and the one in which it was published. In other words, the narrative uses its disguise as a Western to provide critical commentary of some of the social ills of postwar North America, namely its fierce individualism, its hegemonic gender configurations and its lack of empathy. This criticism was relevant at the time of the novel's publication and undoubtedly remains relevant nowadays. With *Welcome to Hard Times*, Doctorow managed to turn the tale of a Western town into a tool to debunk essentialist views of gender and trauma and denounce social injustice through the rejection of the rule of the either/or. Thus, at an ideological level, E.L. Doctorow succeeded in revitalizing the classical Western, bestowing upon it unprecedented literary sophistication and transforming it into a genre capable of yielding meanings which are relevant to contemporary existence even nowadays, more than fifty years after its publication.

Notes

1 Other post-Western novels that followed Doctorow's lead are Thomas Berger's *Little Big Man* (1964), Ishmael Reed's *Yellow Back Radio Broke Down* (1968) and John Schlesinger's *Midnight Cowboy* (1965). Doctorow's subversion of the conventions of the classical Western has been criticized by commentators such as S.L. Tanner, who dismissed *Welcome to Hard Times* as "another unfortunate attempt to debunk the Western" (82).
2 See Genette (179).
3 It is important to keep in mind that E.L. Doctorow's understanding of psychic trauma must have come from a combination of his early knowledge of Freudian theory and his deep understanding of human nature.
4 Further references to the novel will be to the Random House Trade Paperback Edition, published in 2007.
5 In contrast to the Freudian emphasis on drives, Tomkins defines affects as the main motivational system for human beings, which, combined with their complex analytical capacities, guarantees their freedom (Kosofsky Sedgwick and Frank 36–37). The so-called "Tomkins-Ekman paradigm," based on a "Basic Emotions" view of affects, is currently being contested by a number of researchers in the field of affective neuroscience. Nevertheless, this basic emotions paradigm—supported by many of the most influential researchers in the field, such as Antonio Damasio—continues to dominate the discipline, also influencing most discussions of affect in the Humanities (see Leys 439 on this).
6 It is worth highlighting here that Molly's bodily position is described as suggesting moral superiority even though it is a direct consequence of the physical injuries on her back. Yet, it certainly evokes the critical debate on the moral superiority conferred by the status of victim, based on the widespread cultural notion that suffering ennobles people (see Rothe 28).

68 Welcome to Hard Times

7 Blue stands for the artist/writer/historian in *Welcome to Hard Times*, a figure that will recur throughout most of Doctorow's oeuvre. There are, in fact, frequent references to the act of writing and its futility, particularly toward the end of the novel. The book's metafictional concerns have been explored by a number of critics, most prominently by Bevilacqua (1989) and Jaupaj (2008). Jaupaj (2008) has argued that the novel's primary aim is to highlight the failure of narrative to deliver a truthful representation of the past. Similarly, Levine claims that the novel expresses not only Blue's "frustration over the inadequacy of his narrative but perhaps also Doctorow's misgivings about the ability of fiction to convey the truth about life" (30). See also Saltzman (1983) and Harter and Thompson (1990) on this.
8 As the following chapters will discuss, the figure of the victim-perpetrator will reappear in many of Doctorow's later novels, becoming a key element in his literary exploration of human suffering.
9 Numerous critics have focused on the novel's successful subversion of the traditional Western, see for example Bakker 1984 and 1985, Bevilacqua 1990, Freese 1987, Kusnir 2004, and Jaupaj and Shumeli 2012. None of them have focused on how the novel deploys gender issues as a further tool to subvert the classical conventions of the genre.
10 It is worth pointing out that society in the United States was going through a crisis of masculinity at the time of the novel's publication. In the 1950s and 1960s there started to spread a sense of inferiority or diminished manliness with respect to the previous generation of fathers and grandfathers who had fought World Wars I and II. The most relevant text dealing with gender issues at the time is Betty Friedan's *The Feminine Mystique*, but it would not be published until two years later. This points to Doctorow's ability to put into writing the social unrest that he could perceive in US society, anticipating his observations to the posterior influence of gender studies.
11 Many critics have interpreted the novel's revision of the Western as a critique of capitalism and its individualistic ethos. See for example Shelton (1983), Bakker (1985), Gross (1983), Cooper (1993), van der Merwe (2007), and Jaupaj and Shumeli (2012). None of them, however, focus explicitly on the subordination of women as a key dimension of it.
12 We owe the concept of the mask to Joan Riviere's psychoanalytic paper "Womanliness as a Masquerade" (1929). Riviere was the first to present femininity, which she calls "womanliness," as a mask that may be worn by women, an idea that was later on taken up by Lacan as part of his exploration of female sexuality in "The Signification of the Phallus" (583). A similar understanding of gender was defended by the French existentialist Simone de Beauvoir, whose formulation in *The Second Sex* that "one is not born, but rather becomes, a woman" (267) was subsequently reconsidered by feminist critics such as Judith Butler (1990) to forward an anti-essentialist view of gender as a cultural performance.
13 Molly is not the only female character in Doctorow's oeuvre who uses sex as a tool to achieve her aims. As we will see, Evelyn Nesbit, in *Ragtime*, notably resorts to her sex appeal to fulfill her ambitions, even though this eventually leads to her psychological ruination. Similarly, Susan, in *The Book of Daniel*, brandishes her sexuality as a weapon to exert her power over her brother Daniel. The recurrence of this motif achieves a special significance when considered in the light of the comments (quoted in the Introduction) made by Doctorow when asked in an interview about his position with respect to gender and power.
14 By female voice I do not actually refer to the opinions and ideas conveyed by Molly, which as explained above mirror hegemonic gender configurations.

I use the term in a Bakhtinian sense (1981) to refer to the female voice that challenges the novel's authoritative (male) discourse as represented by Blue, regardless of the characters' ideology.
15 In this context, it is particularly surprising to find that the critic John G. Parks pays no attention whatsoever to *Welcome to Hard Times* in his paper "The Politics of Polyphony" (1991), where he approaches Doctorow's early fiction from a Bakhtinian perspective.
16 cf. the dialogue in which Hélène Cixous and Catherine Clément engage in the final section of *The Newly Born Woman* (1986).

References

Arendt, Hannah. "Organized Guilt and Universal Responsibility." *The Portable Hannah Arendt*. Ed. and Intro. Peter Baehr. London and New York: Penguin, 2000. 146–156.
Bakhtin, Michael M. *The Dialogic Imagination: Four Essays*. Ed. Michael Holquist. Austin: University of Texas Press, 1981.
———. *Problems of Dostoevsky's Poetics*. Minneapolis: University of Minnesota Press, 1984.
Bakker, Jan. "The Western: Can it Be Great?" *Dutch Quarterly Review of Anglo-American Letters* 14.2 (1984): 140–163.
———. "E.L. Doctorow's *Welcome to Hard Times*: A Reconsideration." *Neophilologus: An International Journal of Modern and Mediaeval Language and Literature* 69.3 (1985): 464–473.
Berger, Thomas. *Little Big Man*. 1964. New York: Dell, 2005.
Bevilacqua, Winifred F. "The Revision of the Western in E.L. Doctorow's *Welcome to Hard Times*." *American Literature* 61.1 (1989): 78–95.
———. "Narration and History in E.L. Doctorow's *Welcome to Hard Times, The Book of Daniel* and *Ragtime*." *American Studies in Scandinavia* 22 (1990): 94–106.
Bewes, Timothy. *The Event of Postcolonial Shame*. Princeton: Princeton UP, 2011.
Biddle, Jennifer. "Shame." *Australian Feminist Studies* 12.26 (1997): 227–239.
Bloom, Sandra. "Bridging the Black Hole of Trauma: The Evolutionary Significance of the Arts." *Psychotherapy and Politics International* 8.3 (2010): 198–212.
Burrows, Victoria. "The Ghostly Haunting of White Shame in David Malouf's Remembering Babylon." *Westerly* 51 (2006): 124–135.
Butler, Judith. *Gender Trouble: Feminism and the Subversion of Identity*. New York: Routledge, 1990.
Caruth, Cathy, ed. Introduction to Part I. *Trauma: Explorations in Memory*. Baltimore: Johns Hopkins UP, 1995. 3–12.
Cixous, Hélène and Catherine Clément. *The Newly Born Woman*. Trans. Betsy Wing. Minneapolis: University of Minnesota Press, 1986.
Connell, Raewyn W. *Masculinities*. Berkeley and Los Angeles: University of California Press, 2005.
Cooper, Stephen. "Cutting Both Ways: E. L. Doctorow's Critique of the Left." *South Atlantic Review* 58.2 (May 1993): 111–125.
De Beauvoir, Simone. *The Second Sex*. Trans. H. M. Parshley. New York: Penguin, 1972.

Dean, Tim. *Beyond Sexuality*. Chicago and London: University of Chicago Press, 2000.
Doctorow, E.L. *Welcome to Hard Times*. 1960. New York: Random House Trade Paperback, 2007.
———. *The Book of Daniel*. 1971. London: Penguin, 2006.
———. *Ragtime*. 1974. London: Penguin, 2006.
Escudero, Maite. "The Burden of Shame in Sarah Waters' *The Night Watch*." *Trauma in Contemporary Literature: Narrative and Representation*. Eds. Marita Nadal and Mónica Calvo. New York and London: Routledge, 2014. 223–236.
Freese, Peter. "E.L. Doctorow's *Welcome to Hard Times* and the Mendacity of the Popular Western." *Literatur in Wissenschaft und Unterricht* 20.1 (1987): 202–216.
Freud, Sigmund. *Beyond the Pleasure Principle*. 1920. *The Standard Edition of the Complete Psychological Works of Sigmund Freud*, Volume XVIII (1920–1922). Ed. James Strachey. London: Vintage, 2001.
———. *Moses and Monotheism: Three Essays*. 1939 [1934–1938]. *The Standard Edition of the Complete Psychological Works of Sigmund Freud*, Volume XXIII (1937–1939). Ed. James Strachey. London: Vintage, 2001.
Genette, Gérard. "Voice." 1980. *Narratology*. Eds. Susana Onega and José Ángel García Landa. London and New York: Longman, 1996. 172–189.
Gentry, Marshall B. "'Ventriloquists' Conversations: The Struggle for Gender Dialogue in E.L. Doctorow and Philip Roth." 1993. *Modern Critical Views: E.L. Doctorow*. Ed. Harold Bloom. Philadelphia: Chelsea House, 2002. 113–132.
Gilligan, James. "Shame, Guilt, and Violence." *Social Research* 70.4 (2003): 1149–1180.
Gross, David S. "Tales of Obscene Power." *E. L. Doctorow, Essays & Conversations*. Ed. Richard Trenner. Princeton and New York: Ontario Review, 1983. 120–150.
Harter, Carol C. and James R. Thompson. *E. L. Doctorow*. Boston: Twayne, 1990.
Henke, Suzette. *Shattered Subjects: Trauma and Testimony in Women's Life Writing*. London: Palgrave Macmillan, 1998.
Jaupaj, Artur. "The Rise of the New Western in the 1960s: E.L. Doctorow's *Welcome to Hard Times*." *European Journal of American Studies*. Spec. issue 2008. Web. 12 July 2014. <http://ejas.revues.org/3303>.
Jaupaj, Artur and Arjan Shumeli. "Failure of the Myth: The American West as Fraud." Book of Proceedings of the *2nd International Conference on Human and Social Sciences ICHSS*, 2012. 9–15.
Kauffman, Jeffrey. "On the Primacy of Shame." *The Shame of Death, Grief, and Trauma*. Ed. Jeffrey Kauffman. New York and London: Routledge, 2010. 3–24.
Kosofsky Sedgwick, Eve and Adam Frank, eds. *Shame and Its Sisters: A Silvan Tomkins Reader*. Durham and London: Duke UP, 1995.
Kusnir, Jaroslav. "Parody of Western in American Literature: Doctorow's *Welcome to Hard Times*, and R. Coover's *The Ghost Town*." *Theory and Practice in English Studies* 2 (2004): 101–107.

LaCapra, Dominick. *Writing History, Writing Trauma*. Baltimore: Johns Hopkins UP, 2001.
Levi, Primo. *Survival in Auschwitz: The Nazi Assault on Humanity*. Trans. by Stuart Woolf. New York: Simon and Schuster, 1996.
Levinas, Emmanuel. *On Escape*. 1982. Trans. by Bettina Bergo. Stanford: Stanford UP, 2003.
Levine, Paul. *E.L. Doctorow: An Introduction*. New York: Methuen, 1985.
Leys, Ruth. "The Turn to Affect: A Critique." *Critical Inquiry* 37.3 (2011): 434–472.
Morris, Christopher D. ed. *Conversations with E. L. Doctorow*. Jackson: Mississippi UP, 1999.
Parks, John G. "The Politics of Polyphony: The Fiction of E.L. Doctorow." *Twentieth Century Literature* 37.4 (Winter 1991): 454–463.
Reed, Ishmael. *Yellow Back Radio Broke Down*. 1968. London: Allison & Busby, 1995.
Riviere, Joan. "Womanliness as a Masquerade." *The International Journal of Psychoanalysis* 10 (1929): 303–313.
Rothe, Anne. *Popular Trauma Culture: Selling the Pain of Others in the Mass Media*. Piscataway: Rutgers UP, 2011.
Saltzman, Arthur. "The Stylistic Energy of E.L. Doctorow." *E.L. Doctorow, Essays & Conversations*. Ed. Richard Trenner. Princeton and New York: Ontario Review, 1983. 73–108.
Schlesinger, John. *Midnight Cowboy*. 1965. London: ITV, 2002.
Schwab, Gabriele. *Haunting Legacies: Violent Histories and Transgenerational Trauma*. New York and Chichester: Columbia UP, 2010.
Shelton, F.W. "E.L. Doctorow's *Welcome to Hard Times*: The Western and the American Dream." *Midwest Quarterly: A Journal of Contemporary Thought* 25.1 (1983): 7–17.
Starr, Kevin. "Welcome to Hard Times." *The New Republic* (Sept. 6, 1975): 25, 27.
Tanner, S.L. "Rage and Order in Doctorow's *Welcome to Hard Times*." *South Dakota Review* 22.3 (1984): 79–85.
van der Kolk, Bessel A. and Onno van der Hart. "The Intrusive Past: The Flexibility of Memory and the Engraving of Trauma." *Trauma: Explorations in Memory*. Ed. Cathy Caruth. Baltimore: Johns Hopkins UP, 1995. 158–181.
van der Merwe, Philip. "Hard Times as Bodie: the Allegorical Functionality in E.L. Doctorow's *Welcome to Hard Times*." *Literator* 28.2 (2007): 49–73.
Vickroy, Laurie. *Trauma and Survival in Contemporary Fiction*. Virginia: Virginia UP, 2002.
Whitehead, Anne. *Memory*. London and New York: Routledge, 2009.
Williams, John. *Fiction as False Document: The Reception of E. L. Doctorow in the Postmodern Age*. Columbia: Camden House, 1996.
Williams, Wirt. "Bad Man from Bodie." *New York Review of Books* (Apr. 30, 1960): 7.

2 *The Book of Daniel*
A Memoir Gone Awry

Eleven years after the publication of *Welcome to Hard Times*, *The Book of Daniel* was released. Its reception was rather ambiguous at first. A few months after coming out, it had already achieved remarkable critical recognition, becoming a finalist for the National Book Award for fiction. It was praised as "the political novel of our age" (Kauffmann 25), as "a ferocious feat of the imagination" (Prescott 111) and as a "brilliant achievement" (Richmond 628), and Joyce Carol Oates went so far as to call the book a "nearly perfect work of art" (in Williams 21–22). However, it was virtually ignored by the academia for almost ten years. The first readings of the novel tended to either celebrate it or condemn it on the basis of its political content (see Estrin 1975; Stark 1975; Levine 1983), but these early critics' fixation with the novel's politics might have blinded them to the richness of theme and style that it displays. It was only following the critical and commercial success of *Ragtime* that scholarly attention extended to *The Book of Daniel*.

At its simplest, the novel is the fictional rendering of the conviction and execution of the Isaacsons from the viewpoint of their surviving son. The plot is loosely based on the actual trial and execution of the Rosenbergs, the New York communist couple who were convicted and executed in 1953 for conspiracy to commit espionage leading to the development of the Soviet nuclear program. However, as John Parks has noted, *The Book of Daniel* is many "stories" at once (456). It is a *Bildungsroman*, since it tells the story of Daniel Isaacson's struggles as he grows up; it is also a *Künstlerroman*, since it concerns itself with Daniel as a writer who tries to discover his own identity and his relationship with society as he composes a history dissertation;[1] it is the tale of a survivor, since it narrates Daniel's effort to find a narrative that will reconcile him with his traumatic past; it is a revenge story, since it deals with a son's duty to clear his parents' names; and it is a clever political critique since, as Stephen Cooper has argued, it condemns the conservatism of McCarthyism and the Red Scare while at the same time questioning and criticizing the Old Left of the 1930s and 1940s and the New Left of the 1960s (115–117).[2] As we will see, this multiplicity of genre and thematic perspectives is narrated in a highly experimental style, a fragmented hybrid narrative that escapes linearity, interweaves homodiegetic and heterodiegetic narration, and combines features of autobiography and personal memoir with sections of historical description, sociology and political theory, while calling attention to, and assessing, its own status as a (fictional) text.

The Trauma of a Grievous Past

As the reader opens *The Book of Daniel*, it becomes immediately obvious that Daniel Isaacson Lewin is psychologically unwell. "Daniel's Book" (Doctorow, *Daniel* 368)[3]—as he later on renames his narration—is the tale of a survivor, a story of trauma, horror and guilt for staying alive and a desperate attempt to come to terms with the traumatic memories of the past. These memories have returned to haunt Daniel, triggered by his sister's suicide attempt fifteen years after their parents' execution. It is precisely Susan's attempt to end her life that works as a "summons" (37) for Daniel and prompts him to write the story that we read in the book. This section will seek to explore the possibility of reading *The Book of Daniel* as a trauma novel, analyzing the autodiegetic narrator's psychological condition, the status of his memories and the possibility of healing through narration.

Trauma and PTSD

Written about two decades before the rise of trauma studies, *The Book of Daniel* evidences a deep preoccupation with human suffering at both a thematic and a formal level. Indeed, the articulation of the novel's autodiegetic narrator and fictive author allows Doctorow to engage in a fictional exploration of the imagined causes and consequences of psychological trauma. To begin with, the book reveals that the protagonist suffers from many of the symptoms associated with Post-Traumatic Stress Disorder (see American Psychiatric Association, DSM IV-TR 463–468). First of all, Daniel is shown to persistently re-experience the traumatic events in several ways throughout his life. As a young boy he suffered recurrent dreams: "I was afraid to go to sleep. I had terrible nightmares which I couldn't remember except in waking from them in terror and suffocation" (134). Later in his life, the nightmares seem to have given way to a more general obsession with images—"awful visions of his head" (250)—and thoughts that recall his parents' execution. Among these stand out the frequent symbolic references to electricity: Daniel's father is described as tireless and "full of electricity" (59), Grandma's hair is said to resemble "electric wire" (83), he composes an electricity pseudo-poem with "ohm"—the measure of electrical resistance—as its main image, there is a smearing of "electrons on the cellblock" (229), etc.

This fixation suggests that Daniel's mind is helplessly possessed by the not-witnessed event of his parents' execution by electrocution, by the unseen image of their bodies "frying" in the chair (193). As trauma theory tells us it often happens to trauma victims, this image is not fully owned because it was not "abreacted" (Freud and Breuer 8), "not assimilated at the time, only belatedly, in its repeated possession" to borrow Caruth's phrasing of the phenomenon (4–5). This view also finds support in the fact that even the historiographic interludes that interrupt Daniel's narrative of his past and present experiences deal with issues such as Soviet politics, the Cold War, treason and tyranny, traitors and the law, and, most interestingly, traditional forms of execution—topics all of them that evoke the death of Daniel's parents.[4] These historiographic intersections, which would presumably respond to the protagonist's efforts to write his dissertation, play the role of providing emotional relief, since they often interrupt the narrative at times in which writing seems to become too painful for Daniel. That is, they are used as a sort of distraction tool by the fictive author, who employs them to relieve the pain of his own narration. More conspicuously, the novel's alternation of historiographic and autobiographic sections provides a very graphic picture of the functioning of Daniel's mind, which must helplessly and obsessively return to the traumatic events—past and present—when he should be writing a history dissertation.

"Daniel's Book" also reveals that, when exposed to cues that recall his parents' execution, Daniel suffers intense psychological distress. This may be best seen in the fact that he is deeply unsettled when it is suggested that Susan's psychiatrist is going to use shock therapy on her: "He was GONE! A lucky think [sic] too, I would have killed him" (251). Furthermore, when exposed to an event which resembles or reminds him of the traumatic event, Daniel suffers a psychosomatic reaction, which involves breathing difficulties: "I often had spells of difficult breathing. These frightened me. I found that if I ran around and waved my arms like a windmill, I could breathe better for a moment" (195). Daniel is also articulated as showing persistent symptoms of increased arousal and episodes of hypervigilance and paranoia. And so, as his sister lies in the hospital bed, he claims: "[t]o be objective, they are still taking care of us, one by one" (255), which suggests that he is obsessed with the idea that there is a conspiracy to destroy his whole family. Finally, the narrative shows that, as is often reported to occur among trauma victims, Daniel manifests detachment from others and a very restricted range of affect: while he claims to be worried about "establish[ing] sympathy" (8) and metaphorically acknowledges that "heart rejection is a problem" (356), his behavior suggests that he is unable to feel an emotional connection with anyone other than his sister Susan, not even his wife and baby or his adoptive parents. His attitude is one of absolute disrespect for anyone's feelings. Furthermore, Daniel is unable to enjoy any of the activities that are usually found pleasurable by average people, such as hobbies, sexual intercourse, family life or social interaction. This can be illustrated by one of the most distressing passages of the novel, in which Daniel's capacity to turn a beautiful family scene into an insane nightmare becomes manifest:

> In the park I threw Paul in the air and caught him, and he laughed. Phyllis smiled [...]. I tossed my son higher and higher, and now he laughed no longer but cried out. Still I did not stop and threw him higher and caught him closer to the ground. Then Phyllis was begging me to stop. The baby now shut his mouth, concentrating on his fear, his small face, my Isaacson face, locked in absolute dumb dread of the breath-taking flight into the sky and even more terrifying fall toward earth. I can't bear to think about this murderous feeling [...]. I enjoyed the fear in his mother. When I finally stopped she grabbed Paul and sat hugging him. He was white [...]. I took off. (161)

As this quotation suggests, Daniel simply cannot take pleasure in any activity which a healthy person would find enjoyable. More conspicuously, it also points to a destructive, violent nature that leads him to victimize every single person around him, an issue that will be taken up in the second section.

In short, there is a clear case to argue that *The Book of Daniel* engages with the representation of the imagined psychological consequences of trauma for the protagonist. The origin of Daniel's condition is shown to lie at the exposure to his parents' conviction and execution, triggered by his sister's suicide attempt fifteen years later. Yet, it becomes evident as the narrative progresses that, as is often the case among trauma survivors, his psychological response to the event is dramatically worsened by a constellation of traumatic life experiences or cumulative micro-aggressions. And so, Daniel struggles through a childhood of poverty and fear of his insane, cursing grandmother and the black man who lives in the cellar; he watches his father take a beating at the hands of right-wing fanatics; he witnesses the search and dismantling of his home after his parents' arrest, which causes him to wander from hand to hand—from a repulsive, unloving aunt, to a shelter for orphaned children and a foster family that is only interested in the Isaacson children as propaganda for the Communist Party. Finally, he suffers humiliating visits to his parents in jail until he finally finds himself an orphan after the execution which, not having witnessed, he is left to obsessively imagine. This constellation of traumatic micro-aggressions contributes to turning the not-uncommon event of a parent's death into a deeply traumatizing ordeal for the protagonist.

Daniel's suffering is further aggravated by a number of key determining circumstances. First of all, Rochelle and Paul Isaacson are convicted and executed by the state for a crime that they may or may not have committed. This undecidability adds to the traumatic impact of their death, since it denies Daniel any possibility of ever achieving closure as he cannot be certain of their guilt: "I have put down everything I can remember of their actions and conversations in this period prior to their arrests. Or I think I have. Sifted it through my hands. I find no clues either to their guilt or innocence" (159). It is also worth mentioning that the loss of his parents leaves Daniel alone and defenseless in the society whose legal and political institutions have deprived him of his family. In addition, Daniel was very young when his mother and father were taken away from him; as Laurie Vickroy has noted, children are particularly vulnerable to trauma, because it affects the way their psyche develops, impairs their life coping skills and determines how they will relate to other people in the future (14). In short, the arrest, conviction and execution of the Isaacsons render Daniel helpless and disempowered, unable to do anything to change the outcome of events. It is worth pointing out that helplessness has been shown to play a key role in making an experience traumatic (van der Kolk and van der Hart 175). Daniel's lack of agency conspicuously continues to the present day. As he bitterly remarks, his parents' case has deprived him "of the right to be dangerous" (89). He goes on:

> If I were to assassinate the President, the criminality of my family, its genetic criminality, would be established. There is nothing I can do, mild or extreme, that they cannot have planned for. [...] If, on the other hand, I were to become publically militant Daniel Isaacson all their precautions would have been justified. And probably whatever cause I lent myself to could be more easily discredited. (89–90)

Not that he is particularly interested in radical politics after what happened to his family—including Susan. Indeed, some critics have pointed to Daniel's increasing sense of political dissonance as an important factor contributing to his mental illness. Michelle Tokarczyk, for instance, has rightly observed that "Daniel might have had a better foundation for rebuilding [after his parents' death] had he not also lost belief in the ideals that served as touchstones for his parents" (12). Daniel's disillusionment with radical politics manifests itself in the bitter criticism of the Communist Party that underlies his narrative; as he explains, most of the Isaacson's (communist) friends quickly turned their back on Daniel's parents, and the party did not hesitate to erase their names from the membership list right after their arrest, fearing that their conviction would be detrimental to North-American communism. Later on, however, when the Isaacson's potential as tools for political propaganda becomes obvious to the Party, their cause is soon embraced, turning Susan and Daniel into puppets to be exhibited rally after rally, and causing Daniel to eventually lose all faith in radical politics. Susan is convinced, or rather, needs to believe, that "the name Isaacson has meaning" and that "what happened to the Isaacsons is a lesson to this generation" (99). And although Daniel despises her for what he perceives as naïveté, his disillusionment and contempt for radical politics conflicts with his life-long obsession with taking care of his little sister. Daniel's inability to believe in any of the principles for which his parents were executed and that have been enthusiastically endorsed by his sister clashes violently with his perceived sense of family obligation and increases his guilt, as we will see.

The fictive author's traumatic condition not only shapes the novel in terms of theme; it also influences the narrative formally in a number of ways. Geoffrey Harpham, who inaugurated a move away from the debate over history and politics in Doctorow's works to an emphasis on narrative technique, has argued that the master principle of the narrative is electricity. He contends that Daniel's fractured story builds to a recreation of his parents' execution (88). This statement could not be more accurate, since it is possible to argue that Daniel's narration mirrors the "schizophrenic" behavior of the electron: the narrative, like the electron, constantly and quickly leaps in time and space. In point of fact, the constant intrusion of the past into the present results in a narration full of digressions and flashbacks. Key trauma critics agree that the loss of what Anne Whitehead calls "conventional linear sequence" (6) is one of the main characteristics of trauma narratives (see Luckhurst 88, Vickroy 29, Granofsky 17). Laurie Vickroy further claims that anachrony is a common technique for the formal representation of traumatic memories, which are often fragmented and tend to resist normal chronological narration (5). In *The Book of Daniel*, the narrative similarly progresses in a nonlinear manner from one period in Daniel's life to the next and back without warning, by means of apparently chaotic, fragmented leaps in time (and place):

> Perhaps [Phyllis] could summon up my dissertation, actually create it, just by imagining me here in the library. Why not, if her imagination was good enough? One autumn day, with the wind slicing through the chain link fence around the schoolyard, and heavy grey clouds racking into each other over the rooftops of apartment houses, Rochelle went shopping with her son, Daniel, and her baby daughter, Susan. (122)

As this quotation shows, the events do not unfold chronologically in Daniel's tale, but are, rather, rendered in a manner that evokes the way they would come up to the fictive author's mind. Indeed, Daniel admits that he is struggling to "work out the chronology" (193). For instance, at one time he does not even seem to know how old he is or in which year he was born: "We moved there in 1945 when I was four years old. Or maybe in 1944 when I was five years old" (118).

The novel's anachronous feel is further achieved through the use of the present tense to narrate the past. This is the case, for instance, of Daniel's story about the family trip to a concert as a little boy: "In the meantime a yellow school bus has turned into the block. The driver is hunched over the wheel, peering at house numbers" (56). This is a distinctive mark of free indirect style that tends to create the impression of immediacy between narrator and events—and thus between readers and events. To complicate things further, in spite of generally being a retrospective narration in which past events are rendered from Daniel's present-day position, at times the adult focalization gives way to passages where the protagonist seems to withdraw completely to his childhood: "It is Sunday, a warm Sunday morning in September. Everyone is up early. The phone is ringing. I am admonished to hurry up and wash and get dressed. I have to feed stupid Susan while the grownups get dressed" (53). Awkward child-focalized parts like this one further contribute to creating a sense of timelessness. In addition, while most of the events are narrated retrospectively—whether written in the present tense or in the past—at times the narrator tells the story at the very moment in which it occurs:

> This is a Thinline felt tip marker, black. This is Composition Notebook 79C made in U.S.A. by Long Island Paper Products, Inc. This is Daniel trying one of the dark coves of the Browsing Room. Books for browsing are on the shelves. I sit at a table with a floor lamp at my shoulder. [...] I feel encouraged to go on. Daniel, a tall young man of twenty-five, wore his curly hair long. (3–4)

In that sense, following Gérard Genette's analysis of temporal position, *The Book of Daniel* may be defined as an "interpolated narration" (175), since it combines subsequent and simultaneous narration. Interestingly, as Vickroy has noted, interpolation mimics the disorienting effects of trauma (5). It is worth adding that the use of an interpolated narrative style has an obvious effect on the text: the story and the act of narrating become entangled in such a way that the latter has a metafictional effect on the former, and the act of writing becomes a self-conscious effort. These strategies are frequently deployed in trauma fictions to represent formally the discomfiting sense of timelessness often associated with trauma and the problems separating the past from the present that survivors are reported to often encounter.

The novel's time shifts parallel fluctuations in terms of narrative voice. The story teems with random shifts of voice, from first- to third-person narration and back without warning, often from one paragraph, or even from one sentence, to the next: "Less and less did my heart bound in erratic dyssynchronous jumps, like the rubber band balls I used to make. And so Susan and Daniel Lewin slipped into the indolent rituals of teenage middle class" (77). As this quote exemplifies, split voice complicates the analysis of the figure of the narrator, blurring the distinction between homodiegetic (also autodiegetic in this case) and heterodiegetic narration (Genette 184). Yet, as we will see in the second part of this chapter, Daniel remains the only narrating authority in the novel; "Daniel's Book" is his testimony, his primary witness account of the traumatic past events that are responsible for his present condition. Thus, the heterodiegetic voice that emerges at times also belongs to Daniel, since it is also his consciousness that lies behind it. The fragmentation of the narrative voice may be, once again, understood as an attempt to represent formally the dissociation of personality that works as a defense mechanism among some traumatized subjects, as theorized by medical professionals (see for example Herman 43); as Vickroy has noted, split voice mimics the fragmenting and disorienting effect of trauma on victims (27). It is worth adding, in fact, that the shifts from homodiegetic to heterodiegetic narration do not occur at random; as was the case with the historiographic intersections, voice shifts frequently take place when Daniel is narrating a particularly painful memory or event, as the following quotation exemplifies: "And she looked so pale, my God, she is dying and there is nothing Daniel can do" (255).

Similarly, when the events that are being narrated are exceptionally distressing for the fictive author, repetition tends to occur. This may be seen, for instance, in Daniel's recurrent recalling of Susan's last words before she enters a sort of self-inflicted coma: "They are still fucking us. Goodbye, Daniel. You get the picture" (10); "You get the picture. Good boy, Daniel" (82); "THEY ARE STILL FUCKING US. [...] YOU GET THE PICTURE. GOODBYE, DANIEL" (189); and then in Daniel's rendering of his first visit to his parents in jail: "I don't remember who drove the car. It was not Ascher, Ascher was sitting next to me in the back seat. I was in the middle. Susan was on my right" (290–291); "I can't remember who drove. Ascher sat in the back with us. I was between Ascher and Susan. My stomach hurt. My fingers ached" (291). In her study of trauma fiction, Whitehead has claimed that repetition constitutes a powerful formal strategy used by trauma fictions to represent the process of acting out and evoke the troubled mental condition of a character (86). Finally, the narration features repetition also at the level of imagery, which may be best seen in the constant use of metaphors related to electricity, as argued above.

Traumatic Memories

As we have seen, *The Book of Daniel* concerns itself to a great extent with the narration of traumatic memories. These have been triggered by Susan's suicide attempt, prompting Daniel to write. The novel emphasizes the protagonist's problems to retrieve and represent his memories of the traumatic events, which are shown to further complicate his efforts to come to terms with the past. In an influential paper on traumatic memory, Dori Laub and Nanette C. Auerhahn noted that victims' knowledge can emerge in several ways: as transference episodes, in which present experiences are distorted or in some way influenced by the earlier traumatic event, as decontextualized memory fragments, and as overpowering narratives, where the traumatized subject can describe past events but continues to feel buried in the traumatic experience (295). Following Laub and Auerhahn's theorization, "Daniel's Book" as a whole qualifies as an overpowering narrative, since it is plainly evident that Daniel is still buried under the original trauma, despite managing to describe past events in a conscious, even if unintegrated way. Second, decontextualized memory fragments frequently disrupt the narrative line. Among these stands out the episode in which a car smashes a woman against a metallic fence right in front of a very young Daniel's eyes, who sees her blood mixing with the milk from the bottle that she was carrying. This episode is mentioned several times, but neither information about its context nor proof of its veracity are ever provided, and its significance for Daniel can only be guessed. Connecting Doctorow's scenes of complex witnessing with Freud, Naomi Morgenstern calls episodes such as these "primal scenes" in a wider sense of the term, claiming that they are characterized by the fact that they do not require readers to decide over their status as memory or fiction and could be memories that help Daniel "to store, or represent, experiences which defy representation" (72). Finally, there are several transference episodes, the best example probably being Daniel's rendering of his parents' funeral, which abruptly turns into his sister's own funeral, catching the reader off-guard:

> We stand at the side of the graves. An enormous crowd presses behind us. The prayers are incanted. Everyone is in black. I glance at Susan. She is perfectly composed [...]. I feel her warm hand in my hand and see her lovely eye cast down at the open earth at our feet and an inexpressible love fills my throat and weakens my knees. I think if I can only love my little sister for the rest of our lives that's all I will need. The Lewins ride in the rear seat, Phyllis and I in jump seats at their knees. My mother wears a black hat with a veil over her eyes [...]. (365)

It seems apparent, then, that Daniel's determination to write about his traumatic past after his sister's "summons" is not an easy task. Cathy Caruth, relying on the scientific theories of medical professionals such as Judith Herman and Bessel van der Kolk—who have stressed the amnesic and dissociative nature of trauma response—claims that the images of traumatic representation, although often accurate and precise, are largely inaccessible to conscious control (151). In point of fact, some of

Daniel's memories are rendered with astonishing accuracy and in minute detail, to the extent that he even wonders at times: "How do I know this?" (63). He repeatedly calls himself "a little criminal of perception" (37, 41), and remembers with unnatural precision details which are far beyond a child's capacity. For instance, when the FBI starts to investigate his parents, he proves to have a general comprehension of everything that is happening around him:

> Meanwhile, the newspapers have been reporting a chain action of arrests around the world. An English scientist. An American engineer. A half-dozen immigrants in Canada. Secrets have been stolen. The FBI has been finding these people, and convicting them in the same press release. A chain reaction. (133)

This phenomenon has been described by psychiatrist Dori Laub when analyzing his own status as a witness and his awareness as a child survivor. He explains that "it is as though this process of witnessing was of an event that happened on another level, and was not part of the mainstream of conscious life of a little boy" ("Truth and Testimony" 62). Of course, excerpts such as the above might rather be the result of a break of the frame of narration, where the focalization of Daniel the adult infiltrates that of Daniel the little child. Despite his relative success in retrieving the long-repressed memories of his traumatic past, Daniel admits that there are still many things that he has not managed to recover: "I remember nothing of our trip to the Shelter" (197); or "just two or three images left from this period of our life" (183). Van der Kolk and van der Hart have explained that trauma interferes with the capacity to express traumatic events through narrative language (176). The reason for this has been explored by Dori Laub, who argues that trauma evades language because it occurs "outside the parameters of 'normal' reality, [...] outside the range of comprehension, of recounting and of mastery" ("Bearing Witness" 69). Shoshana Felman has further claimed that victims of trauma are *"robbed of a language* with which to articulate [their] victimization" (125; emphasis in the original). Echoing these theories, *The Book of Daniel* substantiates through plot and theme the severe psychological strain involved in attempting to express traumatic memories.

The problems that Daniel faces when trying to render in writing the traumatic experiences of his childhood are also evoked formally. First and foremost, by means of the novel's metafictionality; metafiction draws attention to the violence that, Daniel feels, forcing these events into the narrative conventions of chronology, unity of effect, teleology, cause-effect, characterization, etc. entails. Indeed, the protagonist refers to himself as "the monstrous writer who places one word after another" (300). This contention finds support in Daniel's highly metafictional list of "subjects to be taken up" (19), which he writes as he is trying to cope with the news of his sister's suicide attempt:

1   The old picture poster that I found in Susan's Volvo, in the front seat, in a cardboard tube.
2   The terrible scene the previous Christmas in the Jewish household at 67 Winthrop Rd., Brookline, a two-family house built, in the style of that neighborhood, to look like a one-family.
3   Our mad grandma and the big black man in the cellar.
4   Fleshing out the Lewins [...] Remember that it wasn't until you got into Susan's car that it really hit you. They're still fucking us. You get the picture. Good boy, Daniel.
5   Just as long as you don't begin to think you're doing something that has to be done. I want to make that clear, man. You are a betrayer [...]. (19)

Structurally, this list resembles the typical plan that a writer would elaborate before starting to write—but would probably not include in the final draft—and covers many of the issues that Daniel plans to address in his alleged book. Its significance lies in the fact that it not only draws attention to the act of writing—a common narrative strategy deployed by many of Doctorow's contemporaries; it also highlights the indescribable pain that Daniel suffers when attempting nor merely to narrate the past, but to fit it into an "acceptable" narrative form.

Second, the protagonist's supposed inability to remember certain things results in the creation of silences and gaps. These, as Anne Whitehead reminds us, represent formally the "obstacles to communicating experience" that traumatized subjects find when it comes to rendering the traumatic events that are responsible for their condition (3). A particularly disturbing example of such silences is Daniel's depiction of his first weeks at the Shelter:

> Some of the older boys were into puberty and had hair. There was a lot of homo wrestling. One kid liked to jerk off in the middle of the room where everyone could see him. Once there was an attempted sodomizing. There were always violent confrontations and some kid or other would be discovered with a knife he shouldn't have had. (201–202)

Leaving aside the harshness of this passage, it is more interesting for what it does not say: Daniel is the new boy, and his narration hitherto suggests that he tended to have difficulties when relating to other people. It is possible to assume, then, that it must not have been very easy for Daniel to adapt to his new life at the Shelter. Therefore, one wonders how much of the description above might be a veiled account of his own experience, whether he might have been the victim of that attempted sodomy or the one who was caught with a knife. After all, if things had gone as smoothly at the Shelter as Daniel would have readers believe, he would not have been so utterly desperate to run away. Laurie Vickroy has argued that silences and gaps in a trauma narrative may also represent the traumatic sense of simultaneous knowledge and denial as a result of resistance and repression, and they evoke a conflicted or incomplete relation to memory (29). In keeping with such view, it may be argued that Daniel is blocking information, that he is consciously or unconsciously repressing certain memories. Richard McNally's *Remembering Trauma* (2003), a review of new research that suggests that trauma is, indeed, memorable and representable, raises serious questions about the clinical and scientific foundation on which trauma critics such as Caruth, Hartman, and Felman built their cultural theory. Summarizing McNally's central argument, Joshua Pederson claims that "while victims may *choose* not to speak of their traumas, there is little evidence that they *cannot*" (334; emphasis in the original). The question that naturally follows McNally's—and others'—refutation of one of the founding notions of trauma theory is the following: why may survivors choose not to talk about their trauma? Some sectors within the medical profession have recently started to pay attention to the connection that exists between shame/guilt and silence among traumatized victims. As psychologist Alon Blum explains, victims of trauma often consciously avoid mentioning a significant aspect of their experience "because of the shame it involves and the fear of being exposed and rejected" (93).[5]

Another aspect that deserves consideration is the fact that Daniel's memories are not always reliable. For instance, he admits several times to have simply invented what he has just explained. Furthermore, his unreliability as a narrator is also suggested by the fact that, at times, he seems to be incapable of separating the "real" world from the products of his own imagination:

> Also, a heavy, old diamond shaped microphone from a real radio station. It broadcasts on a secret frequency directly to my father in his jail cell [...] I advise him to be ready and to wait further instructions. Roger, he radios back to me. Roger and out, I reply. (149)

As this quotation suggests Daniel's unreliability appears particularly evident in light of the ironic gap that exists between his story and the ultimate implications of the text: no reader would fail to notice that the statement above cannot be possible true, that it is the product of the protagonist's fantasy of communicating with his father after he has been arrested. Daniel, however, is convinced of its veracity. His unreliability as a narrator is also indicated by the fact that, as the story progresses, he seems to have become mysteriously omniscient. And so, he provides an outright invented narrative of his parents' last moments before their execution, although he was not there to witness it:

> First they led in my father. [...] His legs were weak. He had to be held up. His eyes were red from crying, but he was drained, and now they were dry. [...] When he was seated his breathing became more rapid. He closed his eyes and clenched his hands in his lap. [...] A few minutes after my father's body had been removed on a stretcher, and the floor mopped, and the organic smell of his death masked in the ammoniac scent of the cleanser, my mother was led into the chamber. [...] On her face was a carefully composed ironic smile. (359–362)

The simultaneous need for Daniel to construct a narrative of the past in order to try and establish whether his parents were guilty of the crimes they were executed for and his problems and fears about remembering those extremely painful moments cause him to build an unreliable story made of scraps: his own fragmented but precise memories, the trial transcript, his parents' letters, other accounts by the people involved and his own invented passages. This fact links Daniel's narrative to Sandra Gilbert's notion of "writing wrong" (in Uytterschout 64–65), rendering *The Book of Daniel* what Doctorow himself has termed a "false document." According to Gilbert, who writes about her own personal experiences, "survivors of trauma are left behind with so many questions that all they can (try to) do is filling the gaps of a story [...]. Survivors writing about their experiences are in fact *imagining* what happened" (in Uytterschout 65; emphasis in the original). Gilbert's contention is particularly thought-provoking because, in a way, it points to not only the inherent fictiveness but also the essential truthfulness of survivor accounts. Such a view is also coherent with Doctorow's firm belief in the subjectivity or fictionality of all discourse as expressed in his seminal essay "False Documents." *The Book of Daniel* may be considered a false document for one key reason: its fictional treatment of trauma could well pass for autobiographical writing by a primary witness, and yet, his choice of a well-known topic such as the Rosenberg case effectively excludes this possibility. This contention seconds a point also made by Naomi Morgenstern, who claims that the novel "argues that 'false' memory allows for the only 'true' testimony to trauma" (72).

Interestingly, this understanding of trauma accounts would also cancel out the controversy over who is entitled to write about trauma (see LaCapra 186): the amount of literature written after World War II whose fictional world circles around trauma has led to a complex debate which, as we will see in Chapter 4, has become particularly intense in recent years in the context of Holocaust studies, built upon concerns over the danger of appropriating real victim's experiences for commercial purposes. Scholars Lawrence Langer and Kali Tal among others, who have worked extensively with survivor testimony, have famously put forward the claim that survivor accounts are the only acceptable form of trauma testimony. They object to the "wrongful" appropriation of trauma by secondary witnesses or non-survivors, fearing hidden agendas and attempts to fit the trauma experience into literary conventions such as chronology, description, characterization and the invention of a narrative voice (in Uytterschout 64). After all, as Rothberg has noted, issues of circulation and commodification have proved to be a key issue since the times of postmodernism (13), and more specifically when addressing the fictional representation of trauma. Most scholars and critics, however, concede that trauma is nowadays not only the silent psychic response of an individual to an overwhelmingly painful or terrifying event. They have called attention to the enormous influence of trauma as a symbol of horror in contemporary society, a society that is possessed by the angst of having finally understood the evil which human beings are capable of doing. Thus, most critics are willing to welcome narratives that seek to confront contemporary readers with a reality characterized by social, economic and political structures that potentially create and perpetuate trauma.

Healing?

In spite of his awareness that his narration is fragmented, incomplete, and at times admittedly invented, Daniel feels the need to write the story of his traumatic past. On the one hand, he seeks to relieve his guilt, since he feels that "some of the force that propelled [Susan's] razor was supplied by [him]" (36), thus assuming that it was his betrayal, his refusal to support her in the creation of a foundation bearing their parents' name, that led her to try and end her life. He understands that he has failed to support Susan in her own desperate attempt to find peace through the clearing of their family name. On the other hand, Daniel's guilt also stems from his active rejection of the past all through his adult life, presumably because it was too painful and maybe also mortifying for him to think about what happened to his parents:

> [A]ll my life I have been trying to escape from my relatives and I have been intricate in my run, but one way or another they are what you come upon around the corner, and the Lord God who is so frantic for recognition says you have to ask how they are and would they like something cool to drink, and what is it you can do for them this time. (37)

Daniel's shame is certainly deep as well: as a child, he suffered humiliating visits to his parents at the Death House, where he was confronted with the progressive disintegration of their old selves. In addition, he was also forced to bear the shame of being used as a puppet to be exhibited Communist rally after rally, after being placed in foster care. The feelings of shame and guilt that overwhelm Daniel since his childhood are, undoubtedly, key elements of his traumatic condition. The influence of these affects on survivors' responses to trauma has long been recognized by medical professionals. Among them it is worth bringing to the fore the work of Judith Herman. Aiming at incorporating the experiences of women and children to the newly created PTSD diagnosis, she suggested a new one, "complex PTSD," to account for the symptoms of prolonged, repeated and even chronic trauma where the victim is submitted to totalitarian control (121). In Herman's theorization, guilt and shame are introduced as additional symptoms associated with a majority of long-term traumatic experiences. It is worth adding that these affects have also been proved to play a central role in the chronification of trauma.

As characteristically seems to happen to many trauma victims, Daniel has been silent for years about his parents' execution, troubled by visions that he could not fully own. Now, by allegedly writing the book that we are reading, Daniel is shown to seek to get rid of the burden that troubles his heart in order to find some peace:

> IS IT SO TERRIBLE NOT TO KEEP THE MATTER IN MY HEART, TO GET THE MATTER OUT OF MY HEART, TO EMPTY MY HEART OF THIS MATTER? WHAT IS THE MATTER WITH MY HEART? [...] I, Daniel, was grieved, and the visions of my heart troubled me and I do not want to keep the matter in my heart. (21)

Theorists of trauma such as Judith Herman, Suzette Henke and Dori Laub have stressed the importance of creating a narrative of the event as a strategy to work through trauma and attenuate the damage caused by traumatic memories, or at least to provide some peace to the individual. Indeed, Herman highlights the need for the victim to reorganize "fragmented components of frozen imagery and sensation" into "an organized, detailed, verbal account, oriented in time and historical contents" (177). Similarly, Laub argues that a victim must "re-externalize" the traumatic event by articulating and transmitting the story to an "empathic listener" and then "take it back again, inside" ("Bearing Witness" 68–69). In the same line, Suzette Henke points to autobiography as a form of what she calls "scriptotherapy," which offers the possibility "of writing out and writing through traumatic experience in the mode of therapeutic re-enactment" (xii–xiii). The power of articulating and voicing the traumatic experience as a first step toward the cure of trauma was already promoted by Freud and Breuer in their famous theory of the "talking cure," which allegedly would allow patients to transform their traumatic memories into a coherent narrative (57, 68).

Echoing these theories, "Daniel's Book" may be seen as the fictive author's attempt to write his parents off and overcome the trauma of losing them at the hands of the state. For this, he relies on an empathic reader. Daniel's dependence on the narratee—or narratees—is suggested by his frequent references to them throughout the narrative, an example of which is the following quote: "I suppose you think I can't do the electrocution. I know there is a you. There has always been a you. YOU: I will show you that I can do the electrocution" (359). This quotation not only hints at Daniel's difficulties to narrate the actual event of his parents' execution; it also reveals the explicit "you" to which the narrative is addressed. The explicit or implicit narratee has been widely recognized as an essential element of all types of narrative (see Prince 194). In the case of *The Book of Daniel*, this is certainly a very interesting figure—or figures, rather: Professor Sukenick,[6] Daniel's thesis director, can be assumed to be the addressee of most of the out-of-context encyclopedia-like interludes that interrupt Daniel's narration of the traumatic events of his past. As explained above, these excerpts of varied length deal with topics which, generally speaking, would be considered appropriate for a history dissertation. More importantly, at other times Daniel's narratee is revealed to be Susan, who is explicitly addressed in situations of remarkable psychological strain for Daniel:

> As it is I've done too much for you—and for what? You don't talk, you don't reinforce their sense of you. All they have is my word. I remember your voice, but how can I expect them to remember your voice. You can't write out voices. All I can say about your voice is that it is so familiar to me that I cannot perceive the world except with your voice framing the edges of my vision. It is on the horizon and under my feet. The world has always been washed in Susan's voice. (254)

As this quotation illustrates, Daniel's pain after his sister's suicide attempt causes him to often turn her into the addressee of his narration. What is more, Daniel seems to be writing not only to her but *for* her: it is from her that he seeks understanding and forgiveness, for which he explicitly addresses her, and it is for her that he decides to try and put their traumatic past into writing, perhaps hoping to save the two of them.

Yet, at other times, Daniel seems to direct his alleged text to an unknown narratee, who is addressed frequently and in different terms depending on Daniel's mood at the time. Indeed, the narratee is at times articulated as a sympathetic reader who might be willing to help Daniel in his mourning process:

A NOTE TO THE READER
Reader, this is a note to you. If it seems to you elementary, if it seems after all this time elementary [...] then reader, I am reading you. And together we may rend our clothes in mourning. (67)

88 The Book of Daniel

At other times, however, Daniel reveals a rather antagonistic relationship with the narratee. This is the case when he narrates particularly despicable episodes, such as those where he renders his abusive behavior toward his wife:

> Do you believe it? Shall I continue? Do you want to know the effect of three concentric circles of heating element glowing orange in a black night upon the tender girlflesh of my wife's ass? Who are you anyway? Who told you you could read this? (75)[7]

As Mieke Bal has noted, the reader watches with the focalizer's eyes and will presumably be inclined to accept the vision presented by that character (146), which is arguably the basis of traditional reader identification patterns in literature. As the above quotation suggests, despite Daniel's concern with establishing sympathy among readers, he is well aware that it is an almost impossible task, given his violent behavior. As a result, he seems to self-punishingly fantasize with a narratee that is more of an enemy than a supporter. Once again, this might be best understood in the context of Daniel's traumatic condition. Vickroy has pointed out that victims of trauma often feel isolated and alienated from society because of their differences with others (23). Similarly, Judith Herman has argued that social judgment of traumatized people tends to be very hard (115). Thus, it may be claimed that Daniel is too ashamed of his behavior, too obsessed with his family's traditional victimization and too tired of being judged by others and used as a tool for political propaganda to expect genuine empathy from anyone. A related issue would be whether empathy might be expected from the novel's implied reader, a possibility that will be addressed in the last section of this chapter.

The question that this discussion begs is whether Daniel's relative success in narrating the traumatic memories of the past has eased his condition and healed his ailment. His ability toward the end of the novel to narrate his parents' execution—the single event that has been eluded throughout the narrative and yet unavoidably hovers over it—together with his ability to do so in the past tense, indicates that he has managed, to a certain extent, to "assimilate" the traumatic experience into his model of the world, to borrow Granofsky's phrasing of the phenomenon (8). However, as Daniel himself beautifully puts it, the imprint of Susan's small warm hand in his hand is permanent. After all, as van der Kolk and van der Hart have found,

> in the case of complete recovery [...] the story can be told, it has been given a place in the person's life history. However, the traumatic experience/memory is, in a sense, timeless. It cannot be transformed into a story placed in time, with a beginning, a middle and an end. If it can be told at all, it is still a (re)experience. (177)

And so, the excessiveness of Daniel's behavior at his sister's funeral in the last pages of his account suggests that, although he has managed to re-integrate the past and achieved some sense of closure, he might never get over his unbearable pain; despite his progress toward working through, the wounds left on his mind by the loss of his family have not healed at the end of the novel.

Concluding Remarks

As I hope my analysis has proved, *The Book of Daniel* qualifies as a trauma novel, since it has been shown to explore the causes and consequences of extreme traumatic events not only at a thematic level—as subject matter—but also at a formal one. Like other trauma fictions, the novel has internalized "the rhythms, processes, and uncertainties of traumatic experience within [its] underlying sensibilities and structures" (Vickroy 3). Indeed, some of the formal features described above demonstrate that the novel is coherent with the general tendency among trauma fictions to bring conventional narrative techniques to their limit (see Whitehead 82). Second, Doctorow's novel focuses on the difficulties and problems for victims of trauma to recover and articulate traumatic memories, reflecting on issues of reliability and accuracy, the conflict between knowledge and denial, and the different ways of accessing the traumatic past. Finally, the analysis has considered the possibility of healing through the act of narration, through the creation of a narrative that may allow the protagonist to come to terms with the past.

Gender Oppression and/as Power

The Book of Daniel is a novel full of contradictions which render it a plural text open to multiple readings. Indeed, it is readily apparent that, when read against the grain, Doctorow's novel constitutes an interesting site for feminist revision. For one thing, most of the central characters in the novel are women.[8] This section sets out to examine the novel's attitude toward some key feminist concerns. In what follows, the book's position with regard to female subjectivity and perspective will be explored, assessing as well the existence of gender dialogue. The ascription of gender roles will also be considered. Finally, I will analyze the representation of gender violence and oppression in the novel, while also addressing its ethical implications.

Subjectivity and Gender Dialogue

To begin with, it is key to acknowledge that, being an autodiegetic narration, all the events in *The Book of Daniel* are filtered through Daniel's perspective and voice, much more so since he is also the fictive author of the book that we are reading, as we have seen. There is no other narrative voice in a superior ontological level; Daniel's consciousness hovers over the whole narrative, placed at the level immediately superior to that of the story. The narrator's frequent shifts of voice, discussed in the previous section, do not correspond to shifts in perspective, and Daniel remains the main focalizer in the novel. The only exceptions are some newspaper excerpts, a few letters written by Paul and Rochelle Isaacson from their prison cells, the lawyer Ascher, Daniel's adoptive father, Daniel's Grandma and Susan, and presumably also those rather rare occasions in which Daniel reports another character's words in direct style. In any case, and keeping in mind his unreliability as a narrator, it is through Daniel's perspective that all the events in the novel are presented, always framed by his commentary and interpretation. Daniel's apparent refusal to open his text to other voices deserves thorough examination, much more so when approaching the novel from a feminist critical perspective. After all, a central concern among feminist critics has been to examine the representation of gendered subjectivities and to assess the existence of gender dialogue.

In her study of female characters in *The Book of Daniel*, Mildred Culp aptly claimed that women collectively "prove integral to the novel" due to the guidance that they provide not only to Daniel, but also to the readers (156). On the one hand, his life choices and decisions are shown to be strongly determined by the different relationships established with these key female characters. On the other hand, his treatment of his mother, sister and wife allows readers to understand his disrupted attachments. In other words, it is through analysis of Daniel's relationship to the novel's main female characters that we are given access to, and can better approach, his troubled mind. First of all, Daniel's narration proudly depicts Rochelle Isaacson as a very strong, realistic and intelligent woman. She is an active member of the Communist Party. She faces her trial, conviction and execution with a "composed ironic smile" on her face (363) and is executed last because "they had rightly conceived that [his] mother was the stronger" (359), even needing a second "dose" of electricity to be killed. Notwithstanding Daniel's visible love for his mother, it soon becomes obvious that, as a little boy, he was already starting to begrudge her power and control over the whole family. In fact, Rochelle is at times presented as a castrating woman whose authority Daniel cannot but resent: "My mother directs us all like a military commander" (53) and "nothing is really official without my mother's endorsement" (57). Meanwhile, Daniel's father is reduced to the role of an "irresponsible child," a man too self-obsessed to take care of practical family matters who "couldn't be trusted to make a living" (45). Apart from depriving young Daniel of his mother, Rochelle's arrest and premature death in the electric chair conspicuously prevent Daniel from challenging her overwhelming authority. As an adult, he seems to be caught between feelings of love and rejection that he has been kept from confronting and resolving, leaving him buried under another layer of guilt and shame.

The narrative similarly reveals that Daniel loves Susan deeply. He idolizes his sister to a point that verges upon insanity and measures all the women in his life against her. And so, for instance, it is a fierce fight with her over her decision to create a foundation for revolution with their parents' name on it that makes him aware of "a poverty in his choice of wife" (97). The bond between Daniel and Susan is too complex, too contradictory and yet too strong to be understood outside the context of their mutual traumatic condition: all throughout his life he has taken care of his sister and tends to her lovingly when she is in hospital after her suicide attempt, wanting to become her sole legal guardian; yet, he fights her roughly in every occasion, always trying to exert his power over her; he admits that his life is strongly determined by hers, but he is glad to be the one who survives; he despises her for her ideas about politics, drugs and sex, and yet he admires her deeply for her passion, strength and determination. Their relationship is further complicated by a sort of mutual incestuous attraction, and Daniel seems to be obsessed with his sister's sexuality. And so, he explains that when Susan was thirteen, she "used to work her tentative saucy sex on [him]" (265), and she gave him "glimpses of herself in her underwear" (78). Likewise, Daniel showed her the hair that he was growing around his penis, and he admits that "more than once [he has] asked [him]self if [he'd] like to screw [his] sister" (253). Although his own answer seems to be 'no,' such fixation with each other's sexuality reveals that the traumatic events of their childhood have impaired their way of relating to one another and to other people. Susan's influence over Daniel is so strong that he admits having chosen his wife out of a merely erotic motivation, perhaps seeking to put an end to the unresolved sexual component of his relationship with Susan. Finally, as argued before, it is Daniel's dreadful guilt over being in some way responsible for Susan's decision to take her own life that acts as a summons for him to finally own the memories of his traumatic past and tell the story of their parents' execution. This in effect renders Susan the single propelling force behind the story that we are reading.

In spite of these female characters' structural and thematic relevance, Daniel resists releasing control over his narration. In the case of Rochelle, the following quotation is particularly illuminating of Daniel's narrative practices:

> *She* worries about him [...] He lives on candy bars from the canteen, and advises *her* to do the same. They don't have his cigars so he smokes camels. He smokes too much and is too thin. Dear God, does he really look for justice? Dear God, grant him foresight. Make

> *my* terrible burden lighter [...] *I* lie in this cell and Mama's voice of her curses comes to *me* down the corridor. The cholera the Cossacks. (232–233; emphasis added)

Toward the end of the novel, Daniel not only includes a couple of conversations between his parents and their lawyer, which he certainly could not have witnessed but may have known about later via the lawyer; he conspicuously renders in writing his mother's supposed thoughts and feelings, creating for her a plainly invented internal monologue. Smoothly moving from the third to the first person—without using inverted commas—Rochelle becomes a fictional character at the mercy of an omniscient Daniel, who unapologetically impersonates or appropriates her voice. As for Susan, despite being a central character or at least the subject matter in most of the narrated episodes, it is Daniel's version that the reader has access to, in which Susan is relegated to the role of secondary character whose voice, as Brian Dillon observantly notices, can only be heard three times throughout the narrative (373). Daniel's depiction of his sister allows the reader to get a glimpse of her traumatic condition and her own desperate attempts to cope, but her experience is not available in an unmediated rendering, and can only be inferred from her brother's narration. Aaron DeRosa acknowledges the silencing of Susan in the novel, but blames it on the collective narrative about the Isaacson case, which overwrites her private trauma (474). While he is right in his claim, Daniel's role in Susan's silencing cannot be so easily dismissed. In her passionate letter after their fight—which incidentally is one of the three occasions where readers have unmediated access to Susan's adult focalization—she informs her brother that, as a consequence of his betrayal, he no longer exists for her, as she is writing him out of her mind, which she achieves by eradicating her own consciousness and adopting "the silence of the starfish" (253). Furthermore, while at that time he seems to truly lament the loss of her voice, the narrative reveals that he had long found Susan to be "too bright, too loud, too hysterically self-occupied," "a commanding presence" that was no longer his "little kid sister" (78), but "a moralist, a judge [...] with her aggressive moral openness, with her loud and intelligent and repugnantly honest girlness. And all wrong. Always wrong" (11).

The stubborn refusal on Doctorow's part to incorporate the voices of women may be interpreted as a further strategy to emphasize the protagonist's psychological disorder. Following this line of thought, Daniel's erasure of female subjectivity through the female characters' subjection to the filter of his own mediating perspective could be easily ascribed to a desperate need on his part to counteract his helplessness and regain a sense of agency and an illusion of control over his life. Thus, arguably begrudging the female character's power over him, Daniel's closing of his text to the voices of his mother and sister may be read as a coping mechanism of sorts; that is, it may be construed as a desperate attempt to recover a sense of independence from the pronounced psychological grip that these two female characters have over the protagonist. In the case of Rochelle, after being turned into a character of Daniel's omniscient narration, she can no longer direct him "like a military commander" (53) as she used to when he was a little boy; she has become a character at the mercy of his mental schemes. Alternatively, the novel's inability or unwillingness to truly open itself to the points of view and voices of women may respond to the overbearing power of Daniel's voice as engineered by the author. Doctorow's explanation of the writing process in an interview is quite illuminating in that sense:

> When I had written about 150 pages, and it was not working out, I was very upset. In fact, I was desolate, and when I had just about given up, I sat down at the typewriter recklessly and irresponsibly, full of rage and frustration, just to do something. And I had my book. I was talking in Daniel's voice. [...] I had to go through that kind of emotional upheaval to discover who Daniel was. (in O'Neill 57)

Thus, the author's own experience of writing *The Book of Daniel* and crafting its protagonist would have entailed being possessed by Daniel's ubiquitous voice, leaving little or no space for other (female) perspectives. In any case, it seems apt to conclude that a conscious attempt to open the text to the voices of women has not been conducted. This seconds a point also indirectly made by Marshall B. Gentry, who in his paper "Ventriloquist Conversations" (1993) scanned several of Doctorow's novels in order to determine whether the author succeeded in incorporating gender dialogue, and found none in *The Book of Daniel*. Daniel's silencing of the female characters' voices by his obsessive narrative control also makes it possible to challenge John G. Parks contention that *The Book of Daniel* should be considered a polyphonic novel (455). In his paper, Parks borrows Bakhtin's notion of "polyphony" to argue that the novel is dialogic in that it is "both disruptive or even subversive of regimes of power, and restorative of neglected or forgotten or unheard voices" (455). While he is right in his claim—Parks refers to the neglected, forgotten and unheard voices of the (male) US left—he overlooks the absence of gender dialogue in the novel.

Gender Roles

The novel's representation of gender roles also begs for a critical enquiry. At first sight it may seem that the roles assigned to the female characters in the novel uncritically mirror hegemonic gender configurations. Grandma's life as a Russian immigrant in the United States is described as a routine of sixteen hours sewing on top of the strain of taking care of a home, a husband and three children. Similarly, her daughter Rochelle works as a bookkeeper while carrying the burden of all house and family chores. Then, when the Isaacson family decides that they can do with only one salary, it is Rochelle that gives up her job and retreats into the domestic realm, even though she used to make more money than her husband and was better educated. One generation later the situation is depicted in the exact same terms. Phyllis is a freshman dropout who has given up college to marry Daniel and start a family, while he fulfills his academic aspirations as a doctoral candidate. More importantly, Phyllis is forced to sacrifice her political activism to take care of the baby. The same problem affects Baby—the girlfriend of the revolutionary guru Artie Sternlicht—who subordinates her political involvement to domestic duties, so that he may fight the state that he opposes and which is at large responsible for the subordination of women. As Eric Rasmussen puts it, Sternlicht, the novel's primary figure of the sixties countercultural radicalism, can be viewed as an emblematic representative of the sexism that characterized a large number of members of the New Left (200), and which also defines Daniel.

Interestingly, however, the assignment of domestic roles to the female characters—which after all is nothing but an accurate depiction of the socio-historical climate of the novel's setting (see for example Friedan 1963)—does not preclude an effort at the level of textual implications to emphasize these characters' autonomy and strength. For one thing, it is readily apparent that both Grandma and Rochelle succeed in taking care of their homes and children while also providing for the family in economic terms, which Daniel proudly acknowledges in his narration. In point of fact, Rochelle's courage and determination puts her son and husband to shame. The same holds true for Susan, a leftist revolutionary activist whose main concern is to preserve her independence. In order to do so, she defies her brother and challenges the sexism of the New Left Movement by seeking to create a "Foundation for Revolution" to be run by herself. She goes so far as to confront Sternlicht's macho rhetoric and the subordination of his girlfriend's activism to his own domestic needs. It is her political insight that allows Susan to understand and expose the limitations of the New Left. In short, *The Book of Daniel* presents the reader with a number of strong, educated and courageous female characters to identify with, whose power Daniel's struggle for narrative control cannot completely erase.

Gender Violence and Oppression

When approaching *The Book of Daniel* from a feminist perspective, some of the issues that most immediately capture the critic's attention are, however, the protagonist's fascination with sexual violence and his abusive relationship with Phyllis, his wife. The former is made apparent by the constant use of metaphors related to aggressive sexual intercourse and violence. And so, for instance, after meeting the revolutionary guru Sternlicht and hearing about his ideas, Daniel concludes that "[he] is probably a champion fucker" (187). Similarly, Daniel describes his parents' trial in sexual terms: "[...] there could be no question about the semantics of disaster. They were fucking us. Each new indictment handed down by the Grand Jury perfecting the conspiracy, expanding it, adding to its overt acts, drove it in deeper" (198). Here, the process of building the Isaacson's conspiracy case is presented as a forceful coital penetration. Daniel's obsession with sexual violence materializes in the form of physical and psychological abuse toward his wife. The abusive nature of Daniel's relationship with Phyllis is emphasized from the start, since the moment that he confesses to the "strong erotic content" of his marriage and describes his wife as

> the kind of awkward girl with heavy thighs and heavy tits and slim lovely face whose ancestral mothers must have been bred in harems. The kind of unathletic helpless breeder to appeal to caliphs. The kind of sand dune that was made to be kicked around. (5)

Unlike the characters discussed in the previous subsections, Daniel presents Phyllis as a passive woman whose apparently weak character offers him the possibility of being, for once, the one in control, the victimizer rather than the victim. Indeed, the highly degrading description quoted above not only establishes the power relationship existent between Daniel—the "tormentor"—and his wife, who is defined as a "sex martyr" (7); readers may also see in a statement such as this one a warning of the explicit violence that is to come, the early confession of a sadistic abuser.

Indeed, *The Book of Daniel* incorporates a few rather crude episodes of sexual violence, in which Phyllis's victimization at the hands of her husband is depicted in great detail. The following one, for instance, deserves being quoted at length:

> Daniel instructed Phyllis to kneel on the seat facing her side of the car, and to bend over as far as she could, kneeled and curled up like a penitent, a worshipper, an abject devotionalist. [...] "Don't hurt me. Just don't hurt me, Daniel." He ran his right hand over her buttocks. The small of her back was dewy with sweat. She shivered and the flesh of her backside trembled under his hand. (74)

Leaving aside the obvious potential for scenes like these to trigger off traumatic reenactment among rape or domestic violence survivors, the representation of graphic violence against women in the novel produces, at best, ethical hesitancy. It is widely acknowledged that explicit descriptions of violence arouse strong emotions, ranging from voyeuristic sexual titillation to utter moralistic disgust or revulsion, leaving almost no one indifferent. As Kathryn Hume has aptly claimed, "aggressive fiction tramples reader sensibilities, offends and upsets willfully and deliberately" (8), which might even lead some readers to avert their eyes in disgust or even put the book down (9). What this boils down to in *The Book of Daniel*—as was the case in *Welcome to Hard Times*—is a hesitancy with respect to the ethical appropriateness of the "spectacle" of sexual violence: on the one hand, it may be read as an awareness-raising strategy on the novel's part, arguably intended to warn of the disastrous consequences of psychological trauma, a possibility that will be taken up in the last section of this chapter. On the other hand, what the novel is undoubtedly doing, like all forms of art, is to encourage readers to witness, in this case, sexual violence without an urgent moral imperative to act on it. Alternatively, exposure to explicit violence might eventually cause readers to become desensitized to the suffering of others. This often takes the shape of dissociation of affect, which is characteristic of what Luc Boltanski has termed "distance suffering" due to overexposure (in Hartman 269). This possibility has been widely explored by medical researchers, who have found reliable clinical evidence as to the desensitization to real-world violence resulting from exposure to media violence (see Smith and Donnerstein 176). Although no similar studies have, to my knowledge, been conducted with regard to violence in literature, visualizing violence with your mind's eye is arguably not necessarily less striking than watching it. In any case, both arguments point to the danger of turning violence into a spectacle. One might think here of Baudrillard's famous claim that "[t]he West's great undertaking [...] will turn out rather to have been the aestheticization of the whole world—its cosmopolitan spectacularization, its transformation into images, its semiological organization" (16).

We might find Doctorow's justification for his explicit depiction of gender violence in an interview, in which he reveals "a preoccupation having to do with sex as power, either perhaps using sex as a metaphor for political relations, or helplessly annotating what passes for sex in a society that suffers paternalistic distortions" (in Morris 121). From this perspective, Daniel's overbearing manipulation and erasure of his mother's and sister's subjectivity would in a way parallel his sadistic and violent treatment of his wife. Following this line of thought, Robert Forrey has gone so far as to suggest that Daniel shows unconscious, incestuous, sadistic impulses toward his mother, but his shame causes him to displace them onto his wife (169). Similarly, Naomi Morgenstern, in her psychoanalytic reading of the novel, has argued that "Daniel's sadism may be an attempt to overcome, by force, his own liminal status as the subject of (and subject to) the primal scene" (77). By this she refers to Daniel's obsession as a young child with spying on his parents' sexual activities: "They didn't go so far as to let me watch them fucking, but I did that too one way or another—I was a small criminal of perception" (37). While one may or may not agree with a psychoanalytic reading of Daniel's sadistic drive, and while one may or may not approve of the graphic representation of sexual violence, Daniel's despicable behavior toward his wife does succeed in determining the sort of bond established between himself and his readers, since it already challenges their readiness to identify with an autodiegetic narrator who is capable of such behavior. In other words, Daniel's sadism hampers traditional modes of reader identification. As we have seen, being an autodiegetic narrative *The Book of Daniel* privileges Daniel's subjective experience. Yet, the character-logic that generally encourages identification with the novel's main center of consciousness is challenged at the narratological level. This is due to the fact that the perception of Daniel as a morally responsible and sympathy-deserving character is dramatically affected by his sexual sadism. Thus, the natural bond of identification between the narrator and the reader that the novel form has traditionally favored (see Bal 146) is helplessly undermined in *The Book of Daniel*, which has important implications that will be explored presently.

Concluding Remarks

It seems apt to conclude, then, that *The Book of Daniel* does not prefigure itself as particularly compatible with feminist forms and themes. Put differently, the novel does not incorporate in a straightforward manner any key feminist concerns or demands. Quite the reverse, Daniel's overbearing presence in the novel bans any female subjectivity—or any other subjectivity, for that matter—from expressing itself as a distinct voice; the roles assigned to female characters appear to be nothing but an ultimate submission to the stereotype; and the novel's explicit depiction of sexual violence gives rise, at best, to ethical hesitancy. Yet, the novel's undermining of the traditional character-logic, its articulation of strong and courageous female characters, and its encouragement of alternative forms of reader identification leave room for a more sympathetic reading; after all, these factors may reveal a condemnation at the level of textual implications of Daniel's erasure of female subjectivity and his abusive behavior.

Discussion and Conclusion

Discussion

The analysis conducted so far has sought to unpack the novel's thematic and formal complexity. It has been argued that, as a trauma narrative, *The Book of Daniel* succeeds in rendering and formally representing the contradictions that characterize the protagonist's traumatic condition and his struggle over integration of his traumatic memories as a path toward healing. The second section has assessed the novel's apparent attitude toward certain feminist concerns, bringing to the fore the ethical hesitancy with respect to the explicit representation of violence and addressing its outright refusal to engage in gender dialogue. Before concluding this chapter, it seems in order to discuss a number of issues that surface thanks to the collusion of the analytic tools provided by trauma studies and feminist criticism.

With that purpose in mind, it is worth taking up again Daniel's sadistic behavior toward his wife. In his narrative, Daniel attempts to justify his abuse as a mentoring project to 'educate' Phyllis into suffering. Michelle Tokarczyk is right when she claims that "one of the most demanding burdens survival places upon a person is the sense of a survivor mission—the imperative to reveal what one has endured so others learn a crucial lesson" (7). Indeed, Daniel claims that Phyllis's leftist political leanings—her flower life and her love of peace—are "principles," "political decisions" (7), and so, he feels he must "work on her" (207) to teach her what being a revolutionary and belonging to the American left implies in terms of suffering; after all, their political stance cost his parents their life and Susan and him their mental health. As Daniel puts it, "it is a lot easier to be a revolutionary nowadays than it used to be" (314). Daniel's physical and psychological violence toward his wife may thus be read as part of the process of what LaCapra, following Freud, has termed "acting out" (21). First of all, it mirrors the determination of Daniel's father to indoctrinate his young son in order to instill communist values into him and improve his mind, "teaching [him] how to be a psychic alien" (42), an attitude that Daniel resents, not without guilt. Second, Daniel's behavior evokes his shame and strong sense of humiliation after his parents' arrest, a feeling which would become particularly acute during his visits to them in prison. Furthermore, like James Gilligan's prison inmates who repeatedly refer to a desire for respect as the motive for extreme violence (1149), Daniel seems to resort to aggression to replace the intolerable emotions of shame and guilt with the opposite feelings of pride and self-respect, and of being feared by others. It is worth recuperating Victoria Burrows definition of shame as "toxic, as destructively disorientating, as a moment of heightened and tormenting self-consciousness in which the self is confronted by the self at its most despicable" (126). Echoing such theorization, the feelings of invulnerability and agency that anger and violence bring about counteract Daniel's helplessness. His behavior may be seen as a pathetic way of compensating for the powerlessness that accompanies his status as a traumatized victim, since it allows him to maintain what Laurie Vickroy calls a "sense of agency" (24). Additionally, the violence that Daniel exerts upon his wife may also be read as a projection of the violence to which he perceives he is subjecting the story of his parents' conviction and execution, by attempting to force it into the narrative conventions of chronology, unity of effect, teleology, cause-effect, characterization, etc., as argued above. In this view, the protagonist's physical and psychological abuse of his wife would mirror the cruelty that, he feels, the act of representing his family's traumatic past entails.

This interpretation would point to Daniel's chronic traumatic condition as a likely source for his sadistic behavior. As such, it seconds a point also made by Eric Rasmussen, who has argued that *The Book of Daniel* embodies the fantasy that "sexual violence, as a mode of extreme and dangerous affective communication, can function as an affective technology for the artful transfer of knowledge and be deployed pedagogically for political purposes" (190). While such interpretation appears apt, and while presenting sexual abuse and torture as a desperate call for attention on Daniel's part might indeed have been the novel's purpose, it is worth keeping in mind Avishai Margalit's warning that "it is silly, if not downright obscene, to regard torture as a mere 'communicative act,'" because "torture in our culture constitutes an extreme form of humiliation," which implies "denying the victim's very human mode of existence" (119). Such a view finds further support in the aforementioned unease about whether the explicit representation of extreme forms of sexual violence in literature might not be problematic from an ethical perspective. While retaining certain misgivings about this possibility, the above does not preclude the claim that the novel's formal and thematic rendering of Daniel's traumatic condition problematizes his violent and abusive attitude—though in no way justifies it. Indeed, the novel reveals a tension at play that revolves around the ethics of identification. As contended in the first section of this chapter, the terrible experiences of Daniel's childhood and his loving tenderness for his sister are narrated in full detail, which is clearly articulated as sympathy-provoking. At the same time, as the second section has shown, Daniel is a sadistic perpetrator who narrates also with a wealth of detail the sexual and psychological violence to which he submits his wife. As a result, readers might find themselves torn between feelings of pity and contempt, sympathy and repulsion at different stages of the narrative.

Thus, just as was the case in *Welcome to Hard Times*, *The Book of Daniel* may be said to favor a non-judgmental, anti-categorical narration in which Daniel occupies a liminal position in the continuum that trauma theory establishes between the categories of victim and perpetrator. In other words, Daniel represents the mutual status of victim and perpetrator, deserving neither full sympathy nor absolute rejection, which is arguably connected to his own condition as a childhood trauma survivor. This is precisely one of the key reasons why readers might read violent fiction, according to Kathryn Hume:

> The degree of discomfiture caused by aggressive fiction can free us from our usual mental schemata by making them inoperable. This fiction liberates us from automatic responses. Instead of applying formulas, we must think and test our interpretive templates and try to construct new ones. (169)

Such interpretation might also find support in the fact that Daniel's violent conduct is shown to diminish in intensity and frequency as the fictive writing of his book progresses, as the following quote suggests: "July-August, 1967, I was very careful with Phyllis. We lived in a state of convalescence, waking up each morning to find the marriage somewhat stronger but still in need of hugs and kisses and tender lovemaking" (121). In fact, by the end of the novel Daniel seems to have overcome his sadistic drive and stopped abusing his wife. This would also confirm the reading of Daniel's narrative as a means to "work through" trauma (LaCapra 21), as a path toward healing.

The novel's role as a fictive tool for working through may also be seen in its use of intertextuality. Its most obvious intertext, as Brian Dillon was the first to notice (366), is the biblical *Book of Daniel*, and its significance is suggested not only by the fact that it provides Doctorow's novel with its title, but also because it frames Daniel's narration—both the first epigraph and the final paragraph are quotations taken from the Bible.[9] Daniel Isaacson seems to have a special fondness for his biblical namesake and refers to his story at several points of his narrative:

> In this context it is instructive to pause for a moment over the career of Daniel, a definitely minor, if not totally apocryphal figure (or figures) who worked with no particular delight for a few of the kings in the post-Alexandrine Empires. (13)

On the one hand, Daniel chooses to identify with this biblical figure since, like him, he has engaged in the task of "interpret[ing] and analyz[ing] the awful visions of his head" (250), of "record[ing] weird dreams and visions which have baffled readers for centuries" (6), just like Daniel's baffle us. On the other hand, Daniel's interest in the biblical *Book of Daniel* is connected to the psychological significance that he gives to the "Book of Susanna" in his narrative. In this apocryphal text, the biblical Daniel manages to save a Hebrew woman named Susanna who has been unjustly sentenced to death. Hence, Daniel's own tendency to associate or compare himself with the biblical Daniel, an intertext which Brian Dillon aptly discusses as a symbol of the protagonist's obsession with a flawed judicial system and with saving his sister—his own Susanna, or "Sussyana," as he often calls her—after her suicide attempt. In short, intertextuality functions as a further coping mechanism for Daniel; *The Book of Daniel* enters an intertextual dialogue with the biblical texts that may too be read as a path toward healing.

As a final consideration, it is worth noting that it was Doctorow's decision to make one of the Isaacson children a girl—the Rosenbergs, on whose case the novel is loosely based, had two sons. In light of this discussion, the narrative and thematic significance of such choice appears obvious, since it provides the novel with a much higher degree of structural coherence in many respects. However, it also suggests that, despite the novel's apparent inattention to a majority of feminist concerns, one cannot dismiss the fact that the character of Susan plays a key structural role in the progression of the narrative in the following ways: by being primarily responsible for Daniel's decision to write, by acting as the main narratee, by triggering the return of Daniel's traumatic memories of the past and by finally providing him with the necessary tools to start the process of working through.

Conclusion

By way of conclusion, it may be claimed that *The Book of Daniel* seeks to warn of the disastrous consequences of psychological trauma for the individual, who might eventually end up becoming a perpetrator. The novel explores the causes and consequences of extreme traumatic events not only on a thematic level, but also on a formal one, bringing conventional narrative techniques to their limit. Among these consequences, the dangers of helplessness and lack of agency are emphasized, since they are shown to lock the protagonist in a spiral of violence and self-destruction. The novel also problematizes the relationship between the categories of victim and perpetrator, highlighting the extremely thin line that separates them in the context of psychological trauma. *The Book of Daniel* further stages the difficulties that trauma victims face when attempting to articulate traumatic memories, reflecting on issues of reliability and accuracy, the conflict between knowledge and denial, and the different means through which the traumatic past may be retrieved. Finally, the novel explores the possibility of healing through the mechanisms of intertextuality and narration (scriptotherapy), highlighting the importance of bearing empathic witness to the pain of others. In short, *The Book of Daniel* deals fundamentally with human suffering and the social impact of injustice.

Disguising as fictionalized memoir, *The Book of Daniel* narrates a tale of extreme suffering that exposes a number of social, economic and political structures of the United States as mechanisms of control and alienation that have a strong traumatizing potential and easily render the individual powerless. It depicts a flawed Judiciary system in which people can be convicted and executed without sufficient evidence as to their guilt, and it dramatizes the failure of social structures and institutions to provide for those who inhabit the margins of North-American society. In addition, the novel warns of the disastrous consequences of individualism, which has brought the country to its current level of indifference, advocating our duty to bear witness and urging us to withhold simplistic judgment. These warnings were necessary in the 1970s and unfortunately still seem appropriate nowadays.

Notes

1 For an in-depth analysis of the novel's exploration of the conflict between art and the artist, see Lorsch (1982) and Girardin (2004).
2 See also Schrank (1993) and Irom (2012) for an examination of the novel's radical possibilities and engagement with political issues. An opposite view is held by Carol Iannone, who in her article "E. L. Doctorow's 'Jewish' Radicalism" sees Doctorow's fiction in general, and *The Book of Daniel* in particular, as compromised by the ideological attitudes of the Left (53).
3 Further references to the novel will be to the Penguin Modern Classics edition, published in 2006.
4 When contrasted with the fictional quality of the novel, the reference in these sections to events and issues that are considered to be historically accurate sends an important postmodern message about the similar epistemological status of history and fiction. It is, in fact, E.L. Doctorow's main contention in his celebrated essay "False Documents" (1977) that history and fiction share the same fictional status. Furthermore, although *The Book of Daniel* is a fictional text, it does refer to a historical event, the Rosenberg case. As such, much of its content is based on historical information extracted from letters, newspaper excerpts and the transcript of the trial. This has led critics such as Hamner (2000 [1981]), Levine (1989), Parks (1991) and Tsimpouki (2008) to focus on the novel's relationship to 'verifiable' history.
5 The impact of the affects of shame and guilt on Daniel's condition will be addressed in the following subsection.
6 Doctorow's choice of name for Daniel's history professor and supervisor appears particularly interesting, given its intertextual reference to North-American writer Ronald Sukenick: in his book *The Death of the Novel, and Other Stories* (2003[1969]), Sukenick claimed that "[t]he contemporary writer—the writer who is acutely in touch with the life of which he is a part—is forced to start from scratch: Reality doesn't exist, time doesn't exist, personality doesn't exist" (41).
7 These quotations also illustrate the novel's metafictional concerns as discussed above.
8 For a brief summary-like character description of the female protagonists in *The Book Daniel*, see Culp (1982).
9 Clayton (1983) and Girgus (1984) have explored Daniel's belonging to the tradition of radical Jewish humanism, locating his Jewishness in his American experience.

References

American Psychiatric Association. *Diagnostic and Statistical Manual of Mental Disorders* (4th ed., text rev.), 2000.
Bal, Mieke. *Narratology: Introduction to the Theory of Narrative*. Toronto: Toronto UP, 1985.
Baudrillard, Jean. *The Transparency of Evil: Essays on Extreme Phenomena*. Trans. James Benedict. London and New York: Verso, 1993.
Blum, Alon. "Shame and Guilt, Misconceptions and Controversies: A Critical Review of the Literature." *Traumatology* 14.3 (2008): 91–102.
Caruth, Cathy, ed. Introduction to Part I. *Trauma: Explorations in Memory*. Baltimore: Johns Hopkins UP, 1995. 3–12.
Clayton, John. "Radical Jewish Humanism: The Vision of E. L. Doctorow." *E.L. Doctorow: Essays and Conversations*. Ed. Richard Trenner. Princeton: Ontario Review, 1983. 109–119.

Cooper, Stephen. "Cutting Both Ways: E. L. Doctorow's Critique of the Left." *South Atlantic Review* 58.2 (May 1993): 111–125.
Culp, Mildred. "Women and Tragic Destiny in Doctorow's *The Book of Daniel*." *From Marginality to Mainstream: A Mosaic of Jewish Writers. Studies in American Jewish Literature*, vol. 2. Ed. Daniel Walden. Albany: New York State UP, 1982. 155–166.
DeRosa, Aaron. "Apocryphal Trauma in E.L. Doctorow's *The Book of Daniel*." *Studies in the Novel* 41.4 (Winter 2009): 468–488.
Dillon, Brian. "The Rosenbergs meet Nebuchadnezzar: The Narrator's Use of the Bible in Doctorow's *The Book of Daniel*." *Critique* 40.4 (Summer 1999): 365–378.
Doctorow, E.L. *The Book of Daniel*. 1971. London: Penguin, 2006.
———. "False Documents." 1977. *Jack London, Hemingway, and the Constitution: Selected Essays 1977–1992*. New York: Random House, 1993. 149–164.
Estrin, Barbara L. "Surviving McCarthyism: E.L. Doctorow's *The Book of Daniel*." *The Massachusetts Review* 16.3 (Summer 1975): 577–587.
Felman, Shoshana. *The Juridical Unconscious: Trials and Traumas in the Twentieth Century*. Cambridge: Harvard UP, 2002.
Forrey, Robert. "Doctorow's *The Book of Daniel*: All in the Family." *From Marginality to Mainstream: A Mosaic of Jewish Writers. Studies in American Jewish Literature*, vol. 2. Ed. Daniel Walden. Albany: New York State UP, 1982. 167–173.
Freud, Sigmund and Josef Breuer. "Studies on Hysteria. 1893–1895." *The Standard Edition of the Complete Psychological Works of Sigmund Freud*, Volume II (1893–1895). Ed. James Strachey. London: Vintage, 2001.
Friedan, Betty. *The Feminine Mystique*. 1963. 10th Anniversary Edition. New York: Dell Publishing, 1974.
Genette, Gérard. "Voice." 1980. *Narratology*. Eds. Susana Onega and José Ángel García Landa. London and New York: Longman, 1996. 172–189.
Gentry, Marshall B. "'Ventriloquists' Conversations: The Struggle for Gender Dialogue in E.L. Doctorow and Philip Roth." 1993. *Modern Critical Views: E.L. Doctorow*. Ed. Harold Bloom. Philadelphia: Chelsea House, 2002. 113–132.
Gilligan, James. "Shame, Guilt, and Violence." *Social Research* 70.4 (2003): 1149–1180.
Girardin, Sophie. "E.L. Doctorow's *The Book of Daniel*: A Writer-in-Process". E-reaD [online], 2.2 (2004). Web. 1 March 2013. <http://erea.revues.org/440>
Girgus, Sam B. "A True Radical History: E. L. Doctorow." 1984. *Modern Critical Views: E.L. Doctorow*. Ed. Harold Bloom. Philadelphia: Chelsea House, 2002. 7–26.
Granofsky, Ronald. *The Trauma Novel: Contemporary Symbolic Depictions of Collective Disaster*. New York: Peter Lang, 1995.
Hamner, Eugénie L. "The Burden of the Past: Doctorow's *The Book of Daniel*." 1981. *Critical Essays on E. L. Doctorow*. Ed. Ben Siegel. New York: G. K. Hall & Co, 2000. 160–165.
Harpham, Geoffrey G. "E. L. Doctorow and the Technology of Narrative." 1985. *Modern Critical Views: E.L. Doctorow*. Ed. Harold Bloom. Philadelphia: Chelsea House, 1989. 27–49.

Hartman, Geoffrey. "Trauma within the Limits of Literature." *European Journal of English Studies* 7.3 (2003): 257–274.
Henke, Suzette. *Shattered Subjects: Trauma and Testimony in Women's Life Writing.* London: Palgrave Macmillan, 1998.
Herman, Judith L. *Trauma and Recovery: The Aftermath of Violence – From Domestic Abuse to Political Terror.* New York: Basic Books, 1992.
Hume, Kathryn. *Aggressive Fictions: Reading the Contemporary American Novel.* Ithaca and London: Cornell UP, 2012.
Iannone, Carol. "Doctorow's Jewish Radicalism." *Commentary* 81.3 (Mar. 1986): 53–56.
Irom, Bimbisar. "Between 'Retreat' and 'Engagement': Incomplete Revolts and the Operations of Irony in E.L. Doctorow's *The Book of Daniel.*" *Studies in American Fiction* 39.1 (May 2012): 61–85.
Kauffmann, Stanley. "Wrestling Society for a Soul." *New Republic* (June 5, 1971): 25.
LaCapra, Dominick. *Writing History, Writing Trauma.* Baltimore: Johns Hopkins UP, 2001.
Laub, Dori. "Bearing Witness, or the Vicissitudes of Listening." *Testimony: Crises of Witnessing in Literature, Psychoanalysis, and History.* Eds. Shoshana Felman and Dori Laub. New York and London: Routledge, 1992. 57–74.
———. "Truth and Testimony: the Process and the Struggle." *Trauma: Explorations in Memory.* Ed. Cathy Caruth. Baltimore: Johns Hopkins UP, 1995. 61–75.
Laub, Dori and Nanette C. Auerhahn. "Knowing and Not Knowing Massive Psychic Trauma: Forms of Traumatic Memory." *International Journal of Psychoanalysis* 74.2 (1993): 287–302.
Levine, Paul. "The Conspiracy of History: E. L. Doctorow's *The Book of Daniel.*" *E.L. Doctorow: Essays & Conversations.* Ed. Richard Trenner. Princeton: Ontario Review, 1983. 182–195.
———. "Politics and Imagination." *Modern Critical Views: E. L. Doctorow.* Ed. Harold Bloom. Philadelphia: Chelsea House, 1989. 51–60.
Lorsch, Susan. "Doctorow's *The Book of Daniel* as Künstlerroman: The Politics of Art." *Papers on Language & Literature* 18.4 (Fall 1982): 384–397.
Luckhurst, Roger. *The Trauma Question.* London and New York: Routledge, 2008.
Margalit, Avishai. *The Ethics of Memory.* Cambridge and London: Harvard UP, 2002.
McNally, Richard. *Remembering Trauma.* Cambridge: Harvard UP, 2003.
Morgenstern, Naomi. "The Primal Scene in the Public Domain: E. L. Doctorow's *The Book of Daniel.*" *Studies in the Novel* 35.1 (Spring 2003): 68–88.
Morris, Christopher D. ed. *Conversations with E. L. Doctorow.* Jackson: Mississippi UP, 1999.
O'Neill, Catherine. "The Music in Doctorow's Head." *Conversations with E.L. Doctorow.* Ed. Christopher Morris. Jackson: Mississippi UP, 1999. 53–58.
Parks, John G. "The Politics of Polyphony: The Fiction of E.L. Doctorow." *Twentieth Century Literature* 37.4 (Winter 1991): 454–463.
Prescott, Peter S. "Lion's Den." *Newsweek* (June 7, 1971): 110–111.

Prince, Gerald. "Introduction to the Study of the Narratee." 1980. *Narratology*. Eds. Susana Onega and José Ángel García Landa. London and New York: Longman, 1996. 190–202.
Richmond, Jane. "To the End of the Night." *Partisan Review* 39.4 (Fall 1972): 627–629.
Rothberg, Michael. *Traumatic Realism: The Demands of Holocaust Representation*. Minneapolis: University of Minnesota Press, 2000.
Schrank, Bernice. "Getting the Picture: Radical Possibilities in Doctorow's *The Book of Daniel*." The Changing Mosaic: From Cahan to Malamud, Roth and Ozick. Spec. issue of *Studies in American Jewish Literature (1981-)* 12 (1993): 62–71.
Smith, Stacy L. and Edward Donnerstein. "Harmful Effects of Exposure to Media Violence: Learning of Aggression, Emotional Desensitization, and Fear." *Human Aggression: Theories, Research, and Implications for Social Policy*. Eds. Russell G. Geen and Edward D. Donnerstein. San Diego, California: Academic Press, 1998. 167–202.
Stark, John. "Alienation and Analysis in Doctorow's *The Book of Daniel*." *Critique* 16.3 (1975): 101–110.
Sukenick, Ronald. *The Death of the Novel, and Other Stories*. 1969. Tallahassee: FC2, 2003.
Tokarczyk, Michelle M. "From the Lion's Den: Survivors in E. L. Doctorow's *The Book of Daniel*." *Critique* 29.1 (Fall 1987): 3–15.
Tsimpouki, Theodora. "Fictional Contamination of Hegemonical Texts: History, Fiction and the Rosenberg Case." *The European Legacy: Toward New Paradigms* 2.4 (2008): 781–786.
Uytterschout, Sien. "Visualized Incomprehensibility of Trauma in Jonathan Safran Foer's *Extremely Loud and Incredibly Close*." *ZAA* 56.1 (2008): 61–74.
van der Kolk, Bessel A. and Onno van der Hart. "The Intrusive Past: The Flexibility of Memory and the Engraving of Trauma." *Trauma: Explorations in Memory*. Ed. Cathy Caruth. Baltimore: Johns Hopkins UP, 1995. 158–181.
Vickroy, Laurie. *Trauma and Survival in Contemporary Fiction*. Virginia: Virginia UP, 2002.
Whitehead, Anne. *Trauma Fiction*. Edinburgh: Edinburgh UP, 2004.
Williams, John. *Fiction as False Document: The Reception of E. L. Doctorow in the Postmodern Age*. Columbia: Camden House, 1996.

3 *Ragtime*
Remembering the Future

Published in 1975, *Ragtime* meant E.L. Doctorow's admittance into the North-American contemporary literary canon, representing also his greatest commercial success. More than 230,000 copies were sold within only six months of its publication, and it reached most bestseller lists, such as the ones published in "Publishers Weekly" and "The New York Times," where the novel remained at the top for almost four months (Piehl 406–407).[1] What is more, its paperback reprint rights were bought for the unprecedented sum of $1.85 million (Piehl 407). Soon after its publication, highly favorable reviews appeared in periodicals such as *The New Republic* (Grumbach, July 1975), *The New York Times Book Review* (Stade, July 1975), *Saturday Review* (Kauffmann, July 1975), *Time* (Sheppard, July 1975), *Newsweek* (Clemons, July 1975), *The Village Voice* (Fremont-Smith, July 1975), *The New York Review of Books* (Sale, Aug. 1975) and *Atlantic* (Adams, Aug. 1975), among others.[2] The novel was a nominee for the *Nebula Award for Best Novel* and won the *National Book Critics Circle Award for Fiction* in 1975 and the *American Academy and Institute of Arts and Letters Award* in 1976. Such was its perceived literary worth that *TIME Magazine* would eventually include *Ragtime* in its "TIME best English Language Novels from 1923 to 2005," and the *Modern Library* ranked it number 86 on its list of the "100 best English-language novels of the 20th century." Its success would even lead to an adaptation for a 1981 film directed by Miloš Forman and a 1998 musical with book by Terrence McNally, lyrics by Lynn Ahrens and music by Stephen Flaherty. It is no surprise, then, that Bernard Rodgers defined *Ragtime* as "one of those anomalies of American letters: a serious work of fiction which is greeted by both popular and critical acclaim" (138). The literary critics' early attention toward the novel gave way to considerable critical scrutiny from the academia. The publication of two monographs devoted to the novel (Bloom 2002, 2004)—and intended for undergraduate or perhaps graduate audiences—attests to that fact. It is worth pointing out that the scholars who devoted their efforts to the analysis of *Ragtime* were milder in their praise—or criticism, for that matter—of the novel. A review of the literature reveals that there are a number of issues which have captured scholars' attention reiteratively: the Kleistian intertext of the novel (Kurth-Voigt 1977, Neumeyer 1977, Faber 1980, Gelus and Crowley 1980, Helbing 1980, Ditsky 1983, Sterne 1988, Moraru 1997, Orbán 2003), the novel's attitude toward history and fiction (Lukacs 1975, Strout 1980, Harris 2001, Farca 2013) and the ragtime music metaphor (Foley 1983, Ostendorf 1991, Roberts 2004).

At its simplest, the novel is a historical fiction set in New York which deals with the first years of the twentieth century, the Ragtime Era. It tells the story of three families—one WASP, one Jewish immigrant and one African-American—who interact with a number of historical figures and participate in some of the most transcendental events in North-American history at the turn of the century. Despite its superficial and detached appearance, *Ragtime* contains tales of great suffering and struggle: it narrates the disintegration of an upper-class family that sees its values shattered by the arrival of an impoverished African-American girl and her newborn baby, whom she has attempted to murder. It recounts the quest for justice of a black ragtime musician after a racist attack against his dignity and property whose outrage transforms him into a terrorist. It relates the fight for survival of a Jewish socialist immigrant, who finds himself and his little daughter caught up in the struggles of the labor movement and yet manages to thrive and become a rich entrepreneur. As if this combination of elements was not remarkable enough, *Ragtime* also includes fictionalized episodes of the lives of historical personages such as Harry Houdini, Henry Ford, Evelyn Nesbit, Emma Goldman, J.P. Morgan and Sigmund Freud, among others, who interact with the other characters in surprising and meaningful ways. Most interestingly, the novel manages to merge all these stories into an all-encompassing critique of injustice by means of an unconventional but highly crafted narrative style which has irony and focalization shifts at its core.

Trauma and Resilience

When first approaching *Ragtime*, one might have the feeling that it cannot possibly be about anything serious. This was the unfortunate impression that a number of early reviewers of the novel seemed to have, condemning it for being "all surface" (Sale 21). Yet, any sagacious reader will soon discover that deep emotions and bitter criticism of the status quo underlie the novel's apparent simplicity and its easy flow. As this section will attempt to prove, the novel deals with stomach-turning injustice, unspeakable suffering and outstanding resistance in the face of distress. Thus, I will focus on the novel's representation of trauma and resilience, assessing trauma's potential to act as a transformative power. I will also explore Doctorow's narratological choices and motivations in order to establish how they affect the novel's ideology.

From Trauma to Resilience

Most trauma theorists coincide in describing the nature of traumatic symptoms as an intrusive presence of the past in the present that possesses the individual, allowing for little hope of overcoming it. The analyses carried out in the previous two chapters reveal a similar perspective on Doctorow's part: Molly and Blue in *Welcome to Hard Times* are destroyed by the aftereffects of their trauma; the same happens to Susan in *The Book of Daniel*, whose inability to cope with the traumatic experiences of her childhood leads her to commit suicide. As for Daniel, the narrative suggests that a degree of integration and closure have been achieved through scriptotherapy; yet the obsessiveness of his behavior at the end of the novel brings to mind many trauma theorists' bleak expectations as to complete recovery from chronic trauma symptoms. In contrast to the position held by those who see no way out of trauma, a number of medical professionals have more recently started to dedicate efforts to study the possibility that traumatic experiences may have of generating resilience. They have realized that the standard disease model which has dominated the last two centuries[3] does not fit well, and cannot account for, recurrent observations of resilient individual and communal responses to risk factors. As a result, several significant studies and clinical tests have been carried out in recent years, with the aim of shedding some light on the neurobiological, psychosocial and cultural factors involved in the phenomenon of resilience.[4] Research has also been conducted on cognitive, affective and behavioral models of resilience, focusing on the role of emotions and affects, intelligence, personality traits, and even faith or spirituality in a person's capacity for resilience.[5] According to Zautra et al., this is finally producing a shift in the science paradigm, since the efforts of these and other researchers have led to the articulation of what has been termed "the resilience paradigm" (xi–xii).

In its widest definition, resilience is the ability (of a system) to cope with change. Within the field of materials science and engineering, where the concept originated, resilience refers to the properties of a material on the basis of which it may absorb or avoid damage without breaking or without suffering complete failure. Given its definition, it is no wonder that the term has been successfully transposed to a wide number of disciplines. In the psychological sphere, resilience is concerned with "the positive pole of individual differences in people's response to stress and adversity" (Rutter 316). It is defined as "an outcome of successful adaptation to adversity. [...] People who are resilient display a greater capacity to quickly regain equilibrium physiologically, psychologically, and in social relations following stressful events" (Zautra et al. 4). Feder et al. further define resilience as "the ability of individuals to adapt successfully in the face of acute stress, trauma, or chronic adversity, maintaining or rapidly regaining psychological well-being and physiological homeostasis" (35). Resilience, it is worth adding, is part of our DNA, since it accounts for our success in surviving and thriving in utterly adverse conditions during evolutionary times (see Konner 305).

Medical evidence, thus, seems to suggest that while traumatic responses are a common reaction to situations of extreme stress, human beings have a "self-healing bias" (Konner 300, 309), and the percentage of people who develop a long-term or chronic psychopathology is, in fact, rather small (see Bonanno 20, Shalev 207, Zautra et al. 3). Indeed, basing their studies on scientific evidence that resilient reactions to trauma risk factors are the norm rather than the exception, an increasing number of researchers are beginning to conceptualize trauma as a process that triggers a transformation or metamorphosis which evokes both strengths and vulnerabilities (see Rousseau and Measham 279, Sigal 582). Advancing from foundational work on basic biological processes among children and from developmental topics, these researchers have sought to identify the sources of resilience in adults in neurobiological as well as in broader societal, community-level processes (Zautra et al. xi). The following factors have been identified as contributing to resilience: social and family supports, the experience of self-reliance and survival in challenging environments, cultural framing of stress and responses to stress and the need to help dependants (Konner 322); a strong individual optimistic tendency to make the best out of life, active coping strategies, the capacity for cognitive reappraisal, positive emotionality, an integrated sense of self, a sense of purpose in life, affiliative behavior and spirituality (Feder et al. 36–37); social responsibility, adaptability, tolerance, achievement orientation, the presence of supportive caretakers and community resources (Mayer and Faber 98); and self-confidence, positive future orientation, sublimation, affiliation and empathy (Skodol 113), among others.

Although research on resilience has received an important boost in the last few years, scientists and medical professionals have been for several decades producing studies of which factors exacerbate the impact of trauma and which facilitate its healing and reduce its potential to become a long-term disorder. Freud was the first to draw attention to an "instinct for recovery" in his *New Introductory Lectures on Psychoanalysis* (1933), identifying its phylogenic origins as a residue of the "power of regenerating lost organs" in some lower animals (106). However, his increasing pessimism as he aged and his growing interest in the repetition compulsion and the death drive led to an abandonment of further theorization of this self-healing capacity in human beings. Within contemporary science, Michael Rutter was among the first to use the term "resilience" to refer to protective factors in the face of stress and adversity in his influential paper "Psychosocial Resilience and Protective Mechanisms" (1987). Without explicitly using the term in her seminal essay "Reconstructing the Impact of Trauma on Personality," psychologist Maria Root already added to the trauma equation some factors later identified as related to the phenomenon of resilience when she discussed the role of communal support and empathy in recovery after trauma, both in cases of person-perpetrated and accidental trauma (243).

Given fiction's outstanding capacity to draw from multiple sources and fields and incorporate notions and discourses from diverse disciplines—as the mere existence of the critical framework of trauma studies proves—this section draws on the psychological notion of resilience in order to provide some answers as to the nature of *Ragtime*'s alternative approach to extreme human suffering. In contrast to the inescapability from the effects of trauma that Doctorow's previous novels exemplify, there is a case to argue that *Ragtime* shows a subtle shift toward an emphasis on some of the characters' ability to absorb the damage produced by the inhospitable and unjust society of turn-of-the-century New York without breaking completely. In the novel, a myriad of characters face traumatic stress owing to their condition as what Linda Hutcheon has called "ex-centrics" (61)—that is, due to their marginal race, ethnicity, religion, gender or social class, which makes them vulnerable to what Maria Root famously termed "insidious trauma." In Root's theorization, "insidious trauma" refers to the psychological impact of living in a society in which oppression, discrimination and even violence are a normal part of everyday life for those whose identity is different from what is valued by those in power (239–240). The novel is built around a pattern of repetition and variation comparable to a Benjaminian constellation, in that it presents multiple versions of the damaging consequences of oppression and injustice. Characterization in the novel also echoes Lemelson et al.'s observation that for those who endure abusive contexts "[...] there is layer upon layer of acute response to constantly changing threats" (464). Interestingly for my purposes, the novel also depicts multiple ways of responding to these threats based on the characters' capacity for resilience or lack thereof. Indeed, the characters' resilience, their ability to bend without breaking, is a central thematic concern in *Ragtime*.

A key character in that sense is Sarah, an African-American washwoman who enters the narrative right after a newborn "brown" baby is found semi-buried in Mother's garden (Doctorow, *Ragtime* 58).[6] Despite being described as an "impoverished uneducated black girl with such absolute conviction of the way human beings ought to conduct their lives" (156), it becomes apparent that she has attempted to kill her child. Yet, we soon learn that the baby's cord has been bitten off and he is still bloody, which suggests that Sarah has not been attended during labor. At this point one begins to understand that she must have acted out of intense despair, since one might reasonably expect that only under extreme circumstances would a woman attempt to kill her own newborn baby. And this is precisely the case, since the narrative reveals that Sarah has been abandoned by the father of her child, a rather well-off ragtime player named Coalhouse Walker. The general lack of sympathy for her situation and her sense of helplessness seem to be precisely what have brought her to such desperate state: it is readily apparent that she and her baby could hardly have survived on their own in the deeply unequal and racist society of turn-of-the-century New York that the novel depicts. Mother's compassion saves Sarah and her baby, but the African-American girl pays a high psychological price for her ongoing suffering: "Melancholy had taken the will out of her muscles. She did not have the strength to hold her baby" (91), and she refuses to leave her room or tend to her child.

Sarah's immediate response resembles the common psychological aftermath of exposure to a traumatic blow. Her imagined condition may be best described as resulting from "insidious trauma" (239). Maria Root may be credited with being among the first to call for a reconceptualization of trauma that would broaden the experiences that are considered potentially traumatic in order to include experiences subsumed by gender, race, class, sexual orientation and ability (230). Hers was one of the first attempts to articulate trauma studies with conditions of ongoing exposure to violence, discrimination or abuse, such as are common in the context of homophobia, patriarchal oppression and gender violence, racism, exploitation, ageism and ableism. In order to do so, she put forward in her seminal essay "Reconstructing the Impact of Trauma on Personality" (1992) the notion of "insidious trauma," which she articulates against two other categories of traumatic impact: "direct" and "indirect" trauma (239). In her coinage of the term, insidious trauma—also referred to as "cumulative traumatic experiences" (248) and "constellation of singular traumas" (254)—refers to the type of trauma "usually associated with the social status of an individual being devalued because a characteristic intrinsic to their identity is different from what is valued by those in power" (240). She further characterizes insidious trauma as having cumulative effects, affecting a community of people, and "leav[ing] a distinct threat to psychological safety, security, or survival" (241). Thus, Root in effect usefully introduced a framework for the study of the psychological impact and traumatizing potential of being an 'ex-centric,' of living at the 'wrong' side of the dichotomy, in a society in which oppression, discrimination and even violence are a normal part of everyday life for many (240).

Sarah's characterization not only challenges the event-based model of trauma which Root's theory sought to contest; in contrast to the supposedly chronic nature of trauma that classical theory emphasizes, her imagined condition starts to improve when she recovers a sense of safety and normalcy thanks to the social and family support provided by Mother. Then, after Coalhouse Walker—the baby's father—reappears and seeks to atone for his earlier neglect, her ailment progressively improves to the point that she recovers almost completely. Sarah's capacity to heal, motivated by a sense of purpose in her life (her responsibility toward her son) and the experience of survival in adverse circumstances, may be understood as the first suggestion of the novel's shift of emphasis toward resilience. It is also coherent with the medical evidence suggesting that, while traumatic responses are a common reaction to situations of extreme stress, the human being has a "self-healing bias" (Konner 300, 309). It is worth adding that apart from calling attention to the traumatizing potential of ongoing exposure to discrimination, violence and injustice, and broadening the scope of experiences that are traumatic, one of the main aims that Root's influential essay allegedly pursued was the depathologization of what she describes as normal responses to traumatic stress (237). Furthermore, when Sarah sees later on that the life that she has been building with her fiancé starts to crumble due to racist oppression, she overcomes her previous immobilization and takes action to help him in his quest for justice. This suggests that Sarah's earlier experience of survival has dramatically increased her resilience, transforming her into a self-reliant, determined and empathetic woman who does not hesitate to take her future into her own hands and do what she can to help herself and others. Thus, Sarah's transformation arguably exemplifies an alternative understanding of traumatic experiences as a catalyst in bringing about new individual strengths, a possibility that, as argued above, has become the focus of extended research by medical professionals in recent years. Indeed, Rousseau and Measham have contended that it might be more helpful to conceptualize trauma as a process that prompts a transformation which evokes not only vulnerabilities but also strengths (278).

Another character that stands out for her resilience is the fictionalized historical persona of Evelyn Nesbit. Evelyn is first introduced as a celebrated beauty and artist's model who is married to the millionaire Harry K. Thaw and was once mistress of the renowned architect Stanford White. She is described as a sexual goddess who "had caused the death of one man and wrecked the life of another [...]" (5). This leads one to perceive her as a sort of *femme fatale* who exerts her power in order to manipulate men. However, the reader soon discovers that Evelyn is nothing but a broken toy at the hands of two abusive men, who take advantage of their superior economic position to victimize her. For instance, the narrative reveals that she was drugged and raped by White when she was only a fifteen-year-old chorus girl. Later on, we learn that Evelyn was taken on a trip to Europe by the violent and deranged Thaw, who paid her mother off and then took her to a castle in Germany to rape and torture her without interruptions:

> Their first night in the Schloss he pulled off her robe, threw her across the bed and applied a dog whip to her buttocks and the backs

of her thighs. Her shrieks echoed down the corridors and stone stairwells. [...] Shocking red welts disfigured Evelyn's flesh. She cried and whimpered all night. In the morning Harry returned to her room, this time with a razor strop. She was bedridden for weeks. (21)

We also learn that he further humiliates her by forcing her to perform oral sex while he is in jail for murdering White, as "proof of her devotion" (22). Evelyn's history as victim of sexual and physical abuse since she was a young girl has deeply affected her. For instance, she decides to break off her affair with a tender and loving man, Mother's Younger Brother, because "she wanted someone who would treat her badly and whom she could treat badly" (74). She further projects her distress onto Tateh's Little Girl, an outstandingly beautiful child who struggles to survive in the slums with her father. Evelyn's abandonment by her mother at the hands of two abusive men and her identification with the tragedy of the little girl's prospective future as some man's sexual toy inspire in her a profound infatuation with the child, to a point that verges upon insanity: "She was so desperately in love that she could no longer see properly. [...] She saw everything through a film of salt tears, and her voice became husky because her throat was bathed in the irrepressible and continuous crying which her happiness caused her" (43). However, despite the obsessive nature of Evelyn's attachment to the Little Girl, taking care of her provides the young woman with a new sense of purpose and allows her to reintegrate her sense of self. Furthermore, her experience of self-reliance and survival in deeply challenging and adverse conditions increases her adaptability and provides her with a strong sense of pride: "She had grown up playing in the streets of a Pennsylvania coal town. She was the Gaudens statue Stanny White had put on the top of the tower of Madison Square Garden, a glorious bronze nude Diana" (23). Evelyn's experience of living in the slums with the Little Girl also grants her a new awareness of the needs of others and increases her empathy, inspiring her to use the money that she has received from her abusive husband after their divorce—her "hard-earned fortune" (74)—to help the underprivileged.

The understanding of trauma as a transformative force that produces strengths and vulnerabilities is also particularly relevant for the interpretation of Coalhouse Walker's imagined condition, although for different reasons. Walker is an African-American ragtime player who is described as "dress[ing] in the affectation of wealth to which colored people lent themselves" (129). He first appears in the narrative driving a shiny Model T Ford. The WASP family which has taken Sarah in receives Walker with surprise at his respectful but affected manner. Yet, being the quintessential member of the accommodated upper-middle class,[7] Father soon starts to resent what he perceives as Walker's prudish and obstinate character, which leads him to conclude that "Coalhouse Walker Jr. didn't know he was a Negro" (134):

> And so it happened on the next Sunday that the Negro took tea. Father noted that he suffered no embarrassment by being in the parlor with a cup and saucer in his hand. On the contrary, he acted as if it was the most natural thing in the world. (131)

Leaving aside the heavy irony that these words reveal on the part of the narrator—an issue that will be addressed presently—they point to a marked racist bias among the white members of turn-of-the-century North-American society. Indeed, Father is not alone in taking offense in what he perceives as Walker's lack of submissiveness: one day, as the ragtime player is driving past a fire station, the volunteer firemen stationed there trap him, cheat him and vandalize his car, which ends up "spattered with mud. There was a six-inch tear in the custom pantasote top. And deposited in the back seat was a mound of fresh human excrement" (147–148). The police prove to be no better in that they first advise Coalhouse to take his car and leave as if nothing had happened, and then grow angry when they grasp "the phenomenon of his owning a car in the first place" (148). So when he refuses to leave and insists that he wants the damage repaired and an apology, they have him arrested. The gross injustice committed against Coalhouse throws him into a desperate crusade to seek redress through the courts in order to alleviate his shame. However, far from being successful in achieving justice and restoring his pride, his attempt leads to Sarah's death at the hands of the police while she was trying to secure governmental support for Coalhouse's cause, which buries him in the depths of guilt.

Coalhouse's psychological devastation at the loss of his fiancée and the life that they were building together, his sense of powerlessness, as well as his complete alienation from, and scorn for a society that is capable of committing such racist injustices with impunity, lead him to seek a different kind of compensation: in the manner of James Gilligan's prison inmates, he falls into a spiral of violence and becomes an arsonist and murderer whose sole aim is wreaking vengeance, attempting to diminish his shame and regain a sense of agency through violence. Therefore, Coalhouse's traumatic grief acts as a transformative force that, rather than immobilizing him or throwing him into a melancholic state, causes him to "militarize his mourning" (205). Coalhouse's transformation also resonates with the trajectory of berserk fury which has been widely described by Jonathan Shay as assisting veteran soldiers as a result of their psychopathological conditions (in Farrell 289). As Kirby Farrell explains, the concept of "berserking" alludes to ancient Norse warriors who were supposed to achieve extraordinary power and strength by entering states of wild murderous rage by means of which they sought to take revenge, restore order or mystically replenish life through death (289). Echoing this theory, the heterodiegetic narrator explains that "[Coalhouse's] grief for Sarah and the life they might have had was hardened into a ceremony of vengeance in the manner of the ancient warrior" (205). There has been extensive discussion of the possible benefits of cathartic rage for victims of trauma, since exploiting the feelings of invulnerability and agency that anger brings about could be seen as a way to counteract victimization and helplessness. However, as Farrel has also noted, one cannot deny the fact that rage, even if it is righteous, tends to be total and indiscriminate, with no prospect of natural conclusion (207). This is precisely what happens to Coalhouse, whose indignation helps him overcome the traumatic immobilization that is frequently associated with extreme grief, but whose anger can be appeased only after the death of several innocent people and his own. In short, despite the difficulties to survive and thrive in a deeply hostile and oppressive society, the characterization of Sarah, Evelyn and Coalhouse hints at *Ragtime*'s shift of focus with regard to Doctorow's previous novels toward resilience in the face of extreme suffering, and reveals a concern with the examination of trauma's less frequently explored potential to act as a transformative force that yields not only vulnerabilities, but also strengths.

Trauma and Sublimation

A special character in point when examining *Ragtime*'s alternative attitude toward trauma is Tateh, a Jewish silhouette artist from Latvia who can barely earn a living with his labor in the East End. His family archetypically represents immigrant working class exploitation in the novel. Their traumatic existence fictionally exemplifies J.D. Kinzie's analysis according to which many migrants and refugees suffer "massive, multiple, prolonged and unpredictable physical and psychological trauma" that results from the deplorable living conditions that they experience in their country of origin and which continue in their countries of destination, where they frequently meet economic problems, social discrimination and ongoing violence (197). Much the same as the African-American characters described above, Tateh, Mameh and their Little Girl face layer upon layer of insidious traumatic victimization as a result of perpetual social oppression, economic exploitation and injustice. Thus, for instance, after a grievous existence in New York, Tateh and his daughter travel to Lawrence, MA, to work in the mills, where he "st[ands] in front of a loom for fifty-six hours a week. His pay was just under six dollars" (100). They endure new hardships as a result of a strike in which Tateh plays an active role.[8] On top of that, they face the drama of the "Children's Crusade,"[9] perhaps one of the most traumatic events depicted in the novel: Tateh and the other workers take their children to the train to be sent to other cities to board with families in sympathy with the strike until the struggle ends; but the mill owners send the police:

> They were dragging the mothers kicking and screaming to trucks at the end of the platform. [...] Children were being stepped on. They scattered in all directions. A woman ran by with blood coming from her mouth. [...] The policeman cracked [Tateh] on the shoulder and the head with his stick. What are you doing, Tateh cried. He didn't know what the maniac wanted of him. He moved back into the crowd. He was followed and beaten. [...] In a few minutes the police had swept the platform clean, [...] and only a few sobbing battered adults and weeping children remained. (105–106)

Their survival to such traumatic events marks a turning point in their fate and, remarkably enough, fuels Tateh's transformation: "From this moment, perhaps, Tateh began to conceive of his life as separate from the fate of the working class" (109). When they arrive in Philadelphia, Tateh sells the movie books that he has made for his daughter and a new life begins for them.

As this short plot survey suggests, despite Tateh's traumatic existence, he is portrayed as an extremely resilient character that succeeds in channeling the negative experiences that he has undergone into creative energy. Indeed, his transformation brings to mind one of the most complex concepts of Freudian metapsychology—sublimation.[10] In its broadest psychoanalytical definition, sublimation would be the process by which instinctual urges are transformed into non-instinctual behavior. In "Civilization and Its Discontents" (1930), Freud further described it as "an especially conspicuous feature of cultural development; it is what makes it possible for higher psychical activities, scientific, artistic or ideological, to play such an important part in civilized life" (97). Drawing on this understanding, psychiatrist George Vaillant borrowed the term to refer to a human defense mechanism against extreme stress that he had identified as leading to resilience. In his definition, sublimation is

> the gratification of an impulse whose goal is retained, but whose goal is redirected from a socially unacceptable one to a socially valued one. Sublimation allows aggressive and sexual urges to be redirected, rather than neurotically dammed up or directed to socially unacceptable behaviors. (in Ginzburg 547)

The link between modern psychiatric understandings of sublimation as a coping mechanism and Freud's references to artistic practice as a central dimension in his own understanding of sublimation appears particularly relevant for my purposes in the light of the recent emphasis on the sustaining role of creativity in resilience (see Mayer and Faber 98).

Indeed, Tateh constitutes the fictional embodiment of the sublimating power of creativity, which allows the individual to turn the forces of an insidiously traumatic existence into creative energy by means of which he or she may cope with stress without being shattered or lapsing into antisocial behaviors. Finally, the novel's emphasis on Tateh's capacity to bend without breaking thanks to his creativity is also consistent with the contemporary call for a shift of emphasis, from the victim as passive object to the survivor as agent who strives to put into practice alternative survival strategies in the context of trauma (see Borzaga 74).

Tateh's success in coping with insidious traumatization thanks to creativity appears even more outstanding when pitted against other characters' failure to deal with pain, namely the fictionalized Harry Houdini and the fictional Mother's Younger Brother. Like Tateh, they are artist-figures whose creativity and skill allow them to reach the summit of professional success—Houdini as illusionist and Mother's Younger Brother as inventor. Yet, both are the embodiment of the psychoanalytic notion of melancholia. In "Mourning and Melancholia" (1917), Freud analyzed people's reactions to the loss of a loved one or of a cherished idea whereby a normal state of mourning may involve a period of serious distress and depression, but should be overcome after a certain lapse in time. Melancholia would be the pathology that develops when mourning does not end after a reasonable period of time (243). According to Freud, symptoms of melancholia include

> a profoundly painful dejection, cessation of interest in the outside world, loss of the capacity to love, inhibition of all activity, and a lowering of the self-regarding feelings to a degree that finds utterance in self-reproaches and self-revilings, and culminates in a delusional expectation of punishment. (244)

Echoing Freudian theory, Mother's Younger Brother is shown to be devastated when Evelyn Nesbit abandons him. He turns into a deranged zombie who disconsolately wanders from place to place hoping to see her again. After considering suicide, he uses his creativity to design increasingly deadlier weapons and bombs. His despair causes him to run to Mexico, where he joins the Zapatista revolution and his recklessness finally drives him to his long-sought death. As for Houdini, he is said to be "passionately in love with his ancient mother," "the last of the great shameless mother lovers" (29–30). When she dies, Houdini arranges pictures of her all through the house in order to suggest her continuing presence, becoming obsessed with the possibility of communicating with her through a genuine medium. At the same time, his masterly escapist performances become darker, acting out "his desire for his dead mother" and "his wish for his own death" (170). The condition of these two characters may be best described as melancholic in Freudian terms, since it stems from their incapacity to come to terms with the relatively common experience of losing a relative or a loved one in normal circumstances. Thus, the portrayal of these characters is arguably meant to highlight their psychological vulnerability before a relatively minor stressor in the context of their comfortable and safe upper-middle-class existence. The conclusion that can be reached is that, despite an accommodated existence, they are much more vulnerable to trauma than the characters discussed so far. This may be interpreted as an attempt on the novel's part to highlight the 'ex-centric' characters' outstanding resilience in the face of insidious traumatic experiences as opposed to those who occupy the center of economic, social and racial dichotomies.

From the Individual to the Collective

Apart from exploring *Ragtime*'s shift of perspective where it comes to the representation of trauma, so far the analysis has also revealed a preoccupation at the level of textual implications with issues of social and economic injustice, racism and oppression. Thus, one ponders over Doctorow's reasons to elaborate such distant and apparently superficial narrative style; its seeming lack of psychological depth and its quick and seamless pace arguably hinder the readers' ability to empathize with the suffering of the characters and to become imbued with the novel's implicit ideology. Asked in an interview about his reasons for making such narratological choices, Doctorow explains that he liked the "kind of reality" that a rigorous narrative combined with a certain distance from the characters allowed him to produce and which exists "somewhere between fiction and modern journalism or history, sort of an in between region" (Yardley 9).

The novel's narratological features, however, have another key ideological effect: as Stef Craps has noted, dominant conceptions of trauma have tended to be criticized for their emphasis on the individual psyche, since this leaves unquestioned the social, political and economic conditions that led to the trauma, especially in cross-cultural contexts (28). Craps further explains that the category of trauma in its classical understanding risks pathologizing people—and even countries or cultures—by presenting them as victims of an illness that requires psychological treatment, without taking into consideration the fact that they suffer from conditions which are essentially political, social or economic (28). As Michela Borzaga has put it, "it is always reductive and stigmatizing (and potentially re-traumatizing) to speak about stories of trauma while drawing only on psychiatric vocabulary" (75). Consistent with this line of reasoning, Doctorow's narrative choices turn the focus away from the individual mind, without entirely rejecting characterization as the basis of his novel. Something to that effect has been hinted by Luke Spencer, who argues that Doctorow aims to "keep before us the inescapably situated, communal and, hence, political character of experience, [...] consistently foregrounding the social and ideological dimension of his characters' 'personal' experience" (23–24). And so, *Ragtime*'s chronicle-like distant narrative style would allow Doctorow to present the insidious traumas of racism and working-class discrimination not as individual psychobiological phenomena, but as part of a wider social context of injustice that affects millions of people and which must be transformed at all costs.

The novel's formal approach to the insidious victimization of marginalized groups in the United States is characterized by the ideological deployment of irony,[11] satire and focalization shifts. According to the *Concise Oxford Dictionary of Literary Terms*, irony is defined as "a subtly humorous perception of inconsistency, in which an apparently straightforward statement or event is undermined by its context so as to give it a very different significance" (Baldick 114). In *Ragtime*, the ironic tone—which often verges into the crudest sarcasm—is the most important formal tool at Doctorow's disposal to effectively expose and ridicule the views that he seeks to criticize:

> A union was an affront to God. The laboring man would be protected and cared for not by the labor agitators, said one wealthy man, but by the Christian men to whom God in His infinite wisdom had given the control of property interests of this country. (34)

Statements such as these, which carry a capitalist, racist or white supremacist focalization, beg for an ironic reading, underscoring the narrator's ideology. In addition, it facilitates the readers' concurrence with such system of beliefs, since they probably find their face curled in a half-smile, perhaps even in spite of themselves. *Ragtime*'s ironic tone places Doctorow in the tradition of great political satirists such as Jonathan Swift, with his humorous but grotesque proposal that Irish babies become a part of the English diet to solve the problems in Ireland. Like Swift's "Modest Proposal," statements such as the one above have the incontestable force of pure rationality that is apparently deprived of the burden of affect. Thus, instead of openly condemning these views, the fictive author and narrator chooses to mock them, a much more effective technique of social criticism. As Hutcheon has aptly claimed, "irony may be the only way we *can* be serious today" (39; emphasis in the original).

A key way of investing the narrative with its enormous ironic quality is the elaboration of a dispassionate, cold and distant chronicle-like narration in which straightforward, deadpan claims are undermined at the level of textual implications and contrasted with their own heartlessness. The heterodiegetic narrator appears to be a neutral, detached social chronicler who writes insipid staccato declarative sentences. These are, nevertheless, bustling with indignation and reproof: "One hundred miners were burned alive. One hundred children were mutilated. There seemed to be quotas for these things. There seemed to be quotas for death by starvation" (34). It is also worth pointing out that the narrator moves from one strand of the story to the next in an extremely smooth manner, mainly through association of ideas: "He was passionately in love with his ancient mother. In fact, Sigmund Freud had just arrived in America [...]" (29). As this quotation exemplifies, the result is a fluid narrative style that reminds of a succession of film stills.[12] Furthermore, the novel's apparent narrative simplicity and its seamless pace—resulting from the predominant use of free direct style and heterodiegetic narration—are further reinforced through the creation of abrupt though smooth shifts of focalization:

> They were immediately sensitive to the enormous power of the immigration officials. [...] Such power was dazzling. The immigrants were reminded of home. They went into the streets and were somehow absorbed in the tenements. They were despised by New Yorkers. They were filthy and illiterate. They stank of fish and garlic. They had running sores. They had no honor and worked for next to nothing. They stole. They drank. They raped their own daughters. (13)

As this quote exemplifies, focalization shifts do not alter the flow of the narrative, since at times statements narrated through the focalization of different characters melt into one another from one sentence to the next, while dramatically contributing to the novel's ironic tone. In this case, the narrator's apparently neutral, chronicle-like narration subtly melts into someone else's parochial and racist focalization without further notice.

Finally, the novel resorts to satire as a tool to criticize certain traits and values, such as white supremacy, racism, gender discrimination, double standards, predatory ambition, thirst for power and capitalist oppression. Indeed, the bigotry of characters like Chief Conklin, Mayor Gaynor and District Attorney Whitman is bitingly satirized: Whitman, for example, cannot resist meddling in Coalhouse Walker's case out of sheer ambition for power and visibility, becoming the object of the narrator's satire: "He thought it was his duty as President-to-be. He liked to be photographed at the scene of the action" (228); and then when things do not go as he has planned: "I can't give in to the coon. Even to hang him. I can't afford it. It would finish me. [...] And now the D.A. giving in to a nigger? No, sir! It can't be done" (242). Conklin, the fire chief responsible for Coalhouse's transformation into a terrorist, is likewise mocked by the heterodiegetic narrator for "offer[ing] counsel of the same level of wisdom that had triggered the crisis in the first place. He wanted to go to the black neighborhood and clean all the niggers out once and for all" (183). The industrial and economic elites responsible for the oppression and exploitation of the working class are also subjected to the narrator's most brutal satire. Tateh's mill owners are said to resolve that "[f]or the good of the country and the American democratic system [...] there would be no more children's crusades" (104). Similarly, Henry Ford and J.P. Morgan, two other historical characters whose fictionalized personas appear in *Ragtime*, create a secret society based on the shared idea that they are reincarnated pharaohs. Their megalomania leads Morgan to spend a night inside a pyramid, where he expects to receive a sign from Osiris, but is only greeted by aggressive bedbugs. These characters represent the absolute disregard for the well-being of other human beings, and for those attitudes they are subjected to the narrator's bitter satire, to the extent that it is impossible for us to identify with any of them. This automatically causes the reader to align him- or herself with those oppressed because of their marginal race, class or gender.

A special case in point in this sense is, once again, Tateh's. Despite his representation as the most successful character in terms of his capacity to cope with trauma, as argued above, he is also the object of the novel's satire due to his remorseless dereliction of the socialist cause. After disappearing from the narrative for over one hundred pages, he reappears as a rich and successful moving-picture entrepreneur who calls himself Baron Ashkenazy, has forsaken his socialist beliefs and has, metaphorically speaking, become white thanks to wealth; Tateh's transformation into a self-made rich baron has obvious resonances to the myth of the American Dream, which has led some commentators of the novel to accuse Doctorow of presenting a deeply nostalgic account of the past.[13] It could be argued, however, that Tateh's abandonment of his previous socialist beliefs and his remorseless embrace of capitalism is not an accidental flaw in the novel's otherwise critical attitude toward injustice and oppression. Rather, there is a clear case to argue that Tateh is precisely the greatest object of the narrator's satire: he is mocked on the basis of his reliance on the quintessential North-American myth, which is arguably responsible for the country's extreme individualism: "Thus did the artist point his life along the lines of flow of American Energy" (111). Doctorow's humorous criticism of Tateh may be best appreciated in the outstanding naiveté that this character shows at the end of the narrative: when he sees his daughter, the WASP little boy and Sarah's black baby playing together in the lawn, an idea for a film suddenly forms in front of his eyes:

> A bunch of children who were pals, white black, fat thin, rich poor, all kinds, mischievous little urchins who would have funny adventures in their own neighborhood, a society of ragamuffins, like all of us, a gang, getting into trouble and getting out again. (269–270)

As Christopher Morris has rightly argued, Tateh's "vision" is "a gross misrepresentation of the bulk of the action of *Ragtime*, which tells of violent, incurable racial and ethnic conflict" (94). Taking the argument where Morris drops it, Tateh's idealized, utopian vision of the peaceful cohabitation of different races and ethnicities in the United States begs for an ironic reading, because it is obviously played against the reader's knowledge that racism and working-class inequalities cannot be so easily dissolved, not even by the power of capital. Furthermore, such view of harmonious miscegenation and multiculturalism, as epitomized by Tateh's new family, is effectively undermined by the frequent references to the ideology of the society in which they actually live, a society where hoteliers grow uncomfortable when the black baby sits at the table and the need is felt to have a black maid in order to justify his presence. In short, the deployment of narratological techniques such as irony, focalization shifts and satire forces readers to confront intellectually as well as emotionally the repercussions of brutal economic and social practices that led to racism, discrimination and class exploitation at the turn of the century. Yet, rather than keeping the focus on the individual mind, *Ragtime* highlights the collective dimension of insidious trauma and emphasizes its political implications.

Concluding Remarks

In the preceding two chapters, Doctorow's preoccupation with extreme individual suffering has been clearly established. *Ragtime* is no different in many respects, because it also deals with the devastating effects of (insidious) trauma. Yet, as I hope my analysis has shown, the novel inaugurates a significant shift of emphasis from vulnerability and victimization toward adaptability, agency and resilience in the face of great stress. The focus is on survival and on the transformative power of trauma, which may yield not only vulnerabilities but also strengths. Furthermore, unlike Doctorow's previous novels, *Ragtime* focuses not so much on the individual mind as on the wider effects of insidious injustice and discrimination on certain marginalized communities. Indeed, the analysis above has suggested that the novel's narrative style reinforces the focus on the collective dimension of trauma and forces the reader to reflect on the social ills derived from racism and exploitation.

The Politics of Gender

Perhaps in a more explicit manner than any of Doctorow's previous novels, *Ragtime* offers thought-provoking possibilities from the viewpoint of feminist criticism. First of all, the novel includes a wide number of female characters, several of whom are subjected to oppression or even explicit violence due to their intersecting condition as the sexual and racial or social Other. There are also numerous references to the objectification of the female body. In addition, the book establishes a clear contrast between masculine and feminine models of conduct. Finally, and quite remarkably, *Ragtime* includes the fictionalized persona of the historical Emma Goldman, a feminist activist whose revolutionary ideas are extensively rendered in the novel. As this brief survey suggests, the novel seems to be about gender in very explicit ways. These are, therefore, the issues that this section addresses, seeking to tease out the ideological implications of *Ragtime*'s attitude toward some key feminist concerns.

Oppression and Objectification

To begin with, *Ragtime* places a strong emphasis on the notion that female characters face situations of overt victimization that derive not merely from their socio-economic context but also from their condition as women in a deeply patriarchal society. In her seminal study of masculinity, Raewyn Connell identifies a three-fold model of the structure of gender that relies on relations of power, production and cathexis (74). As she explains, in patriarchal societies, the main axis of power in the contemporary gender order is the overall subordination of women and dominance of men; production relations are based on a gendered division of labor in which the gendered character of capital is a key aspect and the practices that shape and realize sexual desire and interaction are commonly based on coercion and an unequal distribution of pleasure (74). This is precisely the gender order that the novel exposes, as we shall see.

Characterization in *Ragtime* functions as a tool to draw attention to the oppression and, at times, violence that women faced at the turn of the century and which intersects with racial and class discrimination. The best example is probably the character of Sarah. As the previous section has shown, Sarah's victimization cannot be dissociated from the adverse socio-economic forces and racism of US society at the time. Yet, it is also made evident that her gender worsens her living conditions, rendering her vulnerable to further victimization: as a derelict and impoverished single mother with no means to support herself and her baby, she is pushed to make a choice between keeping her child and starving to death or abandoning him to a sure death in order to save her own life. The same may be said of Mameh, a Jewish immigrant from Latvia who struggles to survive in the poorest area of the State of New York. The hardships of her life as a working-class immigrant are notably accentuated by her condition as a woman in a deeply patriarchal culture. Indeed, the novel shows how the terrible circumstances that her family must endure force her to helplessly submit to sexual abuse at the hands of her employer:

> The owner invited her into his office [...]. He counted out the money, adding a dollar more than she deserved. This he explained

was because she was such a good-looking woman. He smiled. He touched Mameh's breast. Mameh fled, taking the dollar. The next time the same thing happened [...]. She became accustomed to the hands of her employer. One day with two weeks' rent due she let the man have his way on a cutting table. He kissed her face and tasted the salt of her tears. (15)

It is possible to deduce from the narrative that Mameh is the one that actually supports her whole family with her sewing wages. Thus, what other (white, male) characters unhesitatingly judge as "moral degeneracy" (15) is undeniably an act of self-sacrifice on Mameh's part. In other words, she tolerates her own sexual victimization to ensure her family's survival in utterly adverse socio-economic circumstances, in effect merging economic and sexual oppression. It is worth adding that, when Tateh finds out that his wife has been 'complying' with her employer's abuse, he casts her away without giving it a second thought, condemning her to an even worse fate of vagrancy, prostitution and, presumably, death. Mameh, thus, becomes a "missing person" in Jenny Edkins's interesting use of the term: like the cases of those disappeared in certain totalitarian regimes, those missing in action during a war or those whose fate is unconfirmed after a major accident, natural disaster or terrorist attack, Mameh is "*ontically* missing": she too has "move[d] out of a context in which [she is] part of [her] recognized social or symbolic system" (129; emphasis in the original). Mameh is metaphorically neither alive nor dead, arguably an extreme act of violence on patriarchal society's, and more specifically Tateh's, part. Indeed, her fate is never revealed in the novel, but this does not prevent Tateh from eventually marrying Mother.

Another character whose representation draws attention to the victimization of women in patriarchal society is the fictionalized Evelyn Nesbit. As discussed in the previous section, Evelyn is nothing but a toy at the hands of two abusive men, who use their superior economic position to take advantage of her. At first sight, however, it may appear that the sort of oppression that she experiences is radically different from the victimization which Sarah and Mameh suffer, due to Evelyn's status as member of the privileged class. It is certainly true that Evelyn's plight differs from those of Sarah and Mameh. For one thing, empathy toward her suffering might be hindered by her overriding economic ambitions: as the fictionalized Emma Goldman later on claims "[she is] nothing more than a clever prostitute. [She] accepted the conditions in which [she] found [her]self and [she] triumphed. But what kind of victory has it been? The victory of a prostitute" (48–49). In that sense, *Ragtime* also levels criticism at the traditional myth of female compliance with their own victimization in an attempt to fulfill economic aspirations. These aspirations, however, are critically shown to be imposed by the capitalist values of the patriarchal society that is also responsible for the oppression of women. Interestingly, the novel seems to leave open another possibility for the interpretation of Evelyn's behavior, which may be alternatively understood as revolutionary: in the only feminist-oriented reading of the novel, Phyllis Jones claims that her analysis of the novel's self-made men had been intended to remind us of the cultural fact that the rise from rags to riches was a possibility only for men (25). Taking up the argument where Jones leaves it, it is possible to claim that Evelyn's determination to take her future into her own hands and do whatever it takes to fulfill her ambitions is in a way presented, and may be read, as a sort of triumph after all, even if it constitutes "the victory of a prostitute" (48). That is to say, in spite of the apparent condemnation at the level of textual implications of Evelyn's means to fulfill her ambition, it is undeniable that she has achieved her aim: obtaining economic independence—a remarkable attainment for a woman at the turn of the twentieth century. Thus, Nesbit's sexualized body becomes an oxymoronic symbol of female empowerment and simultaneous subjection.

The articulation of Evelyn Nesbit further allows *Ragtime* to explicitly address a related source of oppression: the objectification of the female body. It is explained, for instance, that Harry K. Thaw takes Evelyn to Europe because he wants to use her body "without worrying if White was to have his turn when he was through" (19). That is, he demands exclusive property rights. She is further defined as "the first sex goddess in American history" (70) and as the woman who provided the inspiration for the movie star system, because some men in the business community realize that "Evelyn's face on the front page of a newspaper sold out the edition" (71). Thus, Nesbit is described as a mere instrument by means of which more products can be sold, in effect denouncing the birth of the business of sexualized publicity that presents the female body as a passive object of the male gaze and as a commodified product that can be bought and sold. Most interestingly, Evelyn herself willingly complies with the objectification of her own body in the name of an ideal of beauty. Indeed, when at one point in the novel she takes off her underclothes, we learn that "marks of the stays ran vertically like welts around Nesbit's waist. The evidence of garters could be seen in the red lines running around the tops of her thighs" (53). It is worth pointing out that the marks left on her body by her corset are described in the exact same terms as the wounds that Thaw inflicts on her at the German castle. This is certainly a tell-tale analogy: the novel weaves a connection between male physical abuse of women and female physical subjugation to the aesthetic rules set by patriarchal society. Thus, *Ragtime* may be also read as an attempt to highlight the negative effects of internalized sexism as manifested in the compliance with artificial beauty standards and self-objectification. Acting as a sort of spokesperson for the novel's gender ideology, Emma Goldman befittingly claims: "Women kill themselves" (54). In short, the novel arguably condemns the model of gender interaction that is based on the oppression and objectification of women. Despite socio-economic and racial differences, the female characters discussed above are presented as facing parallel discrimination and comparable violence, which is explicitly shown to be a result of their gender within a deeply patriarchal society.

Masculinities and Femininities

In what already seems to be a steady effort to denounce gender discrimination, *Ragtime* also engages with perhaps less harmful but equally widespread ideological forms of oppression through the representation of a well-off WASP family. The characterization of Mother and Father constitutes the central tool to explore and contest the polarization of masculine and feminine models of conduct in North-American society at the turn of the twentieth century. At a first glimpse, the character of Mother seems to represent the highest degree of domestic self-fulfillment: she is conveniently married to a wealthy entrepreneur and enjoys a quiet and comfortable upper-middle-class life. Like the average woman in her social stratum at the time, she has never endured any hardships or suffered physical or sexual abuse. However, her characterization highlights the fact that she is bound by certain cultural and social rules that must be dutifully observed. Mother's subjection to social convention can be best perceived in the novel's emphasis on her modesty and reluctance to engage in sexual intercourse, an attitude which Father very much admires and appreciates. Through her focalization, sex is presented as something distasteful and grotesque but which is, nevertheless, considered to be part of her wifely duties:

> Father was a burly man with strong appetites, but he appreciated his wife's reluctance to assume the indelicate attitudes that answered to his needs. [...] He was solemn and attentive as befitted the occasion. Mother shut her eyes and held her hands over her ears. Sweat from Father's chin fell on her breasts. She started. (10–11)

As this quote illustrates, the WASP household's sexual politics are a source of humor and irony for the narrator, who satirizes the family's submission to patriarchal rules of female behavior at every chance. Mother and Father's attitude toward intercourse appears even more limiting when compared to the unconstrained sexual conduct of the Eskimo women: during his expedition to the Pole, Father must confront a society that is not bound by the same rules of female modesty and submission but which he, nevertheless, considers to be undeveloped. He is at once fascinated and repulsed by what he calls the "primitive woman's claim to the gender," by her "grunts and shouts of fierce joy" (63) during sexual intercourse. He is shocked to see an Eskimo woman "thrusting her hips upwards to the thrusts of her husband" and "pushing back" (63). And he disparagingly compares what he perceives as a shameful attitude to Mother's appropriate "fastidiousness, her grooming and her intelligence" (63).

Father's extremely narrow view of the way women ought to behave earns him an even bigger shock when he returns from the Pole and finds his wife holding a black baby and deeply changed by his absence. Indeed, she seems to have undergone an evolution that started when she was forced to make her first independent decision: keeping Sarah's baby and taking responsibility for the two of them against the advice of the doctor and the policeman—traditionally key representatives of white male authority in Western patriarchal societies. Overcoming her initial despair at being "deserted by the race of males" (57), she manages to remain faithful to her own principles and acts independently of male control, which provides her with a new sense of empowerment. Thus, at Father's return Mother has become a much more autonomous woman, going so far as to have assumed executive responsibilities in the family business: "Mother could now speak crisply of such matters as unit cost, inventory and advertising. [...] She had made changes in certain billing procedures and contracted with four new sales agents in California and Oregon. [...] Father was astounded" (93). On top of that, we learn that Mother is also starting to "claim her gender" (93) in bed. Indeed, Father is shocked to find that "she was in some way not as vigorously modest as she'd been" (93) and, humorously enough, considers her readiness in bed to be God's punishment for his absence. To top it all, he finds on his wife's bedside table a pamphlet dealing with family limitations written by Emma Goldman. More remarkably, Mother's evolution can be best perceived in her attitude toward Sarah and her baby. Overcoming the widespread racism of her society, she treats them with extreme empathy and develops genuine affection for them, to the extent that she does not hesitate to legally adopt the child after Sarah's death.

Mother's newly acquired measure of independence and Father's failure to come to terms with it dramatically deteriorate their relationship, causing Mother to awake to the reality of her husband's parochial shortcomings:

> [...] she was coming to the realization that whereas once, in his courtship, Father might have embodied the infinite possibilities of loving, he had aged and gone dull, made stupid, perhaps, by his travels and his work, so that more and more he only demonstrated his limits, that he had reached them, and that he would never move beyond them. (210)

Mother's estrangement from Father—which is aggravated by her sorrow at the loss of Sarah and which makes Father feel "altogether invisible" (182)—culminates in a new and unprecedented tension between them that may be best qualified as a power struggle. And so, Father reproaches his wife for having taken Sarah in, accusing her of victimizing the family with her "foolish female sentimentality" (175). Father's outbursts are particularly noteworthy, because ever since his return, it is obvious that he has felt enormous displeasure at his wife's newly developed autonomy. But it is interestingly his masculinity that he feels to be demeaned by his wife's empowerment. After all, as Connell explains, hegemonic masculinity relies on gender relations based on subordination (78). Therefore, by deprecating her sentimentality and identifying it as a feminine trait, he might be seeking to reinforce his sense of control and restore his wounded manliness. Father also attempts to exert his power through the sexual subjection of his wife, who feels compelled to comply with her husband's sexual demands by a long-learned sense of wifely duty. And so, when they travel to Atlantic City, we learn that "after-the-swim was soon established by Father as the time for amour. [...] She silently resented the intrusion" (210). The emphasis on Mother's silent submissiveness actually works to undermine Father's success in submitting his wife to his own desires. In addition, Father's recovered sense of power is but illusory: not only has Mother moved from disregard to open animosity, but the bitterness and repulsion that she feels toward her husband drives her into another man's arms, leading to the dissolution of their marriage at the end of the novel. In spite of his efforts to return to the old sexual politics of the upper-middle-class household, Father has been helplessly defeated.

Mother's evolution, and the power struggle that ensues, underscores the novel's preoccupation with hegemonic models of masculinity and femininity as well as gender relations. The reader is led to empathize with a female character that, to a certain extent, has managed to awake to the reality of her own submission and has striven to stand up to the patriarchal ideological stagnation that her husband represents. The latter, on the contrary, stands for a model of masculinity that *Ragtime* openly ridicules and seeks to undermine. His behavior is constantly satirized, which effectively shatters the possibility for readers to identify with his dissatisfaction and confusion. In short, *Ragtime* is extremely critical of the mechanisms through which patriarchal societies build and maintain hegemonic gender configurations.

Feminist Ideology in the Novel

If the analysis carried out so far has hinted at the book's visibilization and support of certain second-wave feminist concerns, the character of Emma Goldman may be claimed to constitute explicit proof of it.

Goldman embodies and acts as spokesperson of the novel's ideology, which the fictive author and narrator renders at every turn. For instance, during a socialist meeting organized in the slums, Goldman claims that marriage as an imposition must be repudiated, because it is a "shallow, empty mockery" (45). We find certain support for such statement at the level of the plot, in the marriage between Mother and Father, as we have seen. Goldman, whose words are worth quoting at length, even rebukes the male audience for their compliance with the subordination of women:

> Can you socialists ignore the double bondage of one half of the human race? Do you think the society that plunders your labor has no interest in the way you are asked to live with women? Not through freedom but through bondage? [...] The truth is, Goldman went on quickly, women may not vote, they may not love whom they want, they may not develop their minds and their spirits, they may not commit their lives to the spiritual adventure of life, comrades they may not! And why? Is our genius only in our wombs? Can we not write books and create learned scholarship and perform music and provide philosophical models for the betterment of mankind? Must our fate always be physical? (46)

As this quotation suggest, the words ascribed to Emma Goldman in the novel constitute an explicit condemnation of the capitalistic model of production and consumption that supports itself on the subordination and reduction of women to a reproductive role. Such model is never contested by the male socialists in the novel, Tateh being one of them. Despite paradoxically attempting to put an end to capitalistic oppression, they do not stop to consider its effects on women or their own compliance with it. Indeed, the (male) socialists in the meeting show outrage at Emma's words, which points to the hypocrisy and sexism for which the Socialist Labor Movement has traditionally been well known.[14]

The rendition of these ideas has earned Doctorow accusations of anachronism (see Luckacs 289). It is certainly true that some of the beliefs ascribed to Goldman in the novel would seem more in keeping with second-wave feminist ideology. However, in spite of Doctorow's well-deserved reputation as a fabulator and his taste for the deliberate blurring of differences between the historical record and fictional accounts, it appears that the representation of Emma Goldman has not been purposefully distorted in *Ragtime*. As Alix Kates Shulman explains, the American anarchist/revolutionary belonged to an ideological trend that based its analysis of gender divisions on a radical critique of the family, and often embraced the sexual radicalism of the birth control and Free Motherhood movements (6). The intention behind the introduction of a character that is so outspoken in her condemnation of patriarchal oppression of women might seem self-evident; Goldman's ideology smoothly complements and reinforces the novel's underlying support of certain second-wave feminist concerns, as shown above. Furthermore, as Phyllis Jones has rightly argued, the novel encourages reader identification with Emma, since she emerges as the only character who succeeds in balancing "individual needs with political demands, personal success with societal compassion" (27). Thus, the novel portrays a specifically feminist character, who is generally in charge of voicing the novel's underlying feminist ideology and plays the role of the educator, not only of the female characters in the novel, but also, perhaps, of the readers. After all, Goldman's demands are regrettably still applicable to female existence in many societies nowadays.

Concluding Remarks

As I hope the analysis has proved, *Ragtime* constitutes an effective critique of the sexual oppression and at times violence that women faced at the turn of the twentieth century in the context of a patriarchal and emerging capitalist society, where using their body as currency appears to have been the only means for their advancement or even survival. The novel articulates gender oppression and (sexual) violence as affecting women regardless of their race, ethnicity or social class. In other words, differences aside, the victimization and oppression that the female characters suffer are shown to cut across race, class and ethnicity, which is made visible by the characters' parallel helplessness in patriarchal society in terms of power, production and cathexis relations. This idea was defended by the second wave of feminists who were writing at the time of Doctorow's coming of age as novelist, although it has been rightly contested by black, Marxist and postcolonial feminist critics ever since. Finally, *Ragtime* emphasizes the damage that milder forms of cultural oppression may also cause in terms of hegemonic models of feminine sexual and social behavior.

Discussion and Conclusion

Discussion

The analysis carried out in this chapter has provided an innovative interpretation of E.L. Doctorow's most celebrated and extensively examined novel. The first section has discussed the novel's subtle shift of perspective toward an emphasis on the transformative power of trauma and the phenomenon of resilience on the one hand, and its simultaneous focus away from the individual mind, on the other. The second section has established *Ragtime*'s open support of a wide number of feminist concerns, such as the denunciation of gender oppression and the objectification of the female body, criticism of hegemonic social conventions of feminine behavior and defense of female empowerment. The last section of this chapter attempts to bring together the results obtained so far in order to discuss some of the implications that the analyses informed by trauma theory and feminist criticism have when considered alongside one another.

In order to do so, it is key to consider, first, the novel's many instances of female bonding. Among these, the most conspicuous ones are Mother's selfless act of kindness toward Sarah and Evelyn's tender dedication to the Little Girl, both discussed above. These, however, are not the only ones. What we arguably find in the novel is a subtly woven network among the female characters, who are all interconnected in a community based on empathy and sisterhood: Mother saves Sarah's life, she reads Emma Goldman's pamphlets and becomes the Little Girl's stepmother after marrying Tateh, substituting Evelyn in that role, who in turn becomes deeply attached to Emma,[15] an outspoken defender of the rights of women regardless of their race or class. Furthermore, Mother's awakening to the reality of her oppression is crucially brought about by her determination to help Sarah and by her love for her. Similarly, Evelyn's experience living in the slums with the Little Girl greatly contributes to her new awareness of the needs of others. More importantly, it is precisely through the female characters' reliance on one another that they manage to develop coping mechanisms by means of which they are better suited to overcome traumatic or otherwise oppressive situations. The examples above illustrate Alex Zautra et al.'s point that social ties and secure kin/kith relations are key resources for resilience (10). Indeed, most medical professionals insist on the importance of social support to promote successful adaptation to stress. Arieh Shalev, for instance, has claimed that "[l]ack of social support and continuous adversities increase the likelihood of developing PTSD after exposure to a traumatic event" (208). Similarly, Derrick Silove has found that "[m]ost persons can be expected to recover spontaneously if the social and cultural environment is supportive" (255). In *Ragtime*, recovery after trauma and resilience are conspicuously articulated as being enhanced by support within a network based on empathy, which attests to the key role of the wider social and interpersonal context in determining individual response to (insidious) trauma. Summarizing and giving voice to the novel's underlying ideology, Goldman says it best: "in the total human fate we are sisters" (52).

Another issue that requires critical inquiry in the light of the analysis carried out so far is Tateh's and Coalhouse's ambiguous position as both victims and perpetrators. As the previous chapters have demonstrated, victim-perpetrator characters are particularly recurrent throughout Doctorow's oeuvre. In the case of Tateh, it is undeniable that he is a victim of utterly adverse social, economic and political structures. Despite the novel's apparently detached narrative style, his extreme suffering is presented with a wealth of detail. Yet, the second section has also confirmed Tateh's contemptible role in his wife's fate. Hence, readers might find themselves torn between feelings of pity and contempt at different stages of the narrative. While the character is subjected to the novel's satire for his ready embrace of capitalistic values of production and consumption, he is never openly judged at the level of textual implications for his decision to abandon his wife to her fate upon finding out that she has submitted to her boss's coercive sexual abuse. This might suggest a refusal on the novel's part to pronounce an ethnocentric judgment of Tateh's culture, which requires him to "mourn [his wife] as [they] mourn the dead" (38). Neither is Coalhouse Walker condemned at the level of textual implications for his share of blame for Sarah's state at the beginning of the novel: after getting her pregnant, the narrative reveals that he abandoned her to her fate too, leaving her in such a desperate condition as to attempt to kill her newborn baby in order to save her own life. Coalhouse's later efforts to make amends and recover Sarah's trust, the brutal injustice committed against him, as well as the sympathetic treatment that the character receives at the level of textual implications, arguably predispose the reader to identify with his pain and hold the openly hostile society of turn-of-the-century United States responsible for Sarah's victimization as well as his. Yet, such view does nothing but obscure the different intersecting levels of oppression to which characters such as Sarah and Mameh are subjected because of their double marginalization (due to their race/class and gender).

Coalhouse Walker's dual position as victim and perpetrator is, however, more explicitly established than Tateh's by the novel: as we have seen, after failing to achieve justice through the legal system, and tormented by guilt for having made the restoration of his pride and self-respect a priority over Sarah's needs, he becomes a terrorist and serial murderer. Coalhouse's transformation provides the occasion for the exploration of the boundary that the novel establishes between the elements of the binary victim/perpetrator, which is, once again, shown to be rather fuzzy. Indeed, although one might reasonably argue that nothing justifies the killing of innocent people and the terrorizing of a whole society, the reader is arguably prone to identify with the ragtime player's cause, since it becomes evident at the level of textual implications that he is threatening the very same society that is responsible for his victimization. As the heterodiegetic narrator rhetorically muses, "[i]s injustice, once suffered, a mirror universe, with laws of logic and principles of reason the opposite of civilization's?" (225). In short, although less so than in the novels discussed in the previous chapters, *Ragtime* seems to favor a non-judgmental, anti-categorical narration in these cases. Both Tateh and Coalhouse occupy a liminal position in the continuum that trauma theory establishes between the categories of victim and perpetrator. What is more, the ethical hesitancy elicited by these characters in terms of their contribution other characters' suffering allows the novel to warn of the dire consequences that the victimization of disenfranchised racial and social groups may have not only for the individual, but also for the collective.

One more issue that the analyses informed by trauma studies and feminist criticism raise is the dilemma that the novel's chronicle-like narration and its shift of emphasis from the individual to the collective poses in terms of voicing. Two separate but related aspects demand critical enquiry in that sense. On the one hand, it is important to keep in mind that E.L. Doctorow was a white, upper-middle-class male author who, as respected writer and university professor, belonged to the academic elite of the United States. Yet, in *Ragtime* most of the characters come from the margins of North-American society and, as such, represent structural disempowerment and potential vulnerability to insidious trauma, injustice and (patriarchal) oppression. The imbalance of power existent between Doctorow and most of his characters cannot but bring to mind the notion of 'ventriloquism.' Gayatri Spivak has famously claimed in her influential *Critique of Postcolonial Reason* (1999) that "[t]he ventriloquism of the speaking subaltern is the left intellectual's stock-in-trade" (255). Although Spivak uses the term in a rather pejorative sense to refer to a certain patronage toward the minority on the part of the (leftist) intellectual elite, it is undeniable that fiction writing always entails certain ventriloquism: characters are not independent beings, but rather the product of a writer's imagination. Thus, as ventriloquist's dummies, characters are always compelled to recite a script drafted by the implied author. This is not only not necessarily bad in itself, but it is, indeed, the basis of fiction writing, since otherwise autobiography would be the only ethically acceptable literary form. Yet, the concept of ventriloquism indeed suggests an imbalance of power between writer, characters and readers/spectators. Therefore, a politically neutral interpretation of the dynamics established between puppeteer and dummies is not possible, especially where it comes to novels whose author and the characters to which he or she is giving voice do not belong to the same side of the binary pair. What makes *Ragtime* different from Doctorow's previous novels is that in *Ragtime* not only the feminine Other is voiced, but also the racial and social ones.

On the other hand, it is important to keep in mind that the most discernible voice in *Ragtime* is the heterodiegetic narrator's, who generally keeps a safe emotional distance from the characters and their plight, as argued above. In addition, the voice of the narrator repeatedly melts into the characters' focalization, which further suggests the ubiquity of ventriloquism. In the cases of Sarah and Mameh, this brings to mind Spivak's claim in her seminal essay that "[i]f [...] the subaltern has no history and cannot speak, the subaltern as female is even more deeply in shadow" ("Subaltern" 287). Hence, what we face in *Ragtime* is a certain ethical hesitancy derived from Doctorow's simultaneous attempt to represent the traditionally disenfranchised members of North-American society and to do so in a distant, overbearing and omnipresent chronicle-like narrative voice that, by keeping the focus away from individual pathology, in effect bans the characters from showing a semblance of subjectivity or self-expression. One cannot rule out the possibility that Doctorow's aim might indeed have been to abstain from creating a distinct voice for his characters in order to precisely avoid accusations of ventriloquism. It is worth pointing out that the term has been applied to Doctorow precisely because of the struggle for genuine gender dialogue that his early novels manifest (see Gentry 1993).

Timothy Bewes has clearly spelt out the ethical dilemma that leftist writers in the United States face when seeking to denounce through their fiction some of the social ills that they could never experience in their flesh due to their belonging to the privileged side of most dichotomies:

> In a global conjuncture in which the very expression of ethical solidarity displays and enacts unprecedented disparities of power, writers of literature are in an ethical and aesthetic quandary: how to write without thereby contributing to the material inscription of inequality? Even to pose such a question can appear as romanticizing, or worse, of the position of the "subaltern" [...] subject, who seems thereby reduced to the status of an object that is merely written about. (11)

Doctorow may be a ventriloquist, but his motivations seem to be entirely ethical. His talent resides in his ability to merge multiple textual voices while privileging the traditionally marginalized and silenced ones, a feature which makes *Ragtime* more polyphonic in a Bakhtinian sense than his previous novels. The analyses carried out in this chapter suggest that *Ragtime* challenges patriarchal, capitalist and white supremacist ideology. The implied author speaks on behalf of the marginalized with a clearly ethical purpose in mind: mobilizing the readers' capacity to witness empathically the suffering of others, regardless of whether they can identify with it—that is, imagine themselves in their situation—an issue to which I will return in Chapter 5.

The analysis of the novel informed by trauma theory and feminist criticism also brings attention to one last key issue: although *Ragtime* is set in the early years of the twentieth century, it clearly establishes a critical dialogue between two ages, the time in which the story was set and the time in which it was written. The novel weaves connections between the two periods in terms of social and economic injustice, discrimination and precariousness of racial and social minorities. It also connects the two epochs through the objectification of the female body and female submission and compliance with patriarchal rules of social and sexual behavior and appearance. There is a clear case to argue that *Ragtime* seeks to parodically draw attention to the neoliberal socio-economic and patriarchal conditions of the 1970s, presenting them as a clumsily concealed repetition of past class, race and gender oppression, and highlighting as well how these conditions regrettably continue to shape contemporary US society. Doctorow's fourth novel forces us to experience intellectually as well as emotionally the repercussions of injustice, making us undergo the present as a repetition of past horrors. Finally, the novel succeeds in drawing the readers' attention to the continuing supremacy of wealth and of the (white, male, upper-middle-class) wealthy in Western societies, especially in the context of recent socio-economic upheavals in Europe and the United States. Doctorow makes visible the issues of class, race and gender inequality in a country where these differences are openly criticized but still persist. Thus, in *Ragtime*, Doctorow turned to a harsh past in order to accentuate the harshness of the present.

Conclusion

As the analysis carried out in this chapter has attempted to show, *Ragtime* is a complex novel that, in spite of its apparent superficiality, engages into unrelenting criticism of some of the most acute ills of turn-of-the-century North-American society. First, the novel inaugurates a shift from the understanding of trauma as a long-term, disabling ailing from which it is almost impossible to recover. It has been argued that the novel's focus is, rather, on resilience and on the capacity to overcome immobilization, helplessness and passivity in the face of insidious traumatization. Trauma becomes, for the first time in Doctorow's oeuvre, a force that fuels a transformation in which not just negative symptoms but also positive survival strategies may be developed, sublimation and the creation of a supporting community based on empathy and cooperation being key ones. Yet, the novel rejects an understanding of (insidious) trauma as an individual pathological disorder that can be solved by exclusively providing medical counsel. Rather, it is articulated as part of a wider context of discrimination and injustice that needs to be dramatically reformed at social, economic and political levels, which may, in so doing, reduce the potential for victims to become perpetrators. Second, *Ragtime* has been proved to imply that if adverse socio-economic conditions are extremely damaging for male members of the racial and class social margins, much more so for the female ones, since their vulnerability to victimization in a deeply hostile and patriarchal society is even greater. Yet, the analysis has also suggested that, in *Ragtime*, oppression, objectification and violence against women cut across race, class and ethnicity, emphasizing also the dangers of 'milder' forms of ideological and cultural sexism.

In conclusion, the novel's engagement with racism, discrimination and injustice plays a crucial role in Doctorow's denunciation of how certain legal, social, political and economic structures may generate and perpetuate conditions of traumatic victimization for the underprivileged and disenfranchised. It further highlights and condemns individualism and how it remains strongly inscribed within North-American laws and social practices, as well as being reflected in its cultural products. Yet, the novel's emphasis on survival and resilience has important social and cultural implications. *Ragtime* deepens also Doctorow's continuing concern with the subtle limits between the categories of victim and perpetrator in the context of trauma, through which the author seeks to warn of the disastrous psychological consequences of traumatic injustice for both the individual and society. Finally, the novel's open support of feminist concerns is entirely coherent with Doctorow's ongoing denunciation of the discrimination of women in North-American society, which was at the time, and is still today, very much biased by patriarchal distortions. With *Ragtime*, Doctorow managed to turn a bitter outcry against oppression, injustice and discrimination into a bestseller that has reached millions of people all over the world.

Notes

1 For other reception studies of the novel, see Berryman (1982) and Chances (1983).
2 Toward the end of the year 1975 a number of mildly negative and even harsh critiques of the novel began to appear, maybe because reviewers assumed that any book that met such commercial success could not have much literary value: see Solokov (July 1975), Hart (Aug. 1975), Marcus (Aug. 1975), Kramer (Oct. 1975), Green (Winter 1975–1976), Todd (1976) and Raban (Feb. 1976).
3 As Zautra et al. explain, beginning in the late eighteenth and early nineteenth centuries, as scholars, scientists and medical practitioners came to deal with certain social and individual phenomena, their focus was on their pathological dimension, on the analysis and treatment of individual and social pathologies (xi).
4 See for example Feder et al. (35), González Castro and Murray (375), Helgeson and Lopez (309), Lemery-Chalfant (55) and Ungar (404).
5 See Boehnlein (266), Mayer and Faber (94), Pargament and Cummings (193), Rafaeli and Hiller (171), and Skodol (112).
6 Further references to the novel will be to the Penguin Modern Classics edition, published in 2006.
7 As Jones has aptly noted, the family's archetypical role as representative of a whole class in the novel is suggested by the omniscience of the narration, the general absence of first-person references and the capitalization of these generic names (20). The same may be said of Mameh, Tateh and the Little Girl.
8 The 1912 Lawrence Textile Strike. By mixing references to historical and fictional events and personages, the novel attests to Doctorow's

conviction—widely theorized in his essays and interviews—that literature and history share a similarly constructed status. Doctorow is well known for highlighting the story in history, and *Ragtime* is probably the best example of his fabulating inclinations.

9 Another real historical event, which is remembered as the "Children's Exodus." Calling it "Children's Crusade," when the episode was never called like that, is unlikely to be a genuine mistake on Doctorow's part. Rather, it presumably responds to Doctorow's determination to highlight the fictionality and constructed nature of the historical record, which may be easily manipulated for ideological purposes. After all, "crusade" is a much more dramatic word than "exodus," and it adds interesting connotations which Doctorow parodically exploits.

10 This further testifies to the importance of Freudian theory for Doctorow. Freud even appears briefly in the novel as a fictionalized character, during his visit to the United States. There, the fictive author and narrator humorously has him ride the Tunnel of Love in Coney Island with his former disciple Carl Jung, which, we learn, marks the beginning of a history of upset stomach.

11 Irony also works in the novel as a tool to give a new meaning to the old genre of the historical chronicle. Such use of irony aligns the novel with the postmodern trend which parodies traditional literary genres, an issue which has been explored in depth by theorists of postmodernism such as Linda Hutcheon (136), as argued in the preliminary analysis carried out in the Introduction.

12 *Ragtime* shares with *Welcome to Hard Times* a strong filmic quality, which presumably owes much to Doctorow's early work for a film company. Several critics have noticed *Ragtime*'s cinematic energy: see for example Dawson (1983), Eidsvik (1989), Rapf (1998) and Hague (2000). Their reading of the novel contrasts that of Laura Barret (2000), who believes that the novel's central trope is, rather, photography, being deeply "anti-cinematic" (815). Finally, Hillary Chute (2008) has notably claimed that *Ragtime* approximates the form of the comic because it privileges the visual in terms of both theme and form. Regardless of the specific visual art on which these critics rely, their papers all testify to the novel's uncanny ability to conjure up sharp images in the readers' minds.

13 See for example Kramer (1975), Green (1975), Hart (1975) and Raja (2007). Phyllis Jones, on the contrary, has portrayed Doctorow as a "radical critic of American dreams about success," cleverly claiming that he "mercilessly 'rags' our nostalgia about bygone 'times'" (19). Similarly, Linda Hutcheon has claimed that "[i]f Doctorow does use nostalgia, it is always ironically turned against itself—and us" (89). Indeed, asked in an interview about nostalgia in *Ragtime*, Doctorow claimed that it "is an inadequate self-deluding emotion," adding that "it is the disposition for nostalgia that *Ragtime* mocks" (in Lubarsky 36).

14 E.L. Doctorow has repeatedly shown himself to be extremely critical of the traditional sexism of the Left, most notably in *The Book of Daniel* (1971), as the previous chapter argued.

15 The explicitly erotic nature of Emma's massage to Evelyn when they first meet (53–54) is perhaps one of the most puzzling passages of the novel. The heterodiegetic narrator describes Evelyn's arousal, which unquestionably gives the encounter a highly sexual tinge. But the wording of their encounter makes it open to several interpretations. One might read it as a further attempt on Doctorow's part to tease the reader's convictions about the relationship between verifiable fact and fiction. Alternatively, it may be understood as a fantasy of the heterodiegetic narrator; much has been said about

who this figure might be, a majority of critics claiming that it is actually the upper-middle-class family's child—referred to as the Little Boy in the novel (see Harter and Thompson 65, Parks 60, Saltzman 95). If this were so, he might have fantasized as a young boy with Nesbit, who was for a while his uncle's lover. Finally, a more symbolic reading would also be possible, in which Evelyn's orgasm during Emma's massage could perhaps imaginatively be interpreted as the metaphorical inauguration of Evelyn's newly found respect for her own body and a new healthier attitude toward sexuality after years of sexual subordination to the wishes of two depraved men.

References

Adams, Phoebe. "*Ragtime*, by E.L. Doctorow." *Atlantic Monthly* (Aug. 1975): 88–92.
Baldick, Chris. *The Concise Oxford Dictionary of Literary Terms*. Oxford and New York: Oxford UP, 1991.
Barret, Laura. "Compositions of Reality: Photography, History, and *Ragtime*." *Modern Fiction Studies* 46.4 (Winter 2000):801–824.
Berryman, Charles. "*Ragtime* in Retrospect." *The South Atlantic Quarterly* 81.1 (Winter 1982): 30–42.
Bewes, Timothy. *The Event of Postcolonial Shame*. Princeton: Princeton UP, 2011.
Bloom, Harold, ed. *E.L. Doctorow's Ragtime. Modern Critical Interpretations*. Philadelphia: Chelsea House, 2002.
———. ed. *E.L. Doctorow's Ragtime*. Bloom's Guides: Comprehensive Research and Study Guides. Philadelphia: Chelsea House, 2004.
Boehnlein, James K. "Religion and Spirituality after Trauma." *Understanding Trauma: Integrating Biological, Clinical and Cultural Perspectives*. Eds. Laurence J. Kirmayer, Robert Lemelson, and Mark Barad. Cambridge and New York: Cambridge UP, 2007. 259–274.
Bonanno, George A. "Loss, Trauma, and Human Resilience: Have We Underestimated the Human Capacity to Thrive after Extremely Aversive Events?" *American Psychologist* 59.1 (Jan. 2004): 20–28.
Borzaga, Michela. "Trauma in the Postcolony—Towards a New Theoretical Approach." *Trauma, Memory, and Narrative in the Contemporary South African Novel: Essays*. Eds. Ewald Mengel and Michela Borzaga. Amsterdam: Rodopi, 2012. 65–91.
Chances, Ellen. "The Reds and *Ragtime*: The Soviet Reception of E. L. Doctorow." *E.L. Doctorow: Essays & Conversations*. Ed. Richard Trenner. Princeton: Ontario Review, 1983. 151–157.
Chute, Hillary. "*Ragtime, Kavalier & Clay*, and the Framing of Comics." *Modern Fiction Studies* 54.2 (Summer 2008): 268–301.
Clemons, Walter. "Houdini, Meet Ferdinand." *Newsweek* (July 14, 1975): 73–76.
Connell, Raewyn W. *Masculinities*. Berkeley and Los Angeles: University of California Press, 2005.
Craps, Stef. *Postcolonial Witnessing: Trauma Out of Bounds*. New York: Palgrave MacMillan, 2013.
Dawson, Anthony. "*Ragtime* and the Movies: The Aura of the Duplicable." *Mosaic* 16.1–2 (1983): 205–214.

Ditsky, John. "The German Source of *Ragtime*: A Note." *E. L. Doctorow: Essays & Conversations*. Ed. Richard Trenner. Princeton: Ontario Review, 1983. 179–181.
Doctorow, Edgar L. *Welcome to Hard Times*. 1960. New York: Random House Trade Paperback, 2007.
———. *The Book of Daniel*. 1971. London: Penguin, 2006.
———. *Ragtime*. 1974. London: Penguin, 2006.
Edkins, Jenny. "Time, Personhood, Politics." *The Future of Trauma Theory*. Eds. Gert Buelens, Sam Durrant, and Robert Eaglestone. London and New York: Routledge, 2014. 127–140.
Eidsvik, Charles. "Playful Perceptions: E. L. Doctorow's Use of Media Structures and Conventions in *Ragtime*." *Literaturwissenschaftliches Jahrbuch Im Auftrage der Görres-Gesellschadft* 30 (1989): 301–309.
Faber, Marion. "Michael Kohlhaas in New York: Kleist and E. L. Doctorow's *Ragtime*." *Heinrich von Kleist Studien / Heinrich von Kleist Studies*. Ed. Alexej Ugrinsky. Berlin: E. Schmidt, 1980. 147–156.
Farca, Paula A. "E.L. Doctorow's *Ragtime* in the Context of Historiographic Metafiction – A Study." *IRWLE* 9.1 (Jan. 2013): 1–10.
Farrell, Kirby. *Post-traumatic Culture: Injury and Interpretation in the Nineties*. Baltimore and London: Johns Hopkins UP, 1998.
Feder, Adriana, Eric J. Nestler, Maren Westphal, and Dennis S. Charney. "Psychobiological Mechanisms of Resilience to Stress." *Handbook of Adult Resilience*. Eds. John W. Reich, Alex J. Zautra, and John Stuart Hill. New York and London: The Guilford Press, 2010. 35–54.
Foley, Barbara. "From *U.S.A* to *Ragtime*: Notes on the Forms of Historical Consciousness in Modern Fiction." *E.L. Doctorow: Essays & Conversations*. Ed. Richard Trenner. Princeton: Ontario Review, 1983. 158–178.
Fremont-Smith, Eliot. "Making Book." *The Village Voice*, July 7, 1975. 41.
Freud, Sigmund. "Mourning and Melancholia." 1917 [2015]. *The Standard Edition of the Complete Psychological Works of Sigmund Freud*, Volume XIV (1914–1916). Ed. James Strachey. London: Vintage, 2001.
———. "Civilization and Its Discontents." 1930 [1929]. *The Standard Edition of the Complete Psychological Works of Sigmund Freud*, Volume XXI (1927–1931). Ed. James Strachey. London: Vintage, 2001.
———. *New Introductory Lectures on Psychoanalysis*. 1933 [1932]. *The Standard Edition of the Complete Psychological Works of Sigmund Freud*, Volume XXII (1932–1936). Ed. James Strachey. London: Vintage, 2001.
Gelus, M. and R. Crowley. "Kleis [sic] in *Ragtime*: Doctorow's Novel, Its German Sources and Its Reviewers." *The Journal of Popular Culture* 14.1 (Summer 1980): 20–26.
Gentry, Marshall B. "'Ventriloquists' Conversations: The Struggle for Gender Dialogue in E.L. Doctorow and Philip Roth." 1993. *Modern Critical Views: E.L. Doctorow*. Ed. Harold Bloom. Philadelphia: Chelsea House, 2002. 113–132.
Gilligan, James. "Shame, Guilt, and Violence." *Social Research* 70.4 (2003): 1149–1180.
Ginzburg, Harold M. "Resilience." *Encyclopedia of Trauma: An Interdisciplinary Guide*. Ed. Charles R. Figley. Los Angeles: Sage, 2012. 547–549.
González Castro, Felipe and Kate E. Murray. "Cultural Adaptation and Resilience: Controversies, Issues, and Emerging Models." *Handbook of Adult*

Resilience. Eds. John W. Reich, Alex J. Zautra, and John Stuart Hill. New York and London: The Guilford Press, 2010. 375–403.
Green, Martin. "Nostalgia Politics." *The American Scholar* 45.1 (Winter 1975–1976): 841–845.
Grumbach, Doris. "Review of *Ragtime*." *The New Republic* (July 5 & 12, 1975): 31.
Hague, Angela. "*Ragtime* and the Movies." *Critical Essays on E. L. Doctorow*. Ed. Ben Siegel. New York: G. K. Hall & Co, 2000. 166–176.
Harris, Stephen. "Myths of Individualism in E. L. Doctorow's *Ragtime*." *Australasian Journal of American Studies* 20.2 (Dec. 2001): 47–61.
Hart, Jeffrey. "Doctorow Time." *National Review*, 15 (Aug. 1975): 892–893.
Harter, Carol C. and James R. Thompson. *E. L. Doctorow*. Boston: Twayne, 1990.
Helbing, Robert E. "E.L. Doctorow's *Ragtime*: Kleist Revisited." *Heinrich von Kleist Studien/Heinrich von Kleist Studies*. Ed. Alexej Ugrinsky. Berlin: E. Schmidt, 1980. 157–167.
Helgeson, Vicki S. and Lindsey Lopez. "Social Support and Growth Following Adversity." *Handbook of Adult Resilience*. Eds. John W. Reich, Alex J. Zautra, and John Stuart Hill. New York and London: The Guilford Press, 2010. 309–330.
Hutcheon, Linda. *A Poetics of Postmodernism: History, Theory and Fiction*. New York: Routledge, 1988.
Jones, Phyllis. "*Ragtime*: Feminist, Socialist and Black Perspectives on the Self-Made Man." *Journal of American Culture* 2.1 (1979): 17–28.
Kauffmann, Stanley. "A Central Vision." *Saturday Review* (July 26, 1975): 20–22.
Kinzie, J.D. "PTSD among Traumatized Refugees." *Understanding Trauma: Integrating Biological, Clinical and Cultural Perspectives*. Eds. Laurence J. Kirmayer, Robert Lemelson, and Mark Barad. Cambridge and New York: Cambridge UP, 2007. 194–206.
Konner, Melvin. "Trauma, Adaptation, and Resilience: A Cross-Cultural and Evolutionary Perspective." *Understanding Trauma: Integrating Biological, Clinical and Cultural Perspectives*. Eds. Laurence J. Kirmayer, Robert Lemelson, and Mark Barad. Cambridge and New York: Cambridge UP, 2007. 300–338.
Kramer, Hilton. "Political Romance." *Commentary* 60 (Oct. 1975): 76–80.
Kurth-Voigt, Lieselotte E. "Kleistian Overtones in E. L. Doctorow's *Ragtime*." *Monatshefte* 69.4 (Winter 1977): 404–414.
Lemelson, Robert, Laurence J. Kirmayer, and Mark Barad. "Trauma in Context: Integrating Biological, Clinical and Cultural Perspectives." *Understanding Trauma: Integrating Biological, Clinical and Cultural Perspectives*. Eds. Laurence J. Kirmayer, Robert Lemelson, and Mark Barad. Cambridge and New York: Cambridge UP, 2007. 451–474.
Lemery-Chalfant, Kathryn. "Genes and Environments: How They Work Together to Promote Resilience." *Handbook of Adult Resilience*. Eds. John W. Reich, Alex J. Zautra, and John Stuart Hill. New York and London: The Guilford Press, 2010. 55–78.
Lubarsky, Jared "History and the Forms of Fiction: An Interview with E.L. Doctorow." *Conversations with E.L. Doctorow*. Ed. Christopher Morris. Jackson: Mississippi UP, 1999. 35–40.

Lukacs, John. "Doctorowurlitzer or History in *Ragtime.*" *Salmagundi* 31/32 10th Anniversary (Fall 1975–Winter 1976): 285–295.
Marcus, Greil. "*Ragtime* and *Nashville*: Failure-of-America Fad." *The Village Voice* 96 (Aug. 4, 1975): 61–62.
Mayer, John D. and Michael A. Faber. "Personal Intelligence and Resilience: Recovery in the Shadow of Broken Connections." *Handbook of Adult Resilience*. Eds. John W. Reich, Alex J. Zautra, and John Stuart Hill. New York and London: The Guilford Press, 2010. 94–111.
Moraru, Christian. "The Reincarnated Plot: E. L. Doctorow's *Ragtime*, Heinrich von Kleist's 'Michael Kohlhass,' and the Spectacle of Modernity." *The Comparatist* 21 (1997): 92–116.
Morris, Christopher D. "Illusions of Demystification in *Ragtime.*" *Modern Critical Views: E.L. Doctorow*. Ed. Harold Bloom. Philadelphia: Chelsea House, 1989. 91–104.
Neumeyer, Peter F. "E.L. Doctorow, Kleist, and the Ascendancy of Things." *CEA Critic* 39.4 (May 1977): 17–21.
Orbán, Katalin. "Swallowed Futures, Indigestible Pasts: Post-apocalyptic Narratives of Rights in Kleist and Doctorow." *Comparative American Studies* 1.3 (2003): 327–350.
Ostendorf, Berndt. "The Musical World of Doctorow's *Ragtime.*" *American Quarterly* 43.4 (Dec. 1991): 579–601.
Pargament, Kenneth I. and Jeremy Cummings. "Anchored by Faith: Religion as a Resilience Factor." *Handbook of Adult Resilience*. Eds. John W. Reich, Alex J. Zautra, and John Stuart Hall. New York and London: The Guilford Press, 2010. 193–210.
Parks, John G. *E. L. Doctorow*. New York: Continuum, 1991.
Piehl, Kathy. "E.L. Doctorow and Random House: The Ragtime Rhythm of Cash." *Journal of Popular Culture* 13.3 (Spring 1980): 404–411.
Raban, Jonathan. "Easy Virtue." *Encounter* 46.2 (Feb. 1976): 71–74.
Rafaeli, Eshkol and Atara Hiller. "Self-Complexity: A Source of Resilience?" *Handbook of Adult Resilience*. Eds. John W. Reich, Alex J. Zautra, and John Stuart Hall. New York and London: The Guilford Press, 2010. 171–192.
Raja, Masood. "Doctorow's *Ragtime*: Inserting Class in a Literary Discussion." *Considering Class: Essays on the Discourse of the American Dream*. Eds. Kevin Cahill and Lene Johannessen. Munster/Hamburg: LIT Verlag, 2007. 105–116.
Rapf, Joanna E. "The Transgressive Energy of *Ragtime* as Novel and Film." *Literature/Film Quarterly* 26.1 (1998): 16–22.
Roberts, Brian. "Blackface Minstrelsy and Jewish Identity: Fleshing out Ragtime as the Central Metaphor in E.L. Doctorow's *Ragtime.*" *Critique* 45.3 (Spring 2004): 247–259.
Rodgers, Bernard. "A Novelist's Revenge." *Chicago Review* 27.3 (Winter 1975–1976): 138–144.
Root, Maria. "Reconstructing the Impact of Trauma on Personality." *Personality and Psychopathology: Feminist Reappraisals*. Ed. Laura S. Brown and Mary Ballou. New York: Guilford, 1992. 229–265.
Rousseau, Cécile and Toby Measham. "Posttraumatic Suffering as a Source of Transformation: A Clinical Perspective." *Understanding Trauma: Integrating Biological, Clinical and Cultural Perspectives*. Eds. Laurence J. Kirmayer,

Robert Lemelson, and Mark Barad. Cambridge and New York: Cambridge UP, 2007. 275–293.
Rutter, Michael. "Psychosocial Resilience and Protective Mechanisms." *American Journal of Orthopsychiatry* 57.3 (July 1987): 316–331.
Sale, Roger. "From *Ragtime* to Riches." *The New York Review of Books* (Aug. 7, 1975): 21–22.
Saltzman, Arthur. "The Stylistic Energy of E.L. Doctorow." *E. L. Doctorow, Essays & Conversations*. Ed. Richard Trenner. Princeton and New York: Ontario Review, 1983. 73–108.
Shalev, Arieh Y. "PTSD: A Disorder of Recovery?" *Understanding Trauma: Integrating Biological, Clinical and Cultural Perspectives*. Eds. Laurence J. Kirmayer, Robert Lemelson, and Mark Barad. Cambridge and New York: Cambridge UP, 2007. 207–223.
Sheppard, R. Z. "The Music of Time." *Time* (July 14, 1975): 64.
Shulman, Alix Kates. "Emma Goldman's Feminism: A Reappraisal." *Red Emma Speaks: An Emma Goldman Reader*. New York: Humanity Books, 1998.
Sigal, John J. "Long-Term Effects of the Holocaust: Empirical Evidence for Resilience in the First, Second, and Third Generation." *Psychoanalytic Review* 85.4 (Aug. 1998): 579–585.
Silove, Derrick. "Adaptation, Ecosocial Safety Signals, and the Trajectory of PTSD." *Understanding Trauma: Integrating Biological, Clinical and Cultural Perspectives*. Eds. Laurence J. Kirmayer, Robert Lemelson, and Mark Barad. Cambridge and New York: Cambridge UP, 2007. 242–258.
Skodol, Andrew E. "The Resilient Personality." *Handbook of Adult Resilience*. Eds. John W. Reich, Alex J. Zautra, and John Stuart Hall. New York and London: The Guilford Press, 2010. 112–125.
Solokov, Raymond. "Review of *Ragtime*." *Book World – Washington Post* (July 13, 1975): 3.
Spencer, Luke. "A Poetics of Engagement in E.L. Doctorow's *Ragtime*." *Language and Literature* 5 (1996): 19–30.
Spivak, Gayatri Chakravorty. "Can the Subaltern Speak?" *Marxism and the Interpretation of Culture*. Eds. Cary Nelson and Lawrence Grossberg. Urbana: University of Illinois Press, 1988. 271–313.
———. *A Critique of Postcolonial Reason: Toward a History of the Vanishing Present*. Cambridge, MA and London: Harvard UP, 1999.
Stade, George. "*Ragtime*." *The New York Times Book Review* (July 6, 1975): 1–2.
Sterne, Richard. "Reconciliation and Alienation in Kleist's 'Michael Kohlhaas' and Doctorow's *Ragtime*." *Legal Studies Forum* 12.1 (1988): 5–22.
Strout, Crushing. "Historicizing Fiction and Fictionalizing History: The Case of E.L. Doctorow." *Prospects* 5 (Oct. 1980): 423–437.
Swift, Jonathan. "A Modest Proposal." 1729. *Gulliver's Travels and Other Writings*. Ed. Miriam Kosh Starkman. New York: Bantam Dell, 2005.
Todd, Richard. "The Most-Overrated-Book-of-the-Year Award, and Other Literary Prizes." *Atlantic Monthly* 237 (1976): 96.
Ungar, Michael. "Cultural Dimensions of Resilience among Adults." *Handbook of Adult Resilience*. Eds. John W. Reich, Alex J. Zautra, and John Stuart Hall. New York and London: The Guilford Press, 2010. 404–423.

Yardley, Jonathan. "Mr. Ragtime." *Conversations with E.L. Doctorow*. Ed. Christopher Morris. Jackson: Mississippi UP, 1999. 7–13.

Zautra, Alex J. John Stuart Hall, and Kate E. Murray. "Resilience: A New Definition of Health for People and Communities." *Handbook of Adult Resilience*. Eds. John W. Reich, Alex J. Zautra, and John Stuart Hall. New York and London: The Guilford Press, 2010. 3–29.

4 *City of God*
With Eyes Past All Grief

Published in 2000, *City of God* is one of E.L. Doctorow's most ambitious, complex and enigmatic novels. It is a highly metafictional book that may be best described as a collection of skillfully interwoven plots and voices that create a kaleidoscopic universe of alternative ontological levels. The reception of the novel was rather polarized. Writing for *The New York Times*, Michiko Kakutani called *City of God* a "novel of ideas that may be packed with ideas but that fails as a satisfying work of fiction" (n.p.). In *Newsweek*, Peter Plagens wrote, however, that it all hangs together "brilliantly" (n.p.). Walter Kirn, writing for *New York*, claimed that "[i]t's an easy book to admire but a hard one to love, perhaps" (n.p.). Yet, commentary on *City of God* regrettably remains rather scarce compared to other of Doctorow's novels, probably due to its philosophical complexity, divided focus and unclassifiable nature.

City of God is mainly concerned with a metaphysical quest for meaning. It revolves around the possibility of reconciliation between Judeo-Christian ethics and twentieth-century brutality, incorporating also a discussion of the traditionally conflicting paradigms of contemporary physics and religion. The main plot recounts the stealing of the crucifix from the altar of the Episcopalian church of Saint Timothy's and Reverend Pemberton's attempts to recover it, only to find it on the roof of a synagogue of Evolutionary Judaism. There Pem, torn by doubt and at the brink of apostasy, meets the rabbinical couple formed by Joshua Gruen and Sarah Blumenthal, who are seeking to rediscover the true essentials of their faith through communal study of the Torah. Soon enough, Pem finds himself in love with Sarah and, two years later, converts to Judaism and marries her after her husband's death.[1] These events, however, are merely one strand in the narrative world of *City of God*. Other interspersed storylines interestingly include the narrator Everett's prose-poem memoirs about his father's and brother's service in World War I and II respectively, a stomach-turning anonymous account of the Vietnam War, a first-person Holocaust story of life in a Lithuanian ghetto, brief references to the fictive author's sexual affairs, ideas for film plots, rabbinical commentary and interpretations of popular songs by the so-called 'Midrash Jazz Quartet,' meditations on scientific issues in the voices of Einstein and Wittgenstein, a retired *Times* reporter's quest to punish non-convicted war criminals, as well as passages of bird-watching and passionate descriptions of the cityscape of New York.

Fictionalizing the Holocaust

This section springs from the assumption that the novel's underlying preoccupation with ethics and injustice is tightly connected to the problematics of Holocaust representation and memorialization. This concern, I contend, hovers over the whole narrative and can be felt as a sort of implicit driving force in most of the storylines that the novel pursues. Thus, the main focus of enquiry in this first section is the novel's attitude toward the Holocaust with regard to issues of memory and representation. The novel's self-conscious discussion of the literary representation of the Holocaust will be explored. This will give rise to questions about the novel's genre, given its fictional approach to (particularly sensitive) historical events. Finally, this section will assess the author's motivations for attempting to engage with the fathomless horror of one of the most despicable events in human history, bearing in mind his secular Jewish-American background.

Self-Conscious Discussion of Holocaust Representation

Among the different storylines that *City of God* pursues, a particularly compelling one from the perspective of trauma studies is the first-person account of a Jewish boy's life in a Lithuanian ghetto during World War II. This little boy, we learn, is supposed to be Sarah Blumenthal's father, a Lithuanian Holocaust survivor whose sole obsession is that the ghetto diaries that he helped hide as a little boy be found. Yehoshua's memoirs have been given to Everett, the fictive author of the mosaic draft that readers encounter in this narrative. Yehoshua's autodiegetic story spans over some fifty pages, in which he narrates the hardships endured by his family at the ghetto, the loss of his parents, his life with a bitter old tailor until he is executed, his job as one of the Council's runners smuggling secret documents, testimonies and photographs collected by one of the Council members, and the final dismantling of the ghetto and transportation on a freight train until arrival to an untold destination, presumably Auschwitz or Dachau. There is no information, however, on how the little boy would have survived and reached the United States.

It is key to point out from the outset that *City of God* not only attempts to represent life in a ghetto during World War II; it does so by engaging in a highly metafictional discussion of the literary representation of the Holocaust. To begin with, a central feature of *City of God*'s approach to Holocaust representation is that this novella within the novel is divided into eight episodes that are regularly interrupted by other strands of the narrative, which in effect frame the Holocaust story in illuminating ways. Among these, one of the most thought-provoking intersections is an oddly focalized one in which an unnamed and ultimately unplaceable voice explores the world's "system of cosmic checks and balances" by means of which "[...] just as we have our sunlit river-running canyons, so does the sea bottom have its deepest trenches" (Doctorow, *City of God* 119).[2] The narrator goes on to claim that in these deepest waters there are forms of life that have adapted to subsist there, explaining that,

> [...] there is a Purpose in this as well which we haven't yet ascertained. But if you believe God's divine judgment and you countenance reincarnation, then it may be reasonably assumed that a certain bacterium living in the anus of a particularly ancient hatchetfish at the bottom of the ocean is the recycled and fully sentient soul of Adolf Hitler glimmering miserably through the cloacal muck in which he is periodically bathed and nourished. (120)

This intersection constitutes a conspicuous frame for the Holocaust story because it ironically expresses a longing for the consolation that the possibility of a fully sentient Hitler reincarnated into an excrement-eating bacterium might provide in terms of universal justice and divine retribution. Such a fantasy acquires a meaningful ironic tinge when contrasted with the bitter reality represented in the Holocaust sections of *City of God*. Another remarkable framing episode is one of the study sessions that Everett and Pem attend at Sarah's Synagogue for Evolutionary Judaism, in which the giving to Moses of the Decalogue is being discussed: "The biblical minds who created the Ten Commandments that have structured civilization...provided the possibility of an ethically conceived life, an awareness that we live in states of moral consequence [...]" (133). The exploration of the possibility of ethical life and moral consequence equally constitutes a provocative frame for Yehoshua's story in that ethics is unambiguously absent from the world that it depicts. Indeed, another key feature of the novel's approach to the Holocaust is that the unspeakable horror of the death camps is only hinted at in Yehoshua's account through veiled references, mainly at the level of mental evocation through the use of highly charged keywords, but never directly addressed. For instance, the little boy conspicuously employs the word 'solution' to refer to the Nazi's decision to burn the ghetto hospital (along with patients and staff) when word reaches them that some of them are ill with typhus. Similarly, in his description of the old pipe that he used in order to smuggle Barbanel's diary, Yehoshua employs words such as 'rats,' 'rotten smell,' 'viscera,' and 'barbed wire,' which unequivocally evoke life at the concentration camp. In addition, he describes his deportation in a freight train as "a long train of boxcars of the packed standing and swaying living dead" (142). This phrase is particularly redolent, because it brings to mind Primo Levi's influential notion of the *Muselmänner*, the "non-men," "the drowned," "an anonymous mass" whose "life is short, but [whose] number is endless" who have not been able to adapt to life in the camp quickly enough and, as a result, "march and labour in silence, the divine spark dead within them" (90). This intertextual and undoubtedly self-conscious link to Levi's testimony of life in the concentration camp provides an illustrative example of Doctorow's skill in conjuring up the Holocaust while respectfully refusing to represent its most vicious aspects explicitly. Indeed, these references evoke the death camps in a distinct and powerful way, while manifesting a firm reluctance to deal head-on with the extreme events that unfolded there.

From a narratological perspective, the importance of these references further resides in the fact that they draw attention to the time of their focalization; that is, while Yehoshua's story is generally focalized from the little boy's perspective, these references would seem to have been narrated from the old man's point of view—now Sarah's father, living in the United States—in effect self-consciously breaking the frame of narration again and again. The same may be said of the little boy's account of the execution of the old tailor with whom he lived as pretend grandson after their respective families were murdered. When the tailor Srebnitsky destroys the tunic that he has just finished and for which a Nazi mayor of the Third Reich refuses to pay, he is beaten up and sentenced to hang in the main square gallows and remain unburied for three days. Instead of helping him, Yehoshua runs away, knowing that when a Jew committed a crime his whole family was doomed. Yet, he cannot easily get over a strong sense of survivor guilt—guilt for remaining alive by refusing the tailor the protection and care that he needs in order to save his own life: "It was at that moment I should have helped him instead of running away. I could have stayed with him for a little while anyway" (90). As this quotation suggests, and echoing Lawrence Langer's description of the notion of 'survivor guilt' ("Survivor Testimony" 38), it seems apt to claim that the moral obligation, the 'should' and 'could' that Sarah's father utters, comes from a later position in life within a safe environment in the United States, where he is sheltered by democracy and human rights, and where "traditional moral explanations of conduct presumably prevail" (Langer, "Survivor Testimony" 38). Yet, we might safely assume that no reader would dare to condemn Yehoshua's behavior. What is more, the Holocaust subplot highlights the problematics of applying concerns over morality and individual agency to survivors.

The above references to the death camps also draw attention to the text's own forgery, its composition by the fictive author Everett, since similar allusions appear throughout the whole novel, in all the interspersed storylines. This provides *City of God* with greater coherence despite its mosaic nature, and at the same time it also suggests that the

Holocaust occupies a central position at the level of textual implications. This becomes particularly obvious through the frequent references to 'the living dead,' especially in the oddly focalized scientific musings that at times interrupt the other storylines: "I think how people numbed themselves to survive the camps. So do astronomers deaden themselves to the starry universe?" (4); and later again: "We are instructed that whatever condition God provides, some sort of creature will invent itself to live in it. There is no fixed morphology for living things. No necessary condition for life" (120). The fact that this quotation is an allusion to Auschwitz is confirmed by a reference to Adolf Hitler and God's justice a few lines later. Thus, it seems apt to claim that the Holocaust and the angst derived from its mere occurrence in history are not only the glue that holds *City of God* together, but also its most powerful and intrusive image, which has helplessly possessed not only Everett's imagination as fictive author, but also the implied author's.

Taken together, these features unmistakably point to what is perhaps the most remarkable aspect of the novel's approach to the Holocaust: its self-reflexivity.[3] The novel's metafictional concerns become apparent in the explicit tension between self-consciousness and documentation that *City of God* displays. This tension may be best perceived in the discussion between Sarah and Everett—who, let us remember, is also a character and autodiegetic narrator at one of the superior ontological levels of the novel—after the former has been given the draft of the Holocaust story that we have just finished reading:

> '[A]nyone familiar with the literature will recognize that this is the Kovno ghetto you're talking about, from the Abraham [sic] Tory diary?' 'Yes, I relied heavily on it.' But the Kovno ghetto was larger than you represent.' 'Yes, I made it not much more than a village. But I wanted that geography. The bridge across the city. The fort.' 'And my father was not from Kovno, of course. He was from a village closer to Poland [...]' 'Yes.' 'And I have to say, you must be careful not to oversimplify the way things were. Certainly in the Kovno ghetto they had clandestine military training, for example [...]' 'Yes,' I said, my heart beginning to sink. (165–166)

The relevance of this quotation lies, first and foremost, in its role in unveiling the novel's self-conscious scheme to draw attention to its own status as an artifact. It reveals that what we have been reading is not the literal testimony of Sarah's father, himself a fictional character, but Everett's doubly fictional construction: as fictive author of a draft also named *City of God*, which is, interestingly enough, based on Yehoshua's (fictional) account and Avraham Tory's (real) diary, published in 1991 under the title *Surviving the Holocaust: The Kovno Ghetto Diary*. From Tory's diary *City of God* draws events such as the burning of the hospital (Tory 42), the public hanging—actually of a young Jew named Meck who was caught trying to escape from the ghetto by crawling under a fence (153)—the deportation of most inmates to labor camps before the Kovno ghetto was burned down and completely destroyed (523), the members of the Council, down to the picture of boy runners wearing a garrison cap and Tory's own personal friend Yankele Bergman who carried Tory's material to a hiding place (295).

The incorporation and explicit reference to the European source of the historical events addressed in the novel also raises questions about the role of intertextuality in Doctorow's approach to the Holocaust and Holocaust literary representation. The importance of intertextuality in Holocaust fiction has been productively explored by Sue Vice in her homonymous book. Vice sees intertextuality as "very likely to be the central element in Holocaust fiction" (160); in order to prove it, she aptly resorts to Bakhtin's notion of 'doublevoiced discourse,' which she defines as "novelistic language which looks seamless but is actually shot through with discourse from all kinds of sources, each of which battles for supremacy with the others" (9). In *City of God*, this battle of which Vice speaks—this "clash of discourses" (9)—results from the juxtaposition of literary and historical sources and remains unresolved: as the quotation above suggests, accuracy, or the lack thereof, is a key issue that Everett and Sarah metafictionally address. Vice has argued that "[h]istorical inaccuracy, of itself, tells us very little about a text or how effective its representation is of the Holocaust" (166). Perhaps unable—or unwilling—to solve this problem in *City of God*, Doctorow chooses to metafictionally refer to the debate of authenticity in one of the ontological levels of the novel. It is worth adding that in his seminal essay "False Documents," he famously claimed that "there is no fiction or nonfiction as we commonly understand the distinction: there is only narrative" (163), a conviction that he maintained all throughout his career.

The *Kovno Ghetto Diary* is not the only literary work to have been self-consciously incorporated into the literary texture of *City of God*. Significantly enough, there are references in the novel to sources as varied as Franz Fanon's *The Wretched of the Earth*, Augustine's *The City of God* and Wittgenstein's *Tractatus Logico-Philosophicus*, to name but a few. These prove particularly illuminating not only of Doctorow's attitude toward the literary representation of the Holocaust, but also of his skill as a writer. First of all, the title of the novel explicitly creates an intertextual link to Augustine's *The City of God*. In it, the existence of evil is ultimately proved to be unintelligible; for Augustine, the epitome of evil is the Devil, a creature who decides of its own to defy God, and whose evil will is the cause of its evil actions (O'Daly 147). This establishes a provocative dialogue between the two texts, since Doctorow's own *City of God* also embarks on a literary quest to understand human evil, and similarly vouches its incomprehensibility. More importantly, however, Augustine's text presents human history as a war between two cities, the 'City of God' and the 'Earthly City'—that is, between God and the Devil—in which God supports those who are with the Christian Church in order to oppose the forces aligned with the Devil (see O'Daly 161–194). Doctorow's decision to intertextually link his novel to Augustine's *The City of God* is particularly thought-provoking, given the novel's engagement with the Holocaust and in the light of the long history of Christian persecution, forced conversion, expulsion and massacre of Jews all over Europe, as well as their silent indifference during the Nazi Holocaust.[4] As Pem rants in his remarks to the Bishop's Examiners, "just as the herd grazes in safety for a time after the lions cut one of them out and devour him, so does humanity feel safer from the nameless formless terrors if one of their number is sacrificed" (79). Second, through explicit allusion to "the migrant wretched of the world" (12) and "the wretched of the earth" (307), *City of God* incorporates Fanon's homonymous book to its textual universe. In it, Fanon reflects on the dehumanizing effects of colonialism. It is important to keep in mind that the Holocaust has often been discussed as the colonialist enterprise brought home to Europe, a trend inaugurated by Hannah Arendt's seminal work *The Origins of Totalitarianism* (123). This is probably related to the fact that, as Yehoshua's story shows, Jews were reduced to non-human status in Nazi Germany, which facilitated the majority of the population's compliance with, or endorsement of, Nazi policies with regard to the Jewish population. Furthermore, the intertextual connection between the two texts calls attention to the Holocaust as part of a continuum of Western oppression against, and persecution of the racial and religious Other. As such, this link in effect reinforces a belief in the Holocaust's firm position within history, an issue that will be taken up again shortly. Finally, the novel's reference to the seventh and last proposition of Wittgenstein's *Tractatus*—"what we cannot speak about we must pass over in silence" (89)—may be understood here, not only as the philosopher's termination of metaphysics, but as Doctorow's additional warning against unethical attempts to represent the Holocaust, an issue that will also be addressed in the third part of this chapter.

As if Doctorow's painstaking efforts to highlight the fictionality of his own text through the explicit mention of his main source and the skillful use of intertextuality were not enough, Everett emphasizes the constructedness of his own characters through the use of metalepsis. And so, for instance, when he meets Sarah to discuss the text that he has allegedly composed based on Yehoshua's account and Tory's diary, he claims: "I think now she is, after all, the Sarah Blumenthal of the Heist section" (164). The achieved effect is that of a kaleidoscope in which some sections seem to be at a superior ontological level than others, as if some were more fictional or forged than others. Another remarkable use of metalepsis in the novel may be found in Everett's narration of

City of God 151

Pem's success in finding the ghetto diaries ('Heist' section). The alleged author mentions a river that Pem has crossed, the Neris, in the following terms: "The Neris. Same river my little runner Yehoshua speaks of" (225). As this quotation suggests, Everett assumes the independence of his fictional character ("speaks of"), while highlighting its fictionality ("my"). Indeed, the finding of Mr. Barbanel's diary—the one that, according to Yehoshua's story, he had helped smuggle out of the ghetto as a little boy and which, we learn, is finally found in Russia and brought back to the United States—is particularly illuminating of Doctorow's self-reflexive ontological games. This diary, which is obviously fictional with respect to Avraham Tory's diary, but which occupies a lower ontological level in terms of fictionality with respect to Yehoshua's account, in effect leaps from one ontological level—that of Everett's fictional Holocaust story narrated by homodiegetic Yehoshua—to another—that of Everett's draft for the novel that we are reading and whose title is also "City of God" (251). Figure 4.1 might offer some clarification.

In the light of the analysis carried out so far, it may be useful to categorize Doctorow's novel as an instance of what Michael Rothberg has termed "traumatic realism" in his homonymous book; *City of God* too "exceed[s] the frameworks of both classical realism and the poststructuralist critique of representation" (*Traumatic Realism* 100), manifesting a sort of realism in which "the claims of reference live on, but so does the traumatic extremity that disables realist representation as usual" (106), and sharing a "distrust of representation with modernist formal experimentation and postmodern pastiche," while it "remains committed to a project of historical cognition through the mediation of culture" (140). An understanding of *City of God* as an instance of traumatic realism also finds support in the novel's emphasis on two opposing tensions: the

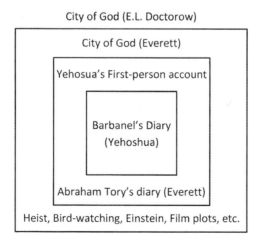

Figure 4.1 Narrative levels.

152   City of God

relationship between the extreme and the everyday, the ordinary and the extraordinary. As Yehoshua explains, "[...] the ordinary unendurable torments we all experienced were indeed exceptional in the way they were absorbed in each heart" (79). Indeed, in Yehoshua's narration of the horrible events that the inmates of the ghetto had to endure, the word "ordinary" keeps intruding: "[...] and with my lips pressed to a thin plane of slatted air of the ordinary, indifferent earth outside" (160). As Rothberg has put it,

> [b]y representing a site of extreme violence as a borderland of extremity and everydayness, traumatic realism attempts to produce the traumatic event as an object of knowledge and to program and transform its readers so that they are forced to acknowledge their relationship to posttraumatic culture. (*Traumatic Realism* 109)

To sum up, *City of God* constitutes Doctorow's first attempt to engage with the Holocaust in writing. However, he seems to have understood that a mimetic approach to it is neither acceptable nor possible in contemporary times, when poststructuralist theories have ruled out naïve understandings of reality and referentiality, and postmodern notions of the commodification of culture have problematized our access to traumatic past events. Thus, the novel may be seen as a self-conscious attempt on the implied author's part to discuss not so much the Holocaust as historical event, but the problems and dangers ascribed to its representation in fiction.

Holocaust Fiction

Holocaust writing has of late become a genre in its own right. Efraim Sicher explains that beginning with the Eichmann trial in 1961 and peaking in the mid-1980s, a body of literature has emerged which has been perceived to generically constitute the so-called 'Holocaust novel' (*Holocaust Novel* xi). As a genre, however, Holocaust fiction begs questions not only about the representation of the Holocaust in fiction, but also about the novel as a mode of writing itself. For one thing, it diffuses the already fuzzy generic boundaries between autobiography and fiction, memoir and fantasy, historical account and realist novel (Sicher, *Holocaust Novel* xii). In addition, a review of the extensive literature produced in recent years regarding this new genre reveals that any fiction dealing with the Holocaust seems to be caught in, and must reconcile, a complex field of forces upon which there is little agreement: between authenticity (the author being related in some way to the Holocaust as survivor or member of the second generation), accuracy (use of historical sources or documents, testimony), verifiability (the role of the imagination, fictionalization vs. fabrication), respect to the claims of unrepresentability (refusing to aestheticize atrocity), and use vs. appropriation (which uses of the Holocaust are ethical and which are not).[5]

As the analysis carried out so far suggests, despite sharing a common theme with other Holocaust stories and bringing out what is most compelling about the Holocaust—the injustices and atrocities perpetrated against innocent human beings and the perversions of an illogic world devoid of morality—*City of God* is not what we would call a conventional Holocaust novel. For one thing, despite being frequently evoked, the Holocaust subplot occupies less than half of a book that is also about a good deal of other things. As one might expect, an indispensable feature of Holocaust fiction is that it deals in some way with the historical events that have come to be termed "the Holocaust"—on this much Holocaust writing scholars seem to agree. In the light of this, and given *City of God*'s explicit allusion to certain events that bear resemblance to historical events that took place in the context of the Nazi genocide, one wonders: is the book a Holocaust novel? It is important to keep in mind that, as the previous section has proved, Doctorow never allows readers to forget that what we are reading is a fiction, which seems to be at odds with a conventional treatment of the historical event that has most dramatically possessed collective imagination in the Western world.

The study of Holocaust literature inevitably raises issues about truth—be it historical, testimonial or fictional truth (Foley 359). Holocaust fiction, Berel Lang claims, is characterized and distinguished from other genres by "its moral connection to the writing of history" (*Holocaust Representation* 20). Yet, in her provocative study about Holocaust fiction, Emily Miller Budick has argued against the premise that literature plays a central role in the preservation of historicity: "Literary texts [...] function in specifically literary ways. And that might well mean that their narrative procedures clash with their historical aspirations" (*Holocaust Fiction* 1). Miller Budick is right when she claims that most critics have tended to read fictions dealing with the Holocaust as fictionalized histories. They have at times disregarded the fact that, by definition, literature is under no obligation to stick to the (historical) facts, and they have refused to acknowledge some of the most important functions of fiction: complicating the relationship between representation and the world that the text purports to be representing, and prompting us to question that world. Thus, although a piece of fiction may have other aims, the text's narrative work should not be dismissed or relegated to a secondary position, regardless of its subject matter (Miller Budick, *Holocaust Fiction* 2–3, 11).

This critical discussion appears particularly relevant for my purposes, given Doctorow's reputation as a fabulator and his unequivocally postmodern attitude toward fact and fiction as established not only in his early novels—as the previous chapters have shown—but also in his

154 City of God

non-fiction. Indeed, Everett's comment that "[f]acts can be inhibiting. Actuality is beside the point" (54) acts as a loud and clear declaration of intent, especially since Everett stands for the figure of the artist in the novel and may be even seen as one of Doctorow's many fictional alter egos. In the author's view, fiction encourages readers to acknowledge the subjectivity of all knowledge. That is, there is no (historical) truth outside the human subject who either experiences events, or writes about them or reads them. If such a view of history is not unproblematic—and indeed it has been widely contested—when dealing with relatively distant historical events (such as the violence implicit in the colonization of the West or the social inequalities of the Ragtime Era), much more so in the case of the Holocaust, due to its apparent ever-presentness in the collective imagination of the United States. Yet, an increasing number of Holocaust scholars have eventually come to share a relativistic view of history. In her provocative paper on Holocaust narratives, Barbara Foley argues that "history is ultimately unknowable, [...] stable general meanings do not inhere in particular instances, and [...] the hypotheses by which we structure our historical understanding cannot aspire to objectivity" (331). Efrain Sicher has similarly claimed that "[f]iction and history are not exclusive. Both, in fact, are narrative constructions" (*Holocaust Novel* xiii).

City of God takes issue with such views—against the Holocaust section's purposefully highlighted fictionality, Sarah claims: "'But I was very moved,' she said. 'It may be inaccurate, but it's quite true. I don't know how, but you caught my father's voice'" (166). Her words seem to support the claim that, in spite of the story's fictive nature—or even forgery—its truthfulness to experience and to history is in no way diminished; its historical force—if not its historical truth—remains.[6] This seconds a point also made years earlier by Paul Levine, who was the first to notice that "Doctorow is more concerned with imaginative truth than with historical accuracy" (56). Furthermore, Sarah's words may be seen as staking a crucial claim about Holocaust representation, especially when considered in the light of those Holocaust commentators who have warned about the moral dangers of fictional representation. Jean Amery put it most bluntly and effectively: "No bridge led from death in Auschwitz to 'Death in Venice'" (in Foley 344). The most frequently put forward argument against the fictional representation of the Holocaust is perhaps Theodor Adorno's often (mis)-quoted ban against poetry after Auschwitz, which has been yielded by a relatively wide number of Holocaust scholars, most famously perhaps by Lawrence Langer (1991) and Kali Tal (1996), to condemn and reject literary—i.e. fictional—renderings of the Shoah. Adorno later wrote that his words never intended a prohibition on Holocaust literature; they were a plea that "pleasure not be squeezed out of the screams of the victims" (in Sicher, *Holocaust Novel* xv; see also Adorno 252). This, nevertheless, raises certain problematic issues:

if the traditional function of literature (poetry) since times of Cicero and Horatio is widely held to have been *docere et delectare*, authors must be extremely careful and write with utmost caution of moral responsibility when dealing with a topic like the Holocaust. Doctorow does not fail to do so. As argued in the previous subsection, the unspeakable horror of the death camps is only hinted at through veiled references; the Holocaust subplot ends at the moment of deportation to a concentration camp, which is also the point at which Tory's diary stops, and which allows Doctorow to avoid any sort of triumphalist narrative of heroic deliverance or to delve into life inside the camp. In other words, Doctorow decided to stay outside the gates of Auschwitz, which arguably speaks volumes of his ethical commitment to be just to the victims.

Furthermore, *City of God* self-consciously reflects on the limits of representation. This may be best seen in the relationship established between Pem, the protagonist of the 'Heist' section, and Everett, who is eventually revealed to be his rather imaginative biographer:

> You write well enough, he says, but no writer can reproduce the actual texture of living life [...]. But now that I see the dissimilarity [between Pem's supposed oral account and what Everett has written] from the inside, so to speak, I think I'll be wary of literature from here on. (53)

Doctorow's ironic warning of the 'power of dissimilarity' again has a special resonance when seen in the light of Holocaust representation. In that sense, there is another subsection in the novel that deserves special attention—Everett's ironic inhabitation of a Nazi officer's voice with regard to the establishment of the "Institute for the Exploration of the Jewish Question":[7] "Reichhsmarschall, I have the honor to report on the status of the work gone forward [...] to establish and maintain a museum for the acquisition, inventory, and ultimate exhibition of items of Judaic historic or anthropologic interest" (212). There follows a two-page-long list of stolen items that resembles a museum inventory appendix.[8] The relevance of this section lies in that, upon reading it for the first time, the unguarded reader may be easily tricked by this skillfully forged example of Nazi euphemism. Thus, this section may be read as a further self-conscious warning on Doctorow's part about the power of discourse to transform reality, which may be used for good or evil purposes. Such a warning is, nevertheless, coherent with E.L. Doctorow's wholehearted defense of the role of creative literature as a cultural product that takes advantage of its wide outreach to improve society, a belief that permeates his whole literary production—as the previous chapters have suggested—and is specifically explored in his collection of essays entitled *Reporting the Universe*. There, Doctorow declares himself to be "one who knows and can attest to the power of the not entirely rationally derived truths of good storytelling to affect mass consciousness and create moral constituencies" (78).

Berel Lang defends that all forms of Holocaust representation, whatever their quality or even their relation to historical truth, carry some value in that they draw attention to the wider issue of the Holocaust itself (*Holocaust Representation* 50). These narratives may not provide any accurate insight into the "why" or the "how" of the Holocaust, but they nevertheless succeed in endowing the reader with a sense of what happened, demanding from him or her not only an emotional, but also an ethical response. As Sicher brilliantly puts it, "[f]iction lies, as Picasso once said of art, but tells the truth" (*Holocaust Novel* xiii). Thus, like Everett's movie plot, the Holocaust story narrated in *City of God* is not about details; it operates "in the abstract realm where practical matters give way to uncanny resonances" (Sicher, *Holocaust Novel* 57) with the truth of the Holocaust. The novelist's claim to veracity may be seen as even stronger than that of the historian, because fiction fleshes out a history inhabited by real victims and perpetrators, with whom readers are compelled to identify through the imagination (see Sicher, *Holocaust Novel* xxi). What the mode of the novel does, as opposed to historical writing, is to enable the imaginative empathy necessary to understand the Holocaust as a real event of enormous atrocity that happened in recent history and at the heart of Western civilization. Therefore, whether *City of God* can be classified as a Holocaust novel, or whether it is merely a novel that touches upon the Holocaust, may be an irrelevant question to ask. In the final analysis, the test that this sort of novels must stand is not whether they deserve belonging to the category of Holocaust fiction, but whether they are good literature and, as such, fulfill a social and cultural role. This issue will be assessed in the last section of this chapter. The question that remains to be asked is the following: why the Holocaust? As Sicher has put it, "[t]he development of the 'Holocaust novel' is a story of both belated impact and of appropriation in popular culture in the West" (*Holocaust Novel* xiii). To an examination of this double powering force we now turn.

Why the Holocaust?

If attempting to represent the Holocaust entails so many difficulties and risks, and must acknowledge so many demands, it is probably worth assessing Doctorow's reasons for finally deciding to engage with it, forty years after starting his career as a novelist. One way to explain it is what has become known as the "Americanization of the Holocaust."[9] Since the late 1970s as historian Peter Novick explains, the Holocaust has come to be thought of as not just a Jewish memory but a North-American one: the teaching of the Holocaust in public schools is legislatively mandated in many states; the North-American armed forces are given specific instructions for conducting "Days of Remembrance," and state-sponsored commemorative ceremonies are annually held; since the 1970s every US President has spoken of the importance of preserving the memory of the Holocaust; and the expenses of the Washington Holocaust Museum have been largely taken over by the Government (Novick 207). Novick is particularly puzzled by the place and timing of American Holocaust consciousness, which since the early 1970s has become increasingly central in American public discourse (1). After all, the Holocaust took place thousands of miles away from the United States, Holocaust survivors and their descendants are a very small fraction of North-American population and very few perpetrators managed to escape to the United States after the war (81). Furthermore, its influence on North-American culture was not immediate—mainly due to geopolitical conditions related to Cold War tensions and postwar repudiation of the status of victim on the part of North-American Jews (121)—and resulted from a very specific political agenda inaugurated with the Eichmann trial (128).

This process of Americanization began with the appropriation of the Holocaust for mass entertainment and its widespread coverage in the media which resulted from the airing of Gerald Green's television serial *Holocaust* (1978)—and all the "Holocaust programming" that accompanied it (see Novick 210). Then, more recently, the release of Steven Spielberg's *Schindler's List* (1993) and the opening the same year of the National Holocaust Museum in Washington DC greatly contributed to expanding Holocaust consciousness.[10] Indeed, the Holocaust "story" has been told and retold, dramatized, novelized and cinematographed in hundreds of aesthetically compelling ways in the United States (Alexander 8). As Sicher has noted, these cultural products introduced the Holocaust into US popular culture, transforming individual memory and collective memory of the attempted extermination of European Jewry by the Nazis into North-American cultural memory ("The Future of the Past" 56). This process of assimilation into the North-American cultural texture has led many (Jewish) commentators to worry over an implicit act of universalization and trivialization of the Holocaust, especially given its potential to be appropriated for all sorts of political agendas.[11] The tendency in the United States has been to locate the Holocaust within a historical framework that includes North-American social problems, and to resort to the language of "Holocaust" to draw attention to a number of social inequalities, which to some constitutes a relativization of the catastrophe brought about by the Nazis. As Alvin Rosenfeld explains, "America's social problems, for all of their gravity, are not genocidal in character and simply do not resemble the persecution and systematic slaughter of Europe's Jews during World War II" (n.p.). This tendency to mingle victims of different historical experiences is growing rapidly, especially within those segments of American culture intent on developing a politics of identity based on victim status (Rosenfeld n.p.; see also Crownshaw vi–vii).

Another issue that deserves critical enquiry is the commercial profit that can be obtained from engaging with certain topics in the context of the contemporary fascination with trauma in the Western world, as the proliferation of the so-called "trauma novels" in the last two decades indicates (see Luckhurst 2). In many of these novels, a narrative aesthetics based on the classical model of trauma arguably appears to have become a profitable template that readers eagerly consume.[12] Many theorists acknowledge that we live in what Kirby Farrell has termed a "posttraumatic culture," a mood that is "belated, epiphenomenal, the outcome of cumulative stresses" and a "fairly straightforward response to the slings and arrows of recent history" which "reflects a disturbance in the ground of collective experience: a shock to people's values, trust, and a sense of purpose; an obsessive awareness that nations, leaders, even we ourselves can die" (3–5). Mark Seltzer similarly speaks of ours as a "wound culture," which he defines as "the public fascination with torn and opened bodies and torn and opened persons, a collective gathering around shock, trauma, and the wound" (3), a symptom of which is, in Setlzer's view, the generalization of trauma (15). This is precisely what Theodor Adorno warned of time and again: "The so-called artistic rendering of the naked physical pain of those who were beaten down with rifle butts contains, however distantly, the possibility that pleasure can be squeezed from it" (252).

In the light of this fascination, Farrell warns, in post-traumatic culture "[p]eople not only suffer trauma; they use it, and the idea of it, for all sorts of ends, good and ill. The trope can be ideologically manipulated, reinforced, and exploited" (21). Dominick LaCapra similarly alerts us of the way in which artifacts of mass culture, such as novels, "may indeed have popular and even critical dimensions either through creative modes of consumption or through more thoroughgoing and even collective procedures in which commodified artifacts are reproduced or refunctioned" (7). The fascination with the spectacle of the pain of the Other does affect not only literary representations of the Holocaust, but also notably 9/11 and slavery among other collective traumas.[13] In short, what these critics do is to acknowledge the importance of being aware of how Holocaust stories and images circulate in literature, in the media and, more broadly, in popular culture, and to what aim. Indeed, *City of God* reveals a self-conscious concern with the economic dimension of writing a novel; as Everett metafictionally muses, "[h]ow can anyone write a proper novel without talking about money?" (296). This reference is particularly problematic when one considers the commercial implications of engaging with a topic like the Holocaust at the turn of the millennium.

While these issues cannot be unproblematically dismissed, there is reasonable proof that E.L. Doctorow's motivations for engaging with the Holocaust may be found elsewhere. First, it is important to consider Doctorow's condition as a secular North-American Jew. John Clayton was the first to claim that Jewish culture is "a deep channel" through which Doctorow's concern with suffering and injustice, with victimization and revenge, flows, and "one of the sources of the vision of E. L. Doctorow" (118). Turning now to the flesh-and-bone author may run the risk of falling into the trap of the so-called biographical fallacy. Yet, while being aware of the dangers of analyzing art in terms of its creator's life and experiences, it seems almost impossible not to do so in this case for a number of reasons. First and foremost, it is worth pointing out that many of the ideas that Sarah expresses in her "Address to the Conference of American Studies in Religion" (288) are included verbatim in Doctorow's collection of essays *Reporting the Universe*, an issue that will be taken up again in the second section of this chapter. Thus, Doctorow's persona might be seen as another agent or participant in the novel, which would provide some justification for resorting to the personal and historical conditions of his life in order to assess his decision to engage with a topic like the Holocaust.

In keeping with such perspective, just as Sarah has grown up haunted by the phantom of what happened to her father—"[y]ou asked about this and asked and asked all through the years of your growing up, and I never wanted to tell you, first because you were too young, and I always wanted you to have your own life, and for it not to be a haunted life" (134)—so Doctorow also belongs to the Jewish-American generation of postmemory (in Marianne Hirsch's broader, cultural understanding of the term).[14] After establishing that "[p]ostmemory most specifically describes the relationship of children of survivors of cultural or collective trauma to the experiences of their parents" ("Surviving Images" 9), Hirsch broadens its application to cultural trauma, describing it as "an intersubjective transgenerational space of remembrance [...] defined through an identification with the victim or witness of trauma, modulated by the unbridgeable distance that separates the participant from the one born after" ("Surviving Images" 10). Indeed, the analysis above suggests that *City of God* enacts Hirsch's claim that "postmemory [...] creates where it cannot recover. It imagines where it cannot recall" ("Past Lives" 664). Hirsch's term refers to "a powerful and very particular form of memory precisely because its connection to its object or source is mediated not through recollection but through an imaginative investment and creation" (*Family Frames* 22).

Many critics acknowledge that, in present-day North America, Jewishness is no longer a self-evident cultural identity, mostly as a result of intermarriage and assimilation (see Shechner 191, Kramer and Wirth-Nesher 4, Novick 185). Yet, when one considers the number of novels written by Jewish-American authors that, if not specifically about the Holocaust, are 'Holocaust-inflected,' it becomes apparent that the

Holocaust occupies a central place within Jewish-American imagination and identity.[15] With the passing of time moral identification with the victims of the Holocaust and their heritage of suffering has become a central element of (American Jewish) identity (see Sicher, "The Future of the Past" 65, Roth 97). As Novick explains, "[t]he only thing that all American Jews shared was the knowledge that but for the immigration of near or distant ancestors, they would have shared the fate of European Jewry" (190). That is, American Jews were acutely aware that it was only a matter of geography that had saved them from the fate of their European brethren. Doctorow is certainly not alone in being deeply affected by the horrible fate shared by six million Jews in Europe, as the work of Saul Bellow, Art Spiegelman, Cynthia Ozick or Philip Roth, among many other Jewish-American writers, suggests. Indeed, few Jewish-American and Israeli postwar novelists have not seen their view of the world affected by the Holocaust or have not had their historical circumstances changed by it (Sicher, *Holocaust Novel* xxi). All these authors seem to have found it impossible *not* to engage with the Holocaust in one way or another through their literary production, as Ozick bitterly implied in her famous reference to her brother's blood drawing and driving her (284). George Steiner goes so far as to claim that "the Shoah, the remembrance of Auschwitz, the haunting apprehension that, somehow, the massacres could begin anew, is today the cement of Jewish identity" (159). As Norma Rosen has put it, "[a]s safe Americans we were not there. Since then, in imagination, we are seldom anywhere else" (in Miller Budick, "Literary Imagination" 212).

It is precisely this perceived sense of moral obligation to avoid the repetition of such horrible events that may have played a determining role in pushing Doctorow to finally engage with the Holocaust.[16] After all, it is a widely accepted truism that history tends to repeat itself. And although another Holocaust—another instance of industrialized mass extermination of a collective—seems implausible, the extremity of human evil and the depth of depravity humans are capable of constitute an important lesson in history that should never be forgotten. Indeed, and echoing Kenneth Seeskin (120), writing is presented in *City of God* as an act of resistance against human forgetfulness; first, through Mr. Barbanel's writing, who becomes "a historian, by necessity" (108):

> [...] the words flying off his pen line after line in his passion to say what happened each day, each moment, of our lives as captives, that supple, deft determination to put it all down, record it indelibly, as something of immense human importance. As it was. As it always will be. (107)

Second, Yehoshua's account and Everett's inclusion of it in his draft of a novel are equally political, because until Barbanel's diaries are found, the former is the only one who can bear witness for those who are dead and cannot speak, those who have been silenced and yet could have provided the truest testimony of all. Then, ultimately, Doctorow's novel is itself an act of resistance: resistance against human evil and against forgetfulness. And so, just as Mr. Barbanel does in Yehoshua's story, Doctorow writes for "the cause of the historical record, the helpless cause of no redress but memory" (117).

The consolation that a degree of retribution could be achieved is metafictionally examined in two of the plot strands. First, in the 'Heist' section, where Mr. Barbanel's recovered diaries and pictures become a tool by means of which escapee Nazi criminals who are hiding in the United States can be identified and brought to justice. In other words, in the universe of *City of God*, memory and testimony become the means for the administration of justice; that is, memorializing the Holocaust also means bringing the guilty ones to justice. Second, the longing for redress is explored through the 'ex-*Times*' guy storyline, a fiction plot devised by Everett that turns into a delirious fantasy in which a retired journalist decides to finish newspaper stories:

> On the other hand, there are major obits, King Leopold's, Hitler's or Stalin's or Pol Pot's, for example, that do not provide closure simply because the subjects died before they could be put on trial. [...] Still, the law could hardly come up with commensurate punishment for such creatures. I myself would send them to the lowest circle of hell and install them at its icy core, where they would be embraced by the scaly arms of Satan, who, over billions of years, would roar his foul excoriating breath into their faces and vomit his foul waste alive with squirmy larvae and dung beetles over them, while, languidly, cell by freezing, exquisitely outraged cell, absorbing them into his hideous being... (210)[17]

That these same words are later on uttered by Pem as part of his wedding speech (at a different ontological level) seems to suggest that Everett shares Pem's outrage and his anguished but undisguised pleasure at the fantastic and remote possibility that criminals such as those might suffer eternal punishment in hell, just like the reader is led to share Doctorow's. To sum up, it may be claimed that the author's decision to engage with the Holocaust responds, on the one hand, to a deeply felt need to impede that the horrors of the Holocaust may fall into oblivion; it responds to the ethical duty to remember, to bear witness. As Israeli novelist Aharon Appelfeld has put it,

> over the years the problem, and not only the artistic problem, has been to remove the Holocaust from its enormous, inhuman dimensions and bring it close to human beings. Without that effort it would remain a distant and unseen nightmare, somewhere off in the distance of time, where it would be easy to forget. (92)

Concluding Remarks

The analysis carried out in this section proves that *City of God* is a very complex novel that self-consciously reflects on the three fundamental demands that have been identified by Michael Rothberg as conditioning contemporary attempts to engage with the Holocaust: "[A] demand for documentation, a demand for reflection on the formal limits of representation, and a demand for the risky public circulation of discourses on the events" (*Traumatic Realism* 7). In other words, as we have seen, the novel takes issue with a lot of Holocaust scholarship and approaches the Holocaust through explicit discussion of the problems and limits of its representation, drawing attention to, and warning about, the act of forgery that underlies all acts of representation, but without rejecting a degree of referentiality to the historical events that are being narrated through the incorporation of testimony, while emphasizing its own status as discourse and as a cultural artifact open to commodification. Ultimately, however, facing so many risks and attending so many demands as pertain to a topic like the Holocaust seems to be worth Doctorow's while.

Voicing Gender

It is by no means infrequent to read comments remarking that the Holocaust tends to overshadow other traumas and other instances of atrocity. In the same way, it often happens that novels dealing with the Holocaust, even if remotely, tend to be discussed exclusively as Holocaust fiction, while other ideological, thematic and narratological aspects are disregarded, due to the Holocaust's overpowering presence in Western collective imagination. This is arguably the case in *City of God*, whose complex engagement with the Holocaust tends to overshadow a number of relevant aspects with regard to gender. Therefore—and with cohesive purposes in mind as well—this section will approach Doctorow's most philosophical novel from the critical perspective provided by feminist theory, exploring the novel's representation of gender models and its attitude toward voice.

Gender Models

City of God features a wide number of female characters, most of them secondary ones, often appearing in no more than a few pages. However, other characters such as Sarah, as the previous section anticipated, are central to the novel in illuminating ways. There is a clear case to argue that, through the representation of a myriad of female characters, the novel engages into a compelling discussion of female gender models. Indeed, it puts forward a kaleidoscopic view of the female that ranges from conservative and submissive to independent and transgressive. At one side of the spectrum we find characters such as Moira, who is introduced to the reader as a passive trophy wife who agrees to meet Everett behind her husband's back. She is described as "a woman of unstudied grace, with none of the coarse ideologies of the time adhered to her" who lives "in some genuine state of integrity" (10) and who "elevate[s] the moral nature of every man around her" (6). As their affair progresses, Everett explains that she becomes dependent on him. This eventually inspires the writer to merge this supposedly biographical subplot into an episodic movie fantasy of complete female submission and dominance: "Movie: Guy begins an affair with this really elegant trophy wife of a business leader [...]. He assumes uncontested control" (37–38). Eventually, the man manages to obtain "the total surrender of her will" (38), which allows him to devise a deranged plan to literally transform himself into Moira's husband and impersonate him before murdering him and presenting his facial skin to his "enslaved" wife (38).

At the other side of the spectrum, there are characters such as Trish (Pem's well-connected ex-wife), Miss Warren (Everett's eloquent and excessive friend), Miss Manderleigh (a character inside Everett's account of his brother's experience fighting in World War II) and especially Miss Margolin (an extremely brave and principled nurse within Yehoshua's story who plays a key role in smuggling Mr Barbanel's ghetto diary, and who risks her own life to help pregnant women secretly give birth in the ghetto). When considered in an isolated manner, these characters might seem of little consequence to the plot or the novel's ideological project, and they can easily go unnoticed, lost within its complex ontological and philosophical universe. However, these characters are sketched as independent and empowered women who in different ways defy hegemonic models of feminine behavior. Thus, despite their secondary role, they in effect serve the purpose of undermining traditionally simplistic, stereotyped or monistic depictions of the female. In other words, they collectively point to an attempt on the novel's part to explore and depict a varied catalogue of femininity. This, as the previous chapters have shown, is not a new concern in Doctorow's literary project, having guided the author's approach to the representation of female characters ever since the creation of Molly.

A special case in point is the character of Sarah, whose relevance in the novel has already been discussed in the previous section. Upon first appearance, Sarah is described as "a beautiful devout" who "needs no make-up," and as the perfect companion for a religious man (32–35). Yet, as the novel progresses, she is shown to be a strong, intelligent and brave rabbi: "She was really good. She was patient and smart and beautiful in a non-sexy rabbinical way, and she was in control" (282). In order to highlight the relevance of Sarah's characterization, a few brief comments about the history of female incorporation to the rabbinate seem in order at this point. First, it is worth pointing out that the first female rabbi in the United States was Sally Priesand, and she was only ordained in 1972 (Jewish Women's Archive n.p.).[18] Since then, no more than three hundred women have become rabbis in the Reform, Reconstructionist and Conservative branches of American Judaism. The Orthodox Rabbinical Council of America, far from officially accepting women in its rabbinate, has recently passed a resolution which denies them the possibility to be ordained or hired into a rabbinic position at an Orthodox institution (Jewish Telegraphic Agency n.p.). Furthermore, women rabbis in all three branches of the denomination continue to struggle in many ways, facing discrimination in aspects such as pay, acceptance at large congregations and maternity leave (The Jewish Week n.p.). Thus, the mere decision of making Sarah a rabbi is in itself a revolutionary act that suggests a critical attitude toward gender stereotypes on the part of the novel. But Sarah is not merely a rabbi. Together with her husband Joshua and then, after his death, on her own, she is also the leader of the fictional Synagogue of Evolutionary Judaism, a congregation that attempts to "redesign, revalidate [their] tradition," which to some "is tantamount to apostasy" (45). Indeed, Sarah is shown to be defying the established branches of Judaism barehanded, by trying to find the essentials of her faith through the study of the Torah, "in order to derive from it the imperatives that would complete the restructuring of the services and eventually [...] provide the theoretical basis for the evolved faith" (130). Thus, Sarah is presented as an empowered intellectual who is fighting to redefine from within a masculinist faith that has traditionally centered on the universal education of men. As she puts it, "[t]he glory of Judaism is its intellectual democracy, though some would try to deny this..." (282). These statements are particularly provocative when seen alongside the novel's references, in Pem's voice, to the possibility that God be female: "To presume [...] to hold Him, circumscribe him, the author of everything we can conceive and everything we cannot conceive... in *our* story of *Him*? *Of Her*? OF WHOM? What in the name of Christ do we think we are talking about!" (16; emphasis in the original), and then again:

> The creator, blessed be His name, who can make solid reality, or what we perceive as reality, out of indeterminate, unpredictable wave/particle functions [...] out of what finally may be the vibration of cosmic-string frequencies...that all this *from Himself, or Herself or Itself*, who is by definition vaster and greater than all this [...]. (286; emphasis added)

Apart from drawing attention to the arbitrariness of having assumed for over two millennia the Christian and Jewish God to possess a male nature, these quotations may be seen as supporting what could be defined as the novel's quiet coup d'état against hegemonic understandings of gender models within the realm of the Judeo-Christian tradition. In short, *City of God* reveals a firm, if by no means central, preoccupation with gender models as well as a strong spirit of subversion of traditional gender configurations in the context of Western religion.

Dialogism and Ventriloquism

The quotations above that allude to God's possible female nature notably raise questions related to voice and focalization in the novel that deserve special consideration. For one thing, when one reads them both alongside, it is easy to assume that they come from the same consciousness or perspective. And yet, at the same time, each has a unique inflection that renders it highly representative of the character that utters them. To wit, the former belongs to one of Pem's last sermons as a priest—a sermon gone awry—while the latter is uttered by Murray Seligman, one of Sarah's congregants, whose voice suspiciously resembles the one responsible for the oddly focalized excerpts about the universe with which the novel puzzlingly opens. Indeed, one of the most outstanding features of *City of God*—certainly one of the features that has captured most early reviewers' attention—is the difficulty for readers to know whose voice and perspective are being favored at each point. As Julia Gracen puts it in her 2000 review for *Salon*, "[a]s soon as we catch one thread of narrative and begin to follow it gratefully, we are twisted around and spun into another story, another era, another life" (n.p.).

The variety of voices, ontological levels and storylines displayed in *City of God* allow for an understanding of the novel as highly polyphonic in Bakhtinian terms. As the novel progresses, readers become acquainted with narrators as varied as a Vietnam veteran, Einstein, Wittgenstein, a Midrash Jazz Quartet, a heretic Episcopalian priest at the brink of apostasy and a Holocaust survivor. To these, the protagonists of Everett's several brief movie fantasies must be added. These narrators, all of them notably male, collectively create a complex narratological kaleidoscope of voices and perspectives. Therefore, the book might be defined as dialogic, since it too would present "a plurality of independent and unmerged voices and consciousnesses, a genuine polyphony of fully valid voices" (Bakhtin 6). Yet, such an interpretation appears problematic for a number of reasons. On the one hand, it often happens that one same phrase or idea is expressed by two different voices at two different ontological levels or subplots of the novel, as the quotations discussed at the end of the previous subsection show. Perhaps the most illuminating example would be the fantasy of punishment in hell for major criminals of history that is deliriously explored by both Pem and the ex-*Times* guy. Another remarkable instance might be the reference to the notion that the soul is "inviolable by circumstance." This phrase is first uttered by the ventriloquized voice of Wittgenstein on page 144 and then by Everett himself in his fictional rendering of his father's experiences during WWI under the heading "Author's Bio," where he "ventures" his father's thoughts at the time (157).[19] It seems apt to claim, therefore, that Everett, as fictive author, is playing ontological and focalization games with the readers, games which self-consciously draw attention to the forgery and ventriloquism implicit in all acts of fictional representation. However, a key effect of this is that Everett's narrative control as fictive author becomes overemphasized. It is important to keep in mind that many of the novel's storylines are filtered through Everett's perspective, and his presence is overbearing and explicitly felt throughout the whole book—in some subplots more strongly than in others, though. He rarely allows other characters to take actual narrative control beyond reporting words in direct style; but even when he does—and in the light of the above—it is almost impossible for readers to know whether he has truly relaxed his grip over the narrative or whether he is merely ventriloquizing them.

On the other hand, despite the wide number of secondary female characters that the novel features, very few of them act as narrators or even focalizers of the different plots and events. This undoubtedly complicates further an understanding of the novel as dialogic, since the voices that are allowed to be heard are almost exclusively male. The one exception is, once again, Sarah. When she first appears in the narrative within the "Heist" subplot, she is presented as a passive object of Pem's, and then Everett's, gaze. However, as the novel progresses, Sarah's voice achieves certain narrative power: it is progressively heard more clearly and seems to be increasingly freer from Everett's mediation, starting from her interview with Everett after she has been given the Holocaust material, up to the sessions of Bible study where she leads her congregation at the Synagogue for Evolutionary Judaism, and culminating in her "Address to the Conference of American Studies in Religion." Despite its short extension—barely over two pages—this passage is particularly interesting when considered from a feminist perspective. Despite the fact that Everett stands in the novel for the figure of the writer, despite his role as fictive author and despite the overpowering presence of his voice and perspective all throughout the narrative, it is Sarah that Doctorow has chosen as spokesperson: in her address to the Conference, which reads as a philosophical treatise, Sarah suggests that the actual place to find God—defined as "Something Evolving"—might be in "our evolved moral sense of ourselves," in our condition as human beings who "live in moral consequence" (290). Now, it is important to keep in mind that Doctorow was a philosophy major who graduated with honors. These words are followed by a warning: "There may not be much time. If the demographers are right, ten billion people will inhabit the earth by the middle of the coming century. Huge megacities of people all over the planet fighting for its resources" (290). That Doctorow is, in fact, using the character of Sarah as the representative of his own ideology is suggested by the fact that these are the words that Doctorow renders in his collection of essays *Reporting the Universe* almost verbatim (118). In short, it is very telling that Doctorow chooses Sarah to express his own views in the novel, and it undoubtedly constitutes a unique and unprecedented act of female empowerment in his literary oeuvre. As Everett puts it, "[...] it all comes of the voice" (251).

The question that remains to be asked in the light of the discussion above is whether the progressive evolution of Sarah's voice in the novel up to a privileged position justifies an understanding of *City of God* as a site of gender dialogue. As argued in this subsection, Everett's narrative control is unquestionable, but Sarah's key ideological role and the powerful voice that she is granted toward the end of the novel arguably allow for an interpretation of the novel as a more or less gender-conscious heteroglossic text: despite featuring a central male narratorial authority and an overwhelming number of male autodiegetic narrators, the text leaves sufficient room for the cohabitation and interaction of a believable female voice that challenges the fictive author's discursive authority and proves to be ideologically and ethically superior to most characters, including Everett himself. Therefore, despite Everett's overbearing presence in most of the novel's ontological levels and storylines, Sarah's powerful ethical voice and her condition as spokesperson of the author prove a certain commitment on Doctorow's part with the opening of his work to the voices of women, a key demand of feminist criticism since the 1970s.

Concluding Remarks

The analysis carried out in this section suggests that, although gender issues are by no means a primary concern in *City of God*, there is enough evidence to support the claim that the novel displays a sympathetic attitude toward certain feminist concerns. On the one hand, it provides a varied catalog of gender models of behavior that undermines traditional simplistic depictions of the female. More remarkably, it performs a radical act of subversion with the characterization of Sarah as a strong rabbi who dares question the precepts of her faith. On the other hand, the novel articulates Sarah as the main representative of Doctorow's ideology, otherwise developed in essay form, which is in itself an important act of female empowerment and allows for an understanding of the novel as a site for gender dialogue.

Discussion and Conclusion

Discussion

The analyses conducted in the previous sections have provided an innovative reading of *City of God*, E.L. Doctorow's highly philosophical and enigmatic work. The first and longest section of this chapter has explored the author's ethical commitment to the representation of the Holocaust, which is characterized by self-consciousness and owes much to the author's status as a member of the generation of postmemory. The second section has attempted to step beyond the overpowering preponderance of the Holocaust in the novel's fictional texture in order to establish its attitude toward gender models and to determine the role of gender dialogue in it. There remains to be assessed whether the novel's overwhelming preoccupation with the Holocaust and its (secondary) engagement with certain feminist concerns allow for broader comments about Doctorow's ethical project in *City of God*. Thus, the last section of this chapter seeks to bring together the results obtained so far in order to discuss some of the implications that the analyses informed by recent Holocaust scholarship and feminist criticism have when seen in the light of each other.

In order to do so, there are a number of issues regarding the novel's approach to the Holocaust that need to be considered. In that sense, it is worth pointing out that, apart from articulating *City of God* as an act of resistance against forgetting, as we have seen, Doctorow's end-of-the-millennium novel confronts those who have contested the Holocaust's firm position *within* history. In other words, the novel seeks to undermine an understanding of the Holocaust as a unique, unintelligible hiatus of human barbarity in an otherwise uninterrupted flux of peaceful cohabitation. This is achieved in two different but related ways. On the one hand, the book locates the Holocaust within a continuum of anti-Semitism. As the impersonated voice of Einstein explains in one of the novel's subsections, the Holocaust may be placed "a moment" after the resentment of "Christian priests and kings that over centuries had demonized and racialized the Jewish people of Europe with the autos-da-fé, pogroms, economic proscriptions, legal encumbrances, deportations, and a culture of socially respectable anti-Semitism" had imploded in the "ears of a thousand, a million children" of Einstein's generation (59). Thus, *City of God* echoes claims raised by scholars such as Jeffrey C. Alexander, who talks about an "oozing anti-Semitic wound that [had] infected modernity" (4):

> Pogroms in the East, the Dreyfus scandal in Republican France, new quotas and old restrictions in the United States, rising anti-Jewish feelings and politics in central Europe. The Nazi monster arose out

of this primordial slime. While the Nazis' anti-Semitic strategy was more ambitious and extreme than had ever before been contemplated, their anti-Semitic feeling was not. (4)

By emphasizing the Holocaust's roots in anti-Semitism and in the economic and social foundations of capitalism and imperialism, *City of God* joins in with those commentators of the Holocaust who have rejected an understanding of the Nazi genocide as unintelligible or incomprehensible.

On the other hand, against Dominick LaCapra's warning that "[c]ertain comparisons may function as mechanisms of denial" (48), the novel presents the Holocaust as one more instance of human barbarity, if a particularly horrid one:

> Nazis goose-stepping, tearing Jews from their homes, Stalin icing millions on the gulags, the Japs practicing beheading techniques on Chinese coolies, the Burmese with their loaded carts jamming the roads out of Ragoon, Italians dive-bombing the Ethiopes waving their spears at the sky, *whole fucking world showing its true humanity*, screaming baby on the railroad track, blood pouring down the mountains, irrigating the deserts, reddening the seas, the world a big bloody circus of human mutilation, with a degree of murderous, insane rage to blast the planet off its axis. (262; emphasis added)

As the above quotation illustrates, *City of God* refers at one point or another to most historical traumas of the twentieth century, namely the two World Wars, Vietnam, Colonialism, Stalinism and the Rwandan and Cambodian genocides. Indeed, the free-verse prose-poem accounts of the three aforementioned wars are among the most skillfully written, powerful and effective subplots of the narrative. Collectively, the three vignettes mourn the damage inflicted on three generations of American men—those of Everett's father, his brother and his own—by US society's refusal to acknowledge that the men they were fighting "were closer to [them] in what they had/to gain or lose/than they were to the generals, and the regal families/who directed them" (154), being as they were "members of the universal working class/that spanned all borders/and was universally enslaved to capitalism/and its monarchical appurtenances/and its nationalist ideologies that were pure/bullshit" (155). Said differently, the novel skillfully blames politics, capitalism and, more generally, the age-old human thirst for power, for humanity's endless quest to destroy its own members. As the ventriloquized voice of Albert Einstein puts it in the novel "[…] what moves not as fast as light but fast enough, and with an accrued mass of such density as not to be borne, is the accelerating disaster of human history" (59).

170   City of God

City of God may thus be read as a rejection of claims of uniqueness which have often been uttered by certain Holocaust scholars as well as secularist historians and rabbis. Doctorow joins Novick and others in their conviction that these claims mean nothing other than a version of the following: "Your catastrophe, unlike ours, is ordinary; unlike ours is comprehensible; unlike ours is representable" (Novick 9).[20] After all, despite the danger of what LaCapra calls a process of "normalization and routinization" (51), it does not seem entirely ethical to rank atrocities, since those rankings might owe more to issues of power and status of the specific 'victim community' involved. Indeed, *City of God* may be also seen as an act of resistance against a supposed Jewish-American tendency toward 'belly-gazing' which, according to some commentators, would result from having embraced—and arguably attempted to monopolize—the status of the victim and the moral authority that traditionally comes with it. As Novick explains, since the 1970s, certain collectives in the United States have tended to define themselves by the Jewish history of victimization, yielding the Holocaust as a tool to maintain their status quo and, in effect, leading to a certain disregard for the suffering of others (183). Echoing this view, Doctorow claims through the voice of Sarah: "We don't accept the ID of victim" (35).

Interestingly, the novel's articulation of the Holocaust as one more—even if outstandingly atrocious—example of human's capacity for evil and injustice is subtly extended to the traditional subordination and oppression of women throughout history. This is achieved by means of one of Everett's odd vignettes supposedly narrated by Pem whose truth-status with regard to the ontologically superior 'Heist' section is, at best, questionable: the subplot is supposed to narrate Pem's autodiegetic recollection of his experiences as a "missionary American Peace Corpser [sic?] with anthropological pretensions" (239). As a missionary, he would have met Tonna mBakita, of the "disfigured, lymphomaed Tobokovo Islanders of the A-test range" (241), who became his supposed child bride. The use of the word "corpser" may not be a typo after all; its satiric bitterness becomes apparent when in the following paragraph Pem passionately explains:

> The sex is in the disparity, from the fourth-century olive-eyed slave dancer of the dusk to the little bought Victorian girls of the working class thrown across the madam's bed eeyowing to have their hymens torn with the shirttailed gentlemen's shilling clutched in their moist hands. Lord, we cannot begin to account Your injustices. (240)

These words, followed by a reference to the "mechanic law" of lust as our "one and only original sin" (240), point to a highly critical attitude toward the traditional subordination of women and the reduction of their value to their sexual organs and wombs. This oppression, despite not being the focus of the novel in ideological terms, is presented as yet another example of injustice and human disregard for other human beings—in this case for no less than one half of the human race.

In spite of the novel's complexity and mosaic nature, the analysis suggests that all the storylines and ontological levels are masterfully interwoven into a meaningful whole through a convergence of genres dealing with a common theme: an underlying concern with (in)justice. This preoccupation is tightly connected to a quest for spirituality that is appropriate for the twentieth century. Indeed, Pem's religious doubts and Sarah's ethical dilemmas equally stem from their awareness of the overwhelming preponderance of injustice and their difficulties in reconciling them with an understanding of a just God. Pem's problem with God, as he rants during his wedding speech, is that "[m]en use You at will for their most hideous purposes. You do not seem to resist—anyone who wants You, and for whatever foul, murderous reason, can have You" (302). Sarah, on her part, has taken it upon herself to convince those who will listen that the quest for the sacred must involve "the expansion of ethical obligation democratically to be directed all three hundred and sixty degrees around, not just upon one's co-religionists" (290); it must entail "a daily indiscriminate and matter-of-fact reverence of human rights" (290), because,

> God is not honored by a mechanical adherence to each and every regulation but by going to the heart of them all, the ethics, and observing those as if your life is at stake, as it may well be, I mean, your moral life, your life of consequence as a good, reflective, just, and compassionate human being. (283)

Keeping in mind that Sarah has been proved to be Doctorow's ideological representative and spokesperson in the novel, it seems apt to claim that the novel's broad engagement with the Judeo-Christian religious tradition, its metaphysical pursuit of meaning and its philosophical quest for God are firmly grounded on ethics.

The possibility of moral progress, the novel suggests, is in each person's acts toward others. Lawrence Wilde is right when he claims that the novel encourages readers to "reach out for reconciliation by accentuating an ethics of compassion" (393), arguing that the novel emphasizes "the preeminence of ethics in religious thought" (401). In other words, we cannot passively and blindly expect justice to come solely from God—who dispassionately tolerated the Holocaust and other instances of human barbarity—not even from our social institutions and governmental structures—which have traditionally failed to protect us humans from ourselves, being as they are run by other imperfect, corruptible, and often essentially selfish and power-thirsty human beings. The novel's main premise may be claimed to be precisely this: we must act ethically and behave onto others as we would have them do onto us, and this is the spirituality that we must aspire to. The religious overtones of such a statement render it particularly apt given Doctorow's own claim in an interview after the publication of his last novel: "I think of my politics as biblical politics: you shouldn't murder, you shouldn't steal, that sort of thing" (in Wolf n.p.). As Sicher explains, "[n]ovels, like all stories, retell the past in order to help us understand the present, and the cataclysmic event called the Holocaust has done a lot to shake the Western world into rethinking its assumptions and beliefs" (*Holocaust Novel* xix). This may have been Doctorow's aim: to force readers to rethink our own lives and beliefs with regard to our attitude toward the others, which is achieved through *City of God*'s engagement with the Holocaust and with other historical instances of major injustice and barbarity.

Conclusion

As I hope the analysis carried out in this chapter has shown, *City of God* is an extremely complex and enigmatic novel that culminates Doctorow's literary engagement with suffering and wholehearted promotion of justice. The book also constitutes the author's first attempt to engage with the Holocaust in writing, an effort which is characterized by a self-conscious understanding of the impossibility of pursuing a mimetic approach. Such awareness leads Doctorow to focus, to a great extent, on issues of fictional representation, which problematizes a straightforward classification of the novel in terms of the contemporary construct "Holocaust fiction." *City of God* further suggests that Doctorow's decision to engage with the Holocaust responds, on the one hand, to his status as a member of the generation of postmemory, and on the other, to a deeply felt need to impede that the horrors of the Holocaust may fall into oblivion. Additionally, although it is by no means a primary concern, the book also undermines traditional simplistic depictions of the female. It also manifests a commitment toward gender dialogue, and it shows a strong spirit of subversion of traditional gender configurations. Finally, *City of God* suggests that Doctorow's decision to engage with the Holocaust and with other instances of human barbarity and injustice stems from his being haunted by the presence of unchecked evil in human history.

In conclusion, *City of God* constitutes an outcry against injustice and a call to memory that 'touches upon' the Holocaust, while ethically refusing to directly attempt to represent the unspeakable horrors of the death camps. Doctorow's concern with the advancement of ethics and social justice—not merely in *City of God*, but as a key element of his literary project—responds to the impossibility of coming to terms with the evil that resides within human nature and the deeply felt moral duty to remember its consequences—the duty to instill in his readers a sense of responsibility toward what Levinas called "the face of the Other," an issue that will be taken up again in the following chapter. So long as the possibility of mass violence against a collectivity remains—and the current global geopolitical climate hardly cancels that possibility—any attempt to understand human potential for barbarity may facilitate the necessary ethical, social and political change that will hopefully render another Holocaust impossible.

Notes

1 This main plot was originally published as a short story with the title "Heist" in *The New Yorker* on April 21, 1997. "Heist" is a truncate autodiegetic account of Reverend Pem's attempts to recover the heisted cross of his church. This plot would be the seed from which *City of God* sprang, and in 2011 it was included as a short story in Doctorow's last collection, *All the Time in the World*.
2 Further references to the novel are to the Abacus Paperback edition, published in 2006.
3 The novel's indebtedness to postmodern aesthetics has been productively explored by Francisco Collado-Rodríguez (2002). In his paper, he aptly claims that postmodern strategies paradoxically contribute to announcing the end of the eclectic postmodern ethos which has dominated the last decades of the twentieth century (59).
4 The silence of Pope Pius XII and his failure to publicly denounce the Holocaust during World War II were brought to the public eye in the early 1960s with the performance in Broadway of *The Deputy*, a play by the German playwright Rolf Hochhuth that was, in Peter Novick's words, "a savage indictment of Pius's inaction" (143).
5 See Foley (1982), Lang (1988, 2000), LaCapra (1994), Rothberg (2000, 2009), Sicher (2000, 2005), Vice (2000) and Miller Budick (2003, 2015).
6 In this sense, *City of God* also evokes the American romance tradition inaugurated by Nathaniel Hawthorne.
7 *Institut zur Erforschung der Judenfrage*: institute set up by Alfred Rosenberg in 1939 to plunder art treasures, archives and libraries from the Jews all over Eastern and Western Europe (AICE, "Rosenberg" n.p.).
8 This list is the one that Doctorow read out loud for a conference hall full of people when invited to discuss Holocaust literature as part of the international conference celebrated at Yale University in 2002 to commemorate the twentieth anniversary of the Fortunoff Video Archive for Holocaust Testimonies. When his time to speak came, Doctorow, without introduction or explanation, began to read his list of items: "Torah (Pentateuch) parchment scrolls handwritten, [...] place settings silver, serving bowls [...], snow sleds children, paint sets children [...]" (212–214). He then sat down before his speaking time had come to an end. As Monica Osborne explains, he could have talked about many things: about survivor testimony, about American-Jewish identity in a post-Holocaust world, about the responsibilities of writers (24). It is extremely difficult to say with any degree of certainty what may have motivated Doctorow to act like that, but one wonders whether his behavior may not be indeed related to a conviction about the importance of respecting the limits of representation where it comes to the Holocaust.

174   City of God

9 For a comprehensive study of the rise of Holocaust consciousness in the United States, see Novick (1999). In his book, he maps the shift of the Holocaust from the margins to the center of American Jewish consciousness, pointing at an "inward turn" that took place in the late 1960s and that inaugurated "an insistence on the defense of separate Jewish interests, a stress on what made Jews unlike other Americans" (170–171).

10 Before that, the only popular cultural products dealing with the Holocaust were Anne Frank's *The Diary of a Young Girl* and its later stage and screen adaptations. These have been accused by some Holocaust scholars and Jewish collectives of universalizing and trivializing the Holocaust experience (see for example Rosenfeld n.p.). Afterward, North-American popular media, particularly television, continued to present the Holocaust with productions such as *Playing for Time, Escape from Sobibor, Triumph of the Spirit* and *War and Remembrance*, which, together with a steady flow of imported foreign films on the topic, contributed to firmly fixing the Holocaust in the North-American collective unconscious (Novick 213–214).

11 Indeed, a critical and self-conscious reflection on the events and their representation has started to emerge, inaugurated by Novick's controversial connection of the rise of memory of the Holocaust with very specific political and sociological purposes. See also Crownshaw (2010), Roth (2012) and Alexander (2016).

12 Even authors as highly reputed as Toni Morrison and Jonathan Safran Foer have been accused of having purposely resorted to this psychoanalytic trauma template in recent years.

13 This appears to be the opinion of one of Doctorow's critics, who claims that the pages devoted to the Holocaust in *City of God* "serve no purpose whatsoever in the novel other than cynically to appropriate the moral authority of the Holocaust and to offer up the suffering of the Jews with all the dignity of a crass poker player flourishing a winning hand" (Bawer 400). Yet, the disproportionate bitterness and spite with which not only *City of God* but Doctorow's whole oeuvre is treated in that paper in effect work to undermine its analytic credibility, especially since no real arguments seem to be provided to justify such negative commentary other than political and religious dissent.

14 See also Rothberg (186).

15 Remembrance is after all a central element of Judaism, with its ethical and historical commandment to remember the Sabbath, or to remember what Amaleq did to the people of Israel, for instance (Sicher, *Holocaust Novel* xxi).

16 At the end of the twentieth century, Holocaust memory regained prominence in the United States, partly because of new evidence suggesting complicity in the Nazi genocide by Vichy France (highlighted by the Barbie, Touvier and Papon trials). The end of the millennium also coincided with important fiftieth anniversaries (particularly of *Kristallnacht* in 1988, the Warsaw Ghetto uprising in 1993 and the liberation of the camps in 1995). And then came the *fin de siècle* itself, with its apocalyptic fixation on calamity and death (Sicher, "The Future of the Past" 57–58). This surge of Holocaust memory may have also influenced Doctorow's decision to openly address the Nazi genocide in his novel.

17 These words vividly recall Dante's description of the Ninth Circle of Hell in his *Divine Comedy*, where the greatest criminals in history are eternally devoured by Satan, trapped in a frozen lake from the waist down. Dante's *Divine Comedy* is indeed another important intertext of Doctorow's *City of God*.

18 Prominent Orthodox feminist thinker, Blu Greenberg, had been advocating for women to become rabbis since the mid-1980s: "Women should be ordained because it would constitute a recognition of their intellectual accomplishments and spiritual attainments; [...] because it offers wider female models of religious life [...]. And because of the justice of it all" (in Hein n.p.).
19 When rendering his brother's experiences in WWII, narrated again under the heading "Author's Bio," Everett similarly draws attention to the act of forgery that fiction writing entails: "But I embellish his account" (195).
20 Novick argues that

> [t]he claim that an event—as opposed to some features of an event—is unique can be sustained only by gerrymandering: deliberately singling out one or more distinctive features of the event and trivializing or sweeping under the rug those features that it shares with other events to which it might be compared. (196)

References

Adorno, Theodor W. *Can One Live After Auschwitz? A Philosophical Reader*. Ed. Rolf Tiedemann. Stanford: Stanford UP, 2003.

Alexander, Jeffrey C. "Culture Trauma, Morality and Solidarity: The Social Construction of 'Holocaust' and Other Mass Murders." *Thesis Eleven* 132.1 (2016): 3–16.

Alighieri, Dante. *The Divine Comedy: Cantica I, Hell; Cantica II Purgatory; Cantica III, Paradise*. Harmondsworth: Penguin Books, 1971.

Appelfeld, Aharon. "After the Holocaust." *Writing and the Holocaust*. Ed. Berel Lang. New York: Holmes & Meier Publishers, 1988. 83–92.

Arendt, Hannah. *The Origins of Totalitarianism*. 2nd enl. ed. Cleveland: The World Publishing Company, 1958.

Augustine. *The City of God. Books I-VII*. Washington, DC: Catholic University of America Press, 2008.

Bakhtin, Michael M. *Problems of Dostoevsky's Poetics*. Minneapolis: University of Minnesota Press, 1984.

Bawer, Bruce. "The Faith of E.L. Doctorow." *The Hudson Review* 53.3 (2000): 391–402.

Clayton, John. "Radical Jewish Humanism: The Vision of E. L. Doctorow." *E.L. Doctorow: Essays and Conversations*. Ed. Richard Trenner. Princeton: Ontario Review, 1983. 109–119.

Collado-Rodríguez, Francisco. "The Profane Becomes Sacred: Escaping Eclecticism in Doctorow's *City of God*." *Atlantis* 24.2 (2002): 59–70.

Crownshaw, Richard. *The Afterlife of Holocaust Memory in Contemporary Literature and Culture*. Basingstroke, Hampshire: Palgrave Macmillan, 2010.

Doctorow, E.L. "False Documents." 1977. *Jack London, Hemingway, and the Constitution: Selected Essays 1977–1992*. New York: Random House, 1993. 149–164.

———. "Heist." *The New Yorker* 21 (Apr. 1997): 82.

———. *Reporting the Universe*. Cambridge, Massachusetts: Harvard UP, 2004.

———. *City of God*. 2000. London: Abacus, 2006.

———. *All the Time in the World*. London: Little Brown, 2011.

Fanon, Franz. *The Wretched of the Earth.* Trans. Constance Farrignton. London: Penguin, 1990.

Farrell, Kirby. *Post-traumatic Culture: Injury and Interpretation in the Nineties.* Baltimore and London: Johns Hopkins UP, 1998.

Foley, Barbara. "Fact, Fiction, Fascism: Testimony and Mimesis in Holocaust Narratives." *Comparative Literature* 34.4 (1982): 330–360.

Gracen, Julia. "City of God, by E.L. Doctorow." *Salon*, Feb. 18, 2000. Web. 30 May 2016. <www.salon.com/2000/02/18/doctorow_2/>

Hein, Avi. "Women in Judaism: A History of Women's Ordination as Rabbis." *Jewish Virtual Library.* Web. 20 Dec. 2015. <www.jewishvirtuallibrary.org/jsource/Judaism/femalerabbi.html>

Hirsch, Marianne. "Past Lives: Postmemories in Exile." *Poetics Today* 17.4 (1996): 659–686.

———. *Family Frames: Photography, Narrative, and Postmemory.* Cambridge, MA: Harvard UP, 1997.

———. "Surviving Images: Holocaust Photographs and the Work of Postmemory." *The Yale Journal of Criticism* 14.1 (2001): 5–38.

Jewish Telegraphic Agency. "Rabbinical Council of America officially bans ordination and hiring of women rabbis." Web. 20 Dec. 2015. <www.jta.org/2015/11/01/news-opinion/united-states/rabbinical-council-of-america-officially-bans-ordination-and-hiring-of-women-rabbis>

Jewish Women's Archive. "Sally Priesand." Web. 20 Dec. 2015. <http://jwa.org/feminism/priesand-sally>

Kakutani, Michiko. "Review of *City of God.*" *The New York Times*, Feb. 15, 2000. Web. 30 May 2016. <www.nytimes.com/2000/02/15/books/books-of-the-times-taking-readers-inside-the-writer-s-notebook.html>

Kirn, Walter. "Heaven Can Wait." *New York*, Feb. 14, 2000. Web. 30 May 2016. <http://nymag.com/nymetro/arts/books/reviews/1928/>

Kramer, Michael P. and Hana Wirth-Nesher. Introduction. *The Cambridge Companion to Jewish American Literature.* Eds. Michael P. Kramer and Hana Wirth-Nesher. Cambridge: Cambridge UP, 2003. 1–11.

LaCapra, Dominick. *Representing the Holocaust: History, Theory, Trauma.* Ithaca: Cornell UP, 1994.

Lang, Berel. *Writing and the Holocaust.* New York: Holmes & Meier Publishers, 1988.

———. *Holocaust Representation: Art within the Limits of History and Ethics.* Baltimore: Johns Hopkins UP, 2000.

Langer, Lawrence. "Interpreting Survivor Testimony." *Writing and the Holocaust.* Ed. Berel Lang. New York: Holmes & Meier Publishers, 1988. 26–40.

———. *Holocaust Testimonies: The Ruins of Memory.* New Haven: Yale UP, 1991.

Levi, Primo. *Survival in Auschwitz: The Nazi Assault on Humanity.* Trans. by Stuart Woolf. New York: Simon and Schuster, 1996.

Levine, Paul. "Politics and Imagination." *Modern Critical Views: E. L. Doctorow.* Ed. Harold Bloom. Philadelphia: Chelsea House, 1989. 51–60.

Luckhurst, Roger. *The Trauma Question.* London and New York: Routledge, 2008.

Miller Budick, Emily. "The Holocaust in the Jewish American Literary Imagination." *The Cambridge Companion to Jewish American Literature.* Eds.

Michael P. Kramer and Hana Wirth-Nesher. Cambridge: Cambridge UP, 2003. 212–230.
———. *The Subject of Holocaust Fiction*. Bloomington, Indianapolis: Indiana UP, 2015.
Novick, Peter. *The Holocaust in American Life*. Boston: Houghton Mifflin, 1999.
O'Daly, Gerard. *Augustine's City of God: A Reader's Guide*. Oxford: Clarendon, 2009.
Osborne, Monica. "The Midrashic Impulse. Reading Cynthia Ozick's *Heir to the Glimmering World* against Representation." *Studies in American Jewish Literature* 26 (2007): 21–34.
Ozick, Cynthia. "Roundtable Discussion." *Writing and the Holocaust*. Ed. Berel Lang. New York: Holmes & Meier Publishers, 1988. 271–290.
Plagens, Peter. "Good God?" *Newsweek* Feb. 20, 2000. Web. 30 May 2016. <www.newsweek.com/good-god-162163>
Rosenfeld, Alvin H. "The Americanization of the Holocaust." *Commentary Magazine* June 1, 1995. Web. 20 May, 2015. <www.commentarymagazine.com/articles/the-americanization-of-the-holocaust/>
Roth, Michael S. *Memory, Trauma and History: Essays on Living with the Past*. New York: Columbia UP, 2012.
Rothberg, Michael. *Traumatic Realism: The Demands of Holocaust Representation*. Minneapolis: University of Minnesota Press, 2000.
———. *Multidirectional Memory: Remembering the Holocaust in the Age of Decolonization*. Standford, CA: Stanford UP, 2009.
Seeskin, Kenneth. "Coming to Terms with Failure: A Philosophical Dilemma." *Writing and the Holocaust*. Ed. Berel Lang. New York: Holmes & Meier Publishers, 1988. 110–121.
Seltzer, Mark. "Wound Culture: Trauma in the Pathological Public Sphere." *October* 80 (1997): 3–26.
Shechner, Mark. "Jewish Writers." *Harvard Guide to Contemporary American Writing*. Ed. Daniel Hoffman. Cambridge and London: The Belknap Press of Harvard University, 1979. 191–239.
Sicher, Efrain. "The Future of the Past: Countermemory and Postmemory in Contemporary American Post-Holocaust Narratives." *History & Memory* 12.2 (Fall/Winter 2000): 56–91.
———. *The Holocaust Novel*. New York: Routledge, 2005.
Steiner, George. "The Long Life of Metaphor: An Approach to the 'Shoah.'" *Writing and the Holocaust*. Ed. Berel Lang. New York: Holmes & Meier Publishers, 1988. 154–171.
Tal, Kali. *Worlds of Hurt: Reading the Literatures of Trauma*. Cambridge and New York: Cambridge UP, 1996.
The American-Israeli Cooperative Enterprise (AICE). *Jewish Virtual Library: Everything You Need to Know from Anti-Semitism to Zionism*. Web. 12 Apr. 2015. <www.jewishvirtuallibrary.org/jsource/Holocaust/Rosenberg.html>
The Jewish Week. "Major Pay Gap for Reform Women." Web. 20 Dec. 2015. <www.thejewishweek.com/news/new-york-news/major-pay-gap-reform-women-rabbis>
Tory, Avraham. *Surviving the Holocaust: The Kovno Ghetto Diary*. Ed. Martin Gilbert. London: Pimlico, 1991.

Vice, Sue. *Holocaust Fiction*. London and New York: Routledge, 2000.
Wilde, Lawrence. "The Search for Reconciliation in E.L. Doctorow's *City of God*." *Religion and the Arts* 10.3 (2006): 391–405.
Wittgenstein, Ludwig. *Tractatus Logico-Philosophicus*. Trans. by D. F. Pears and B. F. McGuinness. Introd. by Bertand Russell. London: Routledge, 1988.
Wolf, David. "E.L. Doctorow: Meet the Author." *The Guardian* 19 Jan. 2014. Web. 8 Feb. 2016. <www.theguardian.com/books/2014/jan/19/el-doctorow-andrews-brain-interview>

5 Discussion
The Ethics and Politics of Literature

"You write in order to change the world, knowing perfectly well that you probably can't, but also knowing that literature is indispensable to the world," wrote North-American novelist James Baldwin (in Romano n.p.). Baldwin had no doubts as to the value of his occupation, convinced as he was that he had dedicated his life to the worthy cause of trying to change the world with his writings. Beginning with the denunciation of indifference expressed by Mayor Blue's complaint that "a man's pride is not to pay attention" (Doctorow, *Hard Times* 4), this book has traced the evolution of E.L. Doctorow's social and ethical commitment as revealed by his engagement with gender and trauma. This has cropped up through the novels' overriding concern with injustice and their engagement with the representation of human suffering in a variety of shapes.

Despite substantial differences in plot, setting, characterization and narrative style, a number of key themes have emerged when approaching the novels from the perspectives of trauma theory and feminist criticism: (1) there is a complex nexus between trauma, shame, guilt and violence, which are connected in an inescapable spiral of destruction; (2) intersectional oppression, discrimination and violence have a strong traumatizing potential; (3) the limits between the categories of victim, perpetrator and bystander are rather fuzzy in the context of psychological trauma; (4) while a psychological condition might be a common result of traumatic experiences, human resilience should not be disregarded, both in its individual and social (i.e. collective) dimensions; (5) hegemonic gender configurations and patriarchal forms of production and consumption are potentially traumatic and affect not only the individual but also the community; (6) there are gender-specific forms of resistance to disempowerment and silencing; (7) unchecked evil abounds in human nature and history, which is shown to be circular and endlessly returning, and human barbarity manifests itself in countless ways. These themes confirm the initial hypothesis from which this project sprang. In light of them, therefore, my aim in this chapter is to discuss Doctorow's ethical commitment and place it within the context of the more general turn to ethics in philosophy and criticism. Contemporary debates regarding narrative empathy and reader response will also be addressed. This will lead to a final reappraisal of Doctorow's literary project, bringing to the fore his fiction's promise for literature and society as a whole.

Beyond Postmodernism: Toward a New Narrative Form

Prior to that, it seems apt take up some of the issues raised in the Introduction. In the light of the analyses carried out in the previous chapters, there is a clear case to argue that Doctorow's early and middle novels mark a transition, or, rather, an evolution from a postmodern ethos toward the recuperation of realistic meaning and the position of the subject in its encounter with the Other. These concerns situate the author relatively apart from the skepticism and uncertainty that characterizes radical postmodernist fiction. More specifically, while remaining thematically and stylistically postmodernist in many ways, as the preliminary analysis suggested, the novels simultaneously endorse and subvert the postmodernist ethos, inaugurating a new literary "non-conformism" that has both an aesthetic and an ethical scope and is based on what Doctorow has called a "poetics of engagement" (in Trenner 48). Thus, considering E.L. Doctorow to be merely a postmodern author, as many of his critics did, risks lapsing into oversimplification. Rather, Doctorow's early and middle books send an important message about the alternative status of the novel in the postmodern era, and he is certainly not alone in doing so.

There seems to be sufficient evidence to support the claim that the return to ethics in philosophy and criticism—which the primacy of feminist criticism and trauma theory in today's critical panorama heralded—has to a certain extent been influenced by a more general move toward a literature of social commitment from the 1970s and 1980s onward. Thus, one might also talk about an ethical turn in literature that has been motivated by the influence on the literary imagination of countless authors of the postcolonial, post-Holocaust, post-Nuclear bomb and post-Vietnam contexts. It is undeniable that experimental texts such as Kurt Vonnegut's *Slaughterhouse-Five, or The Children's Crusade: A Duty-Dance with Death* (1969), Margaret Atwood's *The Handmaid's Tale* (1986) or Toni Morrison's *Beloved* (1987), to name but a few examples, demand to be read ethically. One cannot possibly imagine writers such as these approving a dismissal of the social meanings and ethical implications of their texts. To read these writers in a detached manner—focusing exclusively on the formal elements of their texts and without paying attention to their historical, biographical and cultural context, and societal influence—may be nothing short of cheating them, of breaking the literary contract established between readers and writers by refusing their invitation to reflect on the ethical implications of their works. These ethically oriented postmodern texts confirm, in Hans

Discussion

Bertens view, that "the coexistence of postmodern self-reflexiveness and traditional referentiality is not only possible but also can be a very effective instrument" (308).

Bertens's contention brings to mind Magali Cornier-Michael's pertinent formulation of the notion of "impulse" (5). With it, she seeks to "avoid hypostatizing a collection of plural and dynamic practices" (5). This formulation is particularly useful for my purposes, since it allows drawing attention to

> the variety of strategies or elements located in most fiction (a variety that traditionally is effaced), even when certain ones dominate, and allows for the presence of differing degrees of any given strategy or element. This avoids rigid category markers and the exclusions that result and instead highlights the hybrid nature of fiction. (5)

In other words, what Cornier-Michael is suggesting is to explore the different impulses that co-exist in a text and the relationship established among them. This approach to the analysis of fiction allows for an examination of the intersection and possible collusion of a variety of strategies that have tended to be read as antithetical, as is the case of postmodernism and ethics. Thus, in the light of the analysis carried out so far, it is worth turning now to a reconsideration of the way in which the ethical impulse in Doctorow's novels productively engages and transforms subversive aesthetic strategies usually associated with postmodern fiction to strengthen their ethical edge.

In the case of *Welcome to Hard Times*, postmodernist notions and strategies extend the novel's ethical scope in two central ways. On the one hand, the blurring and reassessment of the traditional conventions of literary genres that became common in times of postmodernism and which sought to replenish fiction through the assimilation of marginal, non-canonical genres paved the way for Doctorow's parodic appropriation of the genre of the Western. The novel's articulation of individual suffering as a direct consequence of the failure of the frontier community benefits to a large degree from the conventions of the Western and the possibility of parodically exploiting them. On the other hand, the critical interrogation of the grand narrative of history and the humanist understanding of it as characterized by endless progress support Doctorow's representation of history as cyclical in the novel, reinforcing a view of violence and trauma as endlessly returning. Additionally, the postmodern distrust of the grand narrative of myth frames Doctorow's attempt to demythologize the American founding illusion of exceptionalism in the novel. Second, the disruption of hegemonic images of masculinity and femininity that the novel performs may have been inspired by the attack against categorical thinking brought about by deconstruction. The postmodern drive toward the destabilization of binaries also facilitates the novel's nonjudgmental narration and the problematization of the limits between the categories of victim, perpetrator and bystander. Finally, the highly self-reflexive mode of writing that was favored in times of postmodernism—characterized by narrative experimentalism and by the simultaneous rejection of objectivity and decentering of subjectivity—stands behind the novel's articulation of the narrator/fictive author as unreliable and creates a space for the polyphonic inclusion of the voices of women.

As for *The Book of Daniel*, the most obvious way in which the novel's ethical undercurrent has benefited from postmodern subversive strategies is in the use of experimental narrative techniques, such as fragmentation, disrupted chronology and repetition. By means of these, the novel succeeds in representing the protagonist's psychic ailment formally, reproducing in the text the disabling effects of trauma on the individual. The novel's ethical engagement with trauma is further supported by a number of postmodern aesthetic strategies, such as intertextuality—which in the novel acts as a tool to work through trauma—and metafictionality, which allow Doctorow to appropriate the conventions of the testimonial mode of writing for ethical purposes. Postmodern self-reflexivity, with its simultaneous decentering of subjectivity and rejection of objectivity, also enhances the unreliability of the narrator/fictive author, emphasizing the disruptive effects of trauma. From a thematic perspective, the postmodern attitude toward history, reality and fiction as equally constructed discourses lies behind *The Book of Daniel*'s redefinition of the past and its opening of it to new and multiple interpretations. Indeed, the postmodern critical interrogation and revision of the universalizing metanarratives of history and politics lies at the core of the novel's deconstruction of assumed official versions of the past by pitting them against the minority perspective of Daniel's family. In addition, the postmodern attack on categorical thinking allows for the novel's problematization of the limits between the categories of victim and perpetrator. Finally, the poststructuralist understanding of the indeterminacy of meaning and the impossibility of truthful representation provide the frame for the novel's emphasis on the overwhelming sense of uncertainty that characterizes contemporary existence.

The postmodern spirit of subversion supports *Ragtime*'s ethical aspirations in the following ways. First of all, the disruption of dichotomies that was favored in times of postmodernism lies behind the novel's representation of three parallel families—one white Anglo-Saxon Protestant, one working-class European immigrant and one African-American—as well as other traditionally marginalized characters. The result is a narrative with multiple centers and no margins that inscribes into fiction and history those that have often been excluded from them. Furthermore, the postmodern rejection of objectivity and decentering of subjectivity that was common in times of postmodernism inspires the plurality of female characters that constitute a repetition with a difference of experiences of oppression, in effect intersecting patriarchal subordination and violence with class, race and ethnicity. Another postmodernist element that facilitates the novel's ethical work is the blurring and reassessment of the traditional conventions of literary genres: in *Ragtime*, the historical chronicle is parodically appropriated, destabilizing and playing against traditional frameworks of generic interpretation. The novel's experimental narrative style, with its dispassionate, cold and distant chronicle-like narration and its use of irony, owes much to postmodernist aesthetics, and facilitates the novel's focus on the collective dimension of trauma, forcing the reader to reflect on the social ills derived from oppression and violence. Finally, the postmodernist critical interrogation and revision of universalizing metanarratives influences the book's attitude toward history, with the constant intermingling of what is generally considered verifiable fact and the author's fictive imagination. This allows Doctorow to redefine the past and open it to new and multiple interpretations.

In the case of *City of God*, the most obvious way in which it benefits from postmodernist subversive strategies is through the experimentalism that characterizes its approach to the representation of the Holocaust. The novel's intertextuality, metafictional self-reflexivity and fragmentation are precisely the strategies that make Doctorow's fictional engagement with the Holocaust possible. Indeed, the postmodern understanding of the indeterminacy of meaning and the impossibility of truthful representation frame the novel's discussion of the demands of Holocaust representation and the tension between documentation and self-consciousness, between truth and fictionality. Specifically, postmodern is also the novel's self-conscious discussion of the circulation of Holocaust stories in post-traumatic culture. Furthermore, the paradoxical decentering of subjectivity and simultaneous rejection of objectivity lie behind the novel's more or less successful commitment to the representation of a plurality of perspectives. Finally, the depiction of a myriad of female characters that creates a kaleidoscopic view of femininity supports itself on the postmodern disruption of categorical thinking and binarism.

To sum up, the novels prove to be highly effective precisely *because* of the combination of postmodernist and ethical impulses. Against Catharine Walker Bergström's claim that "the postmodern narrative techniques that Doctorow often employs are evidence of his desire to stay on top of current critical developments and to be taken seriously by the academic community" (36), I submit that postmodernist and ethical impulses in his novels work together to carry out a subversive critique of Western metaphysics and the Enlightenment tradition in order to open a path toward reconstruction. In the four novels, a space is delineated in which postmodernism and ethics not only can coexist, but also benefit from each other. The texts invite us to read them aesthetically but also ethically; they participate in a radical critique of injustice and oppression, appropriating subversive aesthetic strategies associated with postmodernism and, in so doing, contributing to anchoring postmodernism to its rightful oppositional role.

Mark Busby goes even further, claiming that Doctorow's work has affinities not only with postmodernist and realist literature, but also with modernism (182). Yet, the analysis carried out in this study proves that none of the labels alone does full justice to the complexity of Doctorow's oeuvre. Hans Bertens puts forward the term "postmodern humanism" to refer to those postmodernist novels that succeed in striking a balance between referentiality and non-referentiality, achieving an ethical and far from apolitical mode of writing that would set the base for the ethical turn in literature (305–306). Similarly, Heinz Ickstadt offers the term "postmodernist realism" to group those apparently realist writers who nevertheless include certain elements that reveal their postmodernist allegiances (in Collado-Rodríguez 141). Specifically referring to E.L. Doctorow, T.V. Reed also suggests "postmodernist realism" as the appropriate category to classify the author's early fiction (303). Finally, another possibility would be to adopt Doctorow's own rather ironic term: "I've used certain postmodernist techniques, but for what I think as entirely traditional story telling purposes. What does that make me—a post postmodernist?" (in Morris 193). Whatever label one chooses, however, it remains true that the ethical impulse in E.L. Doctorow's novels simultaneously marks a move beyond the most radical postmodernist features and appropriates them for ethical purposes. The books draw attention to the edges of texts and, consequently, the edges of reality and fiction in Doctorow's overriding desire to communicate truthfully human suffering and injustice. Their hybridity may be interpreted as proof of the writer's efforts to create his own novelistic form, one capable of demystifying received notions of reality and truth while foregrounding the ethical imperative to respond to the pain of the Other.

E.L. Doctorow's Literary Project

Echoing James Baldwin's words quoted above, Doctorow's attempt to create his own literary form, one characterized by the collusion of postmodern and ethical impulses, cannot be divorced from his firm belief that "writing matters, that there is salvation in witness and moral assignment," which is precisely what constitutes what he terms "the passion of [the writer's] calling" ("The Beliefs of Writers" 618). As he explains—and the findings presented so far indeed confirm—his literary project responds to a profound preoccupation with justice: "What is just? What is unjust? That's where it all begins for me" (in Morris 95). It might be useful at this point to recuperate Maria Root's words about the socio-political climate of the 1960s and 1970s quoted in the Introduction: "It was an era marked by a generation's search for meaning and justice" (231). As she further explains,

> [t]he world for which this generation hoped did not exist. Oppression was rampant and affected major portions of the population. The civil rights were being violated daily [...]. Anger and confusion were catalysts for the activism and power of this generation, who spoke about the realities and atrocities of their lives and those of previous generations. (231)

This era, marked by the Vietnam War, international conflict, fear of the Bomb, gay liberation, the second reconstruction of the civil rights movement and the revolution brought about by the Women's Rights Movement, was the ground from which Doctorow's literary project sprouted.

Another important element must be added to this equation: as Barbara Foley rightly explains, Doctorow's consciousness—like that of other contemporary writers—may be also conceptualized as post-Holocaust (356). She specifically refers to Doctorow's postmodern attitude toward fact and fiction, contending that his willful distortion of the past seeks to "convey a chaotic sense of historical process and to suggest the necessarily subjective nature of any attempt to construct a coherent picture of bygone events" (331). Then, she draws attention to what she rightly perceives as a philosophical link between the devastation of the death camps and the solipsistic conception of history as nightmare (331). Extending Foley's insightful argument, one might argue that Doctorow's post-Holocaust consciousness materializes in very specific ways in the four novels discussed. *Welcome to Hard Times* is a tale of devastation that narrates the destruction of a whole community where no one survives to tell their story but Blue. After his own death, the only remnant of this fictional community is his narrative, supposedly the text that we are reading. In *The Book of Daniel* we are presented with a Jewish family who is meticulously destroyed by the state, two of its members murdered and the other two deeply traumatized by the experience. It is worth adding that, as Peter Novick explains, the Rosenberg case was frequently described at the time as the overture to an American holocaust where people would be murdered by state-approved apparatuses as scapegoats (94). As for *Ragtime*, it features a Jewish immigrant who strives to survive in the United States and overcomes discrimination through economic success. He represents those Jews who, like Doctorow's own grandparents, did not die in the Holocaust because they emigrated and later thrived. As Jessica Hillman has argued, Tateh embodies and constantly evokes "an easier kind of survivor, standing in for a much more painful and difficult Holocaust survivor. His immigrant pain and suffering offers a far reduced version of Holocaust suffering [...]" (169). As for *City of God*, the novel's explicit engagement with the Holocaust in a highly self-conscious and bitter manner requires no further remark.

Resorting to the author's own words and socio-historical context to conceptualize his literary project, even if the claims made are supported by textual analysis and close reading, may seem at odds with the debunking of the godlike authority of the writer to legislate meaning that we have witnessed since times of postmodernism. The notion of authorship was badly wounded in the 1970s and 1980s after its death was proclaimed by French theorists Michael Foucault and Roland Barthes. The death of the author was meant to imply "the liberation of the reader" (Felski 57). Indeed, after the influence of these French intellectuals reached the Anglo-American academy, few critics could any longer believe in the possibility of pinning down what a work 'really' meant by appealing to the thoughts, desires or circumstances of the person who had written it. As Rita Felski explains, "[i]nvoking the author was a way of repressing the richness and exuberance of writing by confining it in the straitjacket of a single, original, true meaning" (57). However, a specific effect of trauma theory—with its emphasis on testimony and witnessing—and feminist criticism—given gynocritics' impulse to recuperate women writers and identify manifestations of women's experience in them—among other key contemporary theoretical frameworks, has been a progressive recuperation of the figure of the author. While retaining a firm belief in the independent lives of literary texts, the role of the reader in constructing meanings—an issue that will be discussed presently—and acknowledging the risk of slipping into the trap of the biographical fallacy, the analysis carried out in this book does retain a belief in the figure of the author as a more or less stable subjectivity behind his/her work. Thus, it may be contended that it was Doctorow's post-Vietnam, post-Bomb and post-Holocaust consciousness and his preoccupation with justice that inspired the novels' engagement with ethics.[1]

The question that such conceptualization prompts is undoubtedly the following: is literature a suitable vehicle for ethics? Providing an answer to that question has been the main concern of countless critics. A number of commentators in the so-called aesthetic tradition believe that, regardless of its potential to "convey ideas, opinions, and information, often with great power, [...] the moral content and consequences of a work of literature are irrelevant to its value as literature" (Posner 1). This position, however, betrays a disregard for literature's social meanings and a disinterest in the specificities and singularities of reader response. Critics in the neohumanist tradition, on the contrary, share a firm conviction that "literature needs ethical assessment" (Nussbaum 70), because it "raises ethical questions" (Schwarz 6) and has a "transformative ethical power" (Booth 17). Yet, this understanding in turn suggests a rather naïve belief in universal moral values and could potentially reduce literature to a set of instrumental or utilitarian purposes, or lead to censorship. Most scholars concerned with ethical criticism occupy a reasonable middle ground in that they share a belief in the ethical power of literature and defend the importance of ethical criticism while rejecting the assumption that literature as a whole has a tidy moral, a consistent ethical message that would reduce art to the role of the fable or the political satire.[2] This is precisely the stance that Catharine Walker Bergström takes in her insightful examination of Doctorow's work from the perspective of ethical criticism. Grounding her enquiry in theoretical studies of postmodern and narrative ethics, she concentrates on Doctorow's character-narrators and their "intuition of an autonomous Self with a moral obligation to the Other" (13). In her analysis, the voice of these narrators is that of the postmodern gnostic, who feels a drive to say something truthful that is inscribed with a moral obligation to interpret signs from and for the Other and that is based on an intuition of a responsibility to the Other drawn from a Gnostic myth of pre-originary, but lost, unity—the Over-Soul or collective unconscious (14, 25, 27). Thus, she brilliantly identifies elements of Levinasian ethics, the transcendental philosophical writings of Emerson and Jung, as well as Gnostic mythology and the Kabbalah in Doctorow's novels. Where I cannot fully agree with Walker Bergström, however, is in her rejection of the potential ethical significance of approaching Doctorow's oeuvre from a given particular perspective—she explicitly mentions the feminist and the postcolonial frameworks of interpretation—arguing that they have a narrow focus that cannot lead to an ethical approach to literary texts (16). Such contention must certainly be tightly connected to her rather surprising claim that "the ethical element in Doctorow's fiction is not primarily political" (32), as the agenda of these frameworks undoubtedly is.

A crucial conclusion that emerges from the analysis carried out so far, and this is my key point, is that in Doctorow's literary project the aesthetic, the ethical *and* the political cannot be understood in isolation from one another. Doctorow's literary project not only is ethical, but also has a clearly political dimension, not in the sense of right- or left-wing ideology suggested by early reviewers and commentators, but in that it is a call to action, an invitation to try and change the present in order to avoid the repetition of past mistakes. For one thing, the results obtained by looking at Doctorow's novels through the lenses of feminist criticism and trauma theory make it easier to understand what he meant when he referred to his literary method as a "poetics of engagement" (in Trenner 48). Indeed, in speeches, lectures, essays and interviews Doctorow never tired of complaining about the distinction between the ethical, the political and the literary that was firmly drawn in times of postmodernism, about "an exhaustion of the hope that writing can change anything" ("The Beliefs of Writers" 615).

What can literature in general, and Doctorow's literary project in particular, change, then? Michael Rothberg has claimed that literature, by focusing on the singular, "draw[s] attention to the simultaneously individual and collective nature of history and experience" (*Traumatic Realism* 175). Furthermore, as Todd Davis and Kenneth Womack explain in the Preface to their volume *Mapping the Ethical Turn* (2001), "[t]he act of telling stories—the gesture to represent what all too often is unrepresentable, ineffable—grounds and distinguishes human activity" (ix–x). A similar point has been made by Marshall Gregory, who drawing on Denis Dutton's work about the role of art in human evolution highlights "the socially cohesive functioning and imaginatively stimulating effects of story telling" and their central role in survival (277). Gregory further quotes work done in the fields of cognitive science and evolutionary psychology that suggests that "the brain is now known to change physical structure and functioning [...] on the basis of imaginative and hypothetical input, such as that stimulated by poetry, narratives, and story telling" (277). In the same article, Gregory usefully also puts forward the notion that literary texts have a special agency that he calls "power of invitation" (279). In his view, literary texts extend to readers invitations to feeling (invitations to respond in specifically emotional ways to the story and the characters), to belief (invitations to believe certain notions on which the text relies) and to ethical judgment (invitations to judge which actions, characters, thoughts and speech demand approval or disapproval) (280). Thus, drawing on Gregory's suggestion, one might claim that the way in which we respond to these invitations and the degree to which our responses change us and our outlook on the world will determine the ethical, social and political dimensions of literary texts.

Where it comes to Doctorow's novels, they may be seen as an answer to Michael Rothberg's calls for "better ways of understanding how different forms of suffering and violence may inhabit the same social spaces" (Preface xvii). He further adds that "we need to understand what such overlap entails for the possibilities for resistance, healing, and social change" (Preface xvii). This is precisely how Doctorow's literary project may potentially change things: the novels invite us to confront intellectually and emotionally the damaging effects of injustice and the potential within human nature to hurt others; they demand from us that we bear witness to human suffering in its many forms, highlighting the notion that suffering is a shared human experience that cuts across class, race, gender, religion, ethnicity, etc., while also drawing attention to its uniqueness and specificity in terms of different and/or intersecting subject positions. Finally, the novels compel us to acknowledge history's tendency to repeat itself when past events start to fall into oblivion, forcing us to reflect on the underlying similarities between bygone times and the present in terms of human suffering. To reader's possible responses to Doctorow's ethical and political invitations we now turn.

Narrative Empathy and Reader Response

The analysis carried out so far has extensively discussed concerns about themes and plot (i.e. specific thematic and formal engagements with trauma and gender), values (i.e. social scope) and the figure of the author (i.e. literary project and authorial intention), in *Welcome to Hard Times*, *The Book of Daniel*, *Ragtime* and *City of God*. There is still a key agent in the literary process that has not been considered in sufficient detail: the reader. According to Daniel Schwarz, readers discover a text's significance in relation to their other experiences, including other reading experiences, and in terms of the interpretive communities to which they belong (13). For his part, Marshall Gregory claims that reader response depends on which of the text's invitations we answer affirmatively, which might be determined by "a complex give-and-take relationship" with a number of external pressures (279).[3] Rita Felski similarly suggests that,

> [...] reading is not an all-or-nothing affair, where I must either resist a text fiercely and adamantly or else find myself nodding in agreement with every word. There is a lot of give and take involved in the act of interpretation; [...] Readers are often seduced by what they read; but they may also refuse to be seduced or decide not to go all the way with the work in question. (45–46)

Even Wayne Booth, despite being one of the fiercest champions of the power of literature to ethically change readers, concedes that "[e]ffects on actual behavior are extremely elusive and will [...] never be conclusively demonstrated" (18).

One of the notions traditionally associated with the ethical power of literature to affect readers has been that of narrative empathy, a controversial concept that has generated lively scholarly debates in the context of the turn to ethics in criticism and philosophy. In the traditional view of art, experiencing and identifying with different lives through the act of reading is understood to promote empathy, which in turn leads to ethical improvement and altruism. In more recent versions of this argument, commentators such as Martha Nussbaum, Wayne Booth and Daniel Schwarz defend the claim that "reading complements our experience *by* enabling us to live lives beyond those we live and to experience emotions that are not ours" (Schwarz 10; emphasis in the original). Some of the advocates of the potential of literature to promote empathy are also trauma critics, who share Dominick LaCapra's belief that reading trauma narratives produces what he terms "empathic unsettlement," which "involves a kind of virtual experience through which one puts oneself in the other's position" (722). In her influential book on trauma culture, Ann Kaplan similarly links trauma, witnessing and literature with pro-social, political actions and ethical consciousness as well as injustice (21–23, 120–123). However, some scholars have recently expressed certain misgivings about the notion of narrative empathy. While generally admitting the ethical potential of literature to improve readers' character by means of an affective transaction through the writing and reading of fiction, a major point of disagreement stems from the question of whether literature-produced empathy indeed contributes to making individuals better citizens, more sensitive to the suffering of others and, more importantly, engaged in altruistic behavior (see Amiel-Houser and Mendelson-Maoz 203, Keen 20).[4] In other words, the question is whether reading literature and responding empathically to the plights of the characters might have long-lasting ethical effects on average readers and mobilize strong enough emotions so as to not only inspire them to respond empathically to the pain of real people, but also move them to action toward a more just world.

Two main concerns related to the notion of narrative empathy may be raised: on the one hand, readers encounter literary characters in the privacy and safety of their homes, where they can freely empathize with their suffering without facing a demand to respond ethically in the real world. This release from obligation that fictionality offers may well facilitate empathy by causing readers to put down their psychological defenses to distress (i.e. indifference, skepticism and suspicion), as Suzanne Keen claims (4). Yet, the truth is that literature frees us from the moral imperative to act: we may easily empathize with the suffering of the Joad family while reading *The Grapes of Wrath*, and even shed a few tears, but we may just as easily change the channel to avoid watching a UNHCR campaign during our family dinner or avert our eyes as we walk past a beggar on the street. On the other hand, the notion of narrative empathy has generally relied on the assumption that simulating the inner perspective of the Other—that is, assimilating the Other into the Self—is a key aspect of the ethical process of reading.[5] In other words, the concept of empathy is strongly associated with the projected occupation and experience of the other's subject position. Indeed, moral philosopher Martha Nussbaum is convinced that literary works help cross the hierarchical barriers that society has created by undermining the stereotypes that block us from seeing the humanity of the Other (69). However, evidence suggests that most people usually empathize only with those who are like them. As Suzanne Keen explains, "it turns out in laboratory experiments that we humans, like other primates, tend to experience empathy most readily and accurately for those who seem like us, as David Hume and Adam Smith predicted" (x).[6]

In short, the problem for some critics, among which I include myself, with much traditional commentary on narrative empathy might be, thus, the universalism inherent to it. In other words, retaining the notion of empathy usually implies sharing certain beliefs about the universal nature of human experience and feeling, which has never gone down well with feminist critics, postcolonial theorists and other minority scholars. Yet, it is also true that even those who are most critical with the notion of empathy and its dangerous masking of "our obligation to those people who are not similar to us" (Amiel-Houser and Mendelson-Maoz 207) concede that suffering may be viewed as a shared human experience that does not demand close knowledge of the other person to be plainly recognized.

A possible way out of the narrative empathy dead-end might have been provided by Emmanuel Levinas's theory of the infinite responsibility toward the inaccessible and radically different Other, since it provides a theoretical basis to reconsider empathic response. In *Totality and Infinity* (1961), Levinas puts forward the notion of "imperialism of the same" to refer to the traditional philosophical quest to achieve total knowledge of Being (87). This quest responds to the subject's need to search for coherent structures of meaning, and is achieved by subsuming the particular to the general and reducing the unknown to what Levinas calls the "same" (42). Such a reduction also happens when two people face each other or when a reader faces a fictional character, since in these encounters an empathetic response usually depends on the capacity to understand the other person's/the character's thoughts, motivations, feelings, etc. In Levinasian philosophy, comprehension necessarily involves comparison to the Other, and incorporation of it into the Self (42). In opposition to this process, Levinas claims that the human condition—which is inextricably a social condition where we live together with, and in interaction with, other people—has within it something that is irreducibly other and inaccessibly different (43). For him, it is precisely this radical alterity that dictates an extreme and unconditional responsibility toward the Other to whom the Self stands face to face (36). The face of the Other is then, for Levinas, that which obligates the Self, and that obligation arises out of the Other's need and out of the Other's dignity, its authority (96–97). For Levinas, this obligation is prior to recognition or understanding, takes priority and is extreme, in the sense that there are no limits to it. This responsibility, furthermore, is in his theorization characteristic of human social existence; it is, indeed, a condition of it (178). The ethical challenge is, therefore, to encounter the Other as radically different, totally exterior and fully inaccessible, while nonetheless acknowledging the Self's obligation toward him or her and being able to respond to his or her call for help.

Resisting the "imperialism of the same" and acknowledging our ethical duty to respond to the pain of the Other is, however, not an easy task when dealing with fictional characters in literary texts. For one thing, a number of narrative techniques such as homodiegetic narration and omniscience facilitate character identification and create the illusion of providing readers access to the minds, feelings and personalities of the Other. To avoid this, Jill Bennett brilliantly calls for

> a conjunction of affect and critical awareness [that] may be understood to constitute the basis of an empathy grounded not in affinity (*feeling for* another insofar as we can imagine *being* that other) but on a *feeling for* another that entails an encounter with something irreducible and different, often inaccessible. (10; emphasis in the original)

It is my contention that this conjunction of affect and critical awareness of which Bennett speaks is precisely what characterizes the empathic demands that Doctorow's novels make on readers. After all, Doctorow was convinced that "the presumption of any art is that ordinary messages are insufficient," since they put the writer in "grave danger of becoming didactic" (in Morris 108).

First and foremost, as we have seen, *Welcome to Hard Times*, *The Book of Daniel* and *Ragtime* emphasize the fuzziness of the limits between the trauma categories of victim, perpetrator and bystander. In these novels, Doctorow refuses to provide sufficient ethical guidance for the readers to interpret the main protagonists' behavior and sort out the ethical complexity of their actions. The novels demand from the readers that they respond affectively to the plights of the main characters and bear witness to their suffering, which results not only from unjust socio-economic or political conditions, but also from other characters' disregard for their pain. Yet, their ambiguous role as facilitators or even perpetrators of violence and oppression toward others problematizes their status as victims and forces readers to critically reflect on the dangers of simplistic identification. In other words, these characters' despicable actions hinder the assimilation of the Other into the Self while their simultaneous condition as victims demands from readers an empathic response to their suffering. As a result, readers are caught between feelings of sympathy and scorn; they are unable to fully identify with these characters but are also incapable of dismissing their pain. Thus, by refusing to provide simplistic guidance through the novels' ethical complexity or to offer an easy ethical position for readers to occupy, Doctorow compels us to critically reflect on what it really means to respond empathically to the pain of the Other.

A similar effect is achieved in *City of God*, although in a different manner. As argued in Chapter 4, the fictionality of the plot is constantly highlighted, and readers are not allowed to forget for one minute that they are dealing with imagined characters. This, together with the novel's reference not only to the Holocaust, but also to other particularly brutal and frequently disregarded instances of human barbarity, contributes to complicating reader identification by encouraging critical awareness of our obligation to respond to the suffering of those we have been programmed to empathize with—i.e. Holocaust survivors and war veterans—and of those whose lives seem to matter less to a white North-American audience—i.e. the victims of Pol Pot or of the Rwanda genocide to name but a few. This effect is further achieved by means of narrative technique, namely through the quick interspersion of different plotlines and narrative voices. A similar aim may be claimed to lie behind *Ragtime*'s detached chronicle-like narration. Everything in the novel is narratologically orchestrated to hinder reader identification and simplistic sympathy, since characters are often archetype-like puppets whose suffering gets drowned in the staccato-like voice of the mock historian. Yet, the stark horror of the experiences they go through does force readers to confront intellectually and emotionally the consequences of injustice and inequality without relying on simplistic character identification.

What the four novels undoubtedly share is a determination to expose the darkest effects of the individualistic ethos of contemporary Western societies and to highlight the risks of indifference. The novels' numerous radically different and infinitely demanding faces—a powerless prostitute and rape survivor, a man who struggles to come to terms with the shame and guilt of his compliance with a rapist and murderer, a child victim of trauma who has become a woman batterer and sexual abuser, a woman who is forced to submit to sexual harassment to feed her family, a man who struggles to survive as an immigrant in an unwelcoming country, a woman who attempts to murder her own newborn baby in despair, an arsonist and murderer driven by injustice and shame, an ex-chorus girl raped at age fifteen who willingly endures all sort of sexual humiliations to maintain her economic status, a woman who fights the sexism of the rabbinate from within, a man who risked his life as a child to secure evidence of Nazi crimes and many others—undoubtedly represent the Other of the average middle-class North-American and compel him/her to shake off apathy and respond empathically to their suffering. As Suzanne Keen explains, by doing so, readers will still internalize the experience of empathy toward the face of the Other in a way that promises later real-world responsiveness to his or her needs (xiii–xiv).

In short, by withdrawing excessive ethical guidance, Doctorow's novels encourage critical awareness and intellectual distance while also inspiring powerful emotional responses to the suffering of the Other, compelling readers to experience outrage in the face of injustice and, hopefully, helping them internalize their ethical response. Although this perspective cannot demonstrate how the literary experience of immersing oneself in Doctorow's ethical and political literary project may improve average readers' personality or make them better moral agents, it suggests that the experience offers opportunities for empathic response to the pain of radically others that are more difficult to encounter in real life.

194 *Discussion*

Concluding Remarks

I would like to conclude by quoting Martha Nussbaum's insightful reflection about the power of literature: "I do think that all citizens ought to think about justice, and it seems to me that reading certain novels offers assistance in that task" (77). Asked in an interview about his social ideals Doctorow explains that "there is a presumption of universality to the ideal of justice—social justice, economic justice. It cannot exist for a part or class of society; it must exist for all" (in Trenner 55). This belief, together with his conviction that "a book can affect consciousness—affect the way people think and therefore the way they act" (in Trenner 43), speaks volumes about the author's own view of what truly constitutes "the passion of [the writer's] calling" ("The Beliefs of Writers" 618). The analysis carried out in this chapter has aimed at showing that Doctorow's literary project is not only eminently aesthetic and ethical, but also political. In his novels, the writer resorts to all the available techniques and strategies to challenge readers to take responsibility for the history of injustice that we have inherited, compelling us to actively resist the repetition of past mistakes. Such an analysis of the ethical and political agenda of Doctorow's literary project contests the dark destiny for novels predicted by John Barth, who in his essay "The Novel in the Next Century" (1992) foresaw that reading fiction would become a highly specialized and anachronistic activity, a "more or less elite taste, akin to chess or equestrian dressage" (223).

Notes

1 Such a belief is not, I contend with Felski, incompatible with recognizing that a text "is a zone of unstable, oscillating, and often clashing interpretations" (63).
2 See for example Gibson (1999), who turns to the work of Emmanuel Levinas for a "relevant, sophisticated, many-sided, non-foundational ethics [...] in the service of an ethical literary theory and criticism" (16), and Gregory (2010), who puts forward a framework for ethical criticism based on literature's power of ethical invitation (279), as we will see presently.
3 See also Phelan (2001), who similarly puts forward the notion that reader response depends on the ethical "position" that results from the interaction of four ethical situations: that of the characters within the story world, that of the narrator in relation to the telling and to the audience, that of the implied author in relation to the authorial audience and that of the flesh and blood reader in relation to the set of values, beliefs and locations that the narrative invites one to occupy (95–96).
4 Needless to say, the main implication of such a contention would be that writers, literary critics and professors of literature are the most altruistic and ethically committed members of society, which is certainly not (necessarily) the case.
5 See for example Schwarz (6), Smith (108), Sicher ("The Future of the Past" 66) and Coplan (143). Murray Smith argues that "[w]hen we empathize with another person, we extend our mind to incorporate part of his or her mind"

(108). Similarly, Efrain Sicher claims that literature "summons the imaginative empathy of affinity with the Other" ("The Future of the Past" 66).
6 To understand and share their misgivings, one only needs to watch UNICEF's recent experiment—which is part of their #FightUnfair Campaign—where a six-year-old girl is placed in the middle of the street alone, first wearing clean, elegant clothes and afterward dirty rags while the camera records average people's reactions to her.

References

Amiel-Houser, Tammie and Adia Mendelson-Maoz. "Against Empathy: Levinas and Ethical Criticism in the 21st Century." *Journal of Literary Theory* 8.1 (2014): 199–218.
Atwood, Margaret. *The Handmaid's Tale*. 1986. New York: Anchor Books, 1998.
Barth, John. "The Novel in the Next Century." *Conjunctions* 19 (1992): 213–228.
Bennett, Jill. *Empathic Vision: Affect, Trauma, and Contemporary Art*. Stanford: Stanford UP, 2005.
Bertens, Hans. "Postmodern Humanism." *Canadian Review of Comparative Literature/Revue Canadienne de Littérature Comparée* 39.3 (2012): 299–316.
Booth, Wayne C. *The Company We Keep: An Ethics of Fiction*. Berkeley: University of California Press, 1988.
Busby, Mark. "E.L. Doctorow's *Ragtime* and the Dialectics of Change." *Critical Essays on E. L. Doctorow*. Ed. Ben Siegel. New York: G. K. Hall & Co, 2000. 177–183.
Collado-Rodríguez, Francisco. "Chaotic Borders, Unstable Historicity: A Search for Margins in Contemporary American Fiction." *Margins in British and American Literature, Film and Culture*. Eds. Marita Nadal and Dolores Herrero. Zaragoza: Grupo Milán, 1997. 133–146.
Coplan, Amy. "Empathic Engagement with Narrative Fictions." *The Journal of Aesthetics and Art Criticism* 62.2 (Spring 2004): 141–152.
Cornier-Michael, Magali. *Feminism and the Postmodern Impulse: Post World War II Fiction*. Albany: State University of New York Press, 1996.
Davis, Todd F. and Kenneth Womack, eds. Preface. *Mapping the Ethical Turn: A Reader in Ethics, Culture, and Literary Theory*. Charlottesville and London: University of Virginia Press, 2001. ix–xiv.
Doctorow, E.L. *Welcome to Hard Times*. 1960. New York: Random House Trade Paperback, 2007.
———. *The Book of Daniel*. 1971. London: Penguin, 2006.
———. *Ragtime*. 1974. London: Penguin, 2006.
———. "The Beliefs of Writers." *Michigan Quarterly Review* 24 (Fall 1985): 609–619.
———. *City of God*. 2000. London: Abacus, 2006.
Felski, Rita. *Literature after Feminism*. Chicago: University of Chicago Press, 2003.
Foley, Barbara. "Fact, Fiction, Fascism: Testimony and Mimesis in Holocaust Narratives." *Comparative Literature* 34.4 (1982): 330–360.

Gibson, Andrew. *Postmodernity, Ethics, and the Novel*. London and New York: Routledge, 1999.
Gregory, Marshall W. "Redefining Ethical Criticism. The Old vs. the New." *Journal of Literary Theory* 4.2 (2010): 273–301.
Hillman, Jessica. "Rags and Ragtime." *Echoes of the Holocaust on the American Musical Stage*. Ed. Jefferson: McFarland & Company, 2013. 141–171.
Kaplan, E. Ann. *Trauma Culture: The Politics of Terror and Loss in Media and Literature*. New Brunswick, New Jersey, and London: Rutgers UP, 2005.
Keen, Suzanne. *Empathy and the Novel*. Oxford: Oxford UP, 2007.
LaCapra, Dominick. "Trauma, Absence, Loss." *Critical Inquiry* 25.4 (Summer 1999): 696–727.
Levinas, Emmanuel. *Totality and Infinity: An Essay on Exteriority*. 1961. Trans. by Alphonso Lingis. The Hague: Martinus Nijhoff Publishers, 1979.
Morris, Christopher D. ed. *Conversations with E. L. Doctorow*. Jackson: Mississippi UP, 1999.
Morrison, Toni. *Beloved*. 1987. London: Vintage, 1997.
Novick, Peter. *The Holocaust in American Life*. Boston: Houghton Mifflin, 1999.
Nussbaum, Martha. "Exactly and Responsibly: A Defense of Ethical Criticism." *Mapping the Ethical Turn: A Reader in Ethics, Culture, and Literary Theory*. Eds. Todd F. Davis and Kenneth Womack. Charlottesville and London: University of Virginia Press, 2001. 59–79.
Phelan, James. "Sethe's Choice: *Beloved* and the Ethics of Reading." *Mapping the Ethical Turn: A Reader in Ethics, Culture, and Literary Theory*. Eds. Todd F. Davis and Kenneth Womack. Charlottesville and London: University of Virginia Press, 2001. 93–109.
Posner, Richard A. "Against Ethical Criticism." *Philosophy and Literature* 21.1 (1997): 1–27.
Reed, T.V. "Genealogy/Narrative/Power: Questions of Postmodernity in Doctorow's *The Book of Daniel*." *American Literary History* 4.2 (Summer 1992): 288–304.
Romano, John. "James Baldwin Writing and Talking." *The New York Times* Sept. 23, 1979. Web. 25 May, 2015. <www.nytimes.com/1979/09/23/archives/james-baldwin-writing-and-talking-baldwin-baldwin-authors-query.html>
Root, Maria. "Reconstructing the Impact of Trauma on Personality." *Personality and Psychopathology: Feminist Reappraisals*. Ed. Laura S. Brown and Mary Ballou. New York: Guilford, 1992. 229–265.
Rothberg, Michael. *Traumatic Realism: The Demands of Holocaust Representation*. Minneapolis: University of Minnesota Press, 2000.
———. "Preface: Beyond Tancred and Clorinda—Trauma Studies for Implicated Subjects." *The Future of Trauma Theory*. Eds. Gert Buelens, Sam Durrant, and Robert Eaglestone. London and New York: Routledge, 2014. xi–xviii.
Schwarz, Daniel R. "A Humanistic Ethics of Reading." *Mapping the Ethical Turn: A Reader in Ethics, Culture, and Literary Theory*. Eds. Todd F. Davis and Kenneth Womack. Charlottesville and London: University of Virginia Press, 2001. 3–15.
Sicher, Efrain. "The Future of the Past: Countermemory and Postmemory in Contemporary American Post-Holocaust Narratives." *History & Memory* 12.2 (Fall/Winter 2000): 56–91.

Smith, Murray. "Empathy, Expansionism, and the Extended Mind." *Empathy: Philosophical and Psychological Perspectives*. Eds. Amy Coplan and Peter Goldie. Oxford and New York: Oxford UP, 2011. 99–117.
Trenner, Richard, ed. *E.L. Doctorow: Essays and Conversations*. Princeton: Ontario Review, 1983.
Vonnegut, Kurt. *Slaughterhouse-Five, or the Children's Crusade: A Duty-Dance with Death*. 1969. London: Vintage, 2000.
Walker Bergström, Catharine. *Intuition of an Infinite Obligation: Narrative Ethics and Postmodern Gnostics in the Fiction of E. L. Doctorow*. Frankfurt: Peter Lang, 2010.

Conclusion

This book opened with the sentence "beginnings are usually hard." Although it referred to E.L. Doctorow's struggles to succeed as a writer after a widely ignored first novel and a rather embarrassing second one, the phrase also self-reflexively alluded to this project and to the difficulties of finding the right words to start. If beginnings are hard, endings are probably much more so, since they imply finally letting go. This book started from the premise that, despite the fact that he had generally been considered a postmodernist writer—by some even a minor one—E.L. Doctorow's literary project, as represented by *Welcome to Hard Times*, *The Book of Daniel*, *Ragtime* and *City of God*, was eminently ethical and had a distinct social scope. The results obtained confirm this initial hypothesis: Doctorow's four novels engage with collective historical traumas such as racism, working-class discrimination, political persecution, gender oppression and the Holocaust, representing thematically and formally the imagined psychological aftereffects of extreme individual and collective suffering. The novels also highlight the destructive power of the affects of shame and guilt and their tight connection with violence and trauma response. Collectively, the books draw attention to the disastrous consequences of trauma not only for the individual but also for the community. Yet, they also underscore the human potential to heal and to develop positive survival strategies after trauma. Additionally, the books problematize the categories of victim, perpetrator and bystander by emphasizing the fuzzy and fluid limits that separate them, favoring a non-categorical stance. Furthermore, the novels subvert hegemonic representations of the masculine and the feminine, pointing to their social and cultural constructedness and countering them with a more nuanced understanding of gender identity. They denounce the prevailing model of gender domination, subordination and objectification by exposing their damaging effects through the use of narrative devices such as irony, the undermining of traditional character-logic and reader-identification patterns, and satire. Indeed, the novels incorporate not only themes but also narrative forms compatible with feminism. In addition, they undermine traditional associations of gender, power and violence by staging complex power struggles in their pages. Finally, the books incorporate, to a certain extent, the voices of women and act as sites of gender dialogue, providing the opportunity for the female characters to become empowered and contest the (male) narrators and fictive authors' narrative authority.

More generally, *Welcome to Hard Times*, *The Book of Daniel*, *Ragtime* and *City of God* share an underlying concern with injustice and powerlessness, which they denounce through the representation of different forms of discrimination and suffering which characters that are at the margins of North-American society and history are shown to face as a result of their non-privileged gender, class, race, political stance or religion. The novels perform a critique of the individualistic ethos of North-American society, emphasizing how certain social, legal, political and economic structures generate and perpetuate inequality and oppression for the social, racial, political or sexual Other. Furthermore, they highlight the danger of forgetting past mistakes by putting forward a circular view of history as nightmare. They also draw attention to the potential healing power of the community and the dramatic consequences of its failure for the individual and the collective. In short, the books force us to confront emotionally and intellectually the destructive power of indifference and its far-reaching effects. Such concerns emerge, primarily, from Doctorow's post-Holocaust consciousness and the shock of realizing human capacity for evil.

Doctorow's literary project has, therefore, a clear political dimension, not in the sense suggested by some early reviewers and commentators, but in that it is a call to action, a call to arms against the structures, forces and ideologies that are responsible, or provide a justification, for the oppression and injustice to which those at the margins of society—those who have traditionally been denied power by hegemonic political, social, economic and patriarchal structures—have been, and continue to be, subjected. His novels draw attention to the socio-historical forces that shape the society of the United States. Furthermore, they bring to the fore the multiple shapes that human suffering may take. By doing so, they seek to awaken readers' conscience, and compel us to respond empathically to the pain of others while highlighting their ultimate alterity and uniqueness. In other words, Doctorow's novels bridge the gap between "we" and "they" without reducing the Other to the Same. Thus, the author's ultimate aim is to improve society by calling attention to its defects. His literary project demands from us that we assess critically the ideology, the structures and the institutions that surround us, and that we overcome indifference. *Welcome to Hard Times*, *The Book of Daniel*, *Ragtime* and *City of God* make direct ethical and political claims upon readers with the hope that they may be heard.

Tens of thousands of children around the world die of malnutrition and preventable diseases every day. Political dissidents and sexual minorities are attacked, imprisoned or even murdered—often by their governments—on an everyday basis in many countries of the world. Our current aggressive capitalism is responsible for the exploitation and death of millions every year in third-world factories. Capital circulates the world more freely than people, while refugees are kept in detention centers and camps behind barbed-wired walls and fences. Racism and racial violence are rampant, and some lives continue mattering more than others. Rape culture threatens the integrity of women all over the world, many of whom face not only discrimination and subordination on account of their gender, but also violence on an everyday basis. Upper-middle-class privileges in the Western world are sustained by a system of violence of which we are something more than bystanders and less than perpetrators, but from which we certainly benefit. The political response, however, has often been at best indifference and at worst a turn to the discourse of fear and hate of the Other. A pessimist might say that we have completely failed to learn the lessons of history. An optimist like E.L. Doctorow, as the novels explored in this study suggest, seemed to have retained a belief in the oppositional role of literature, in the power of the aesthetic to inspire the necessary ethical and political change to make a more just and less indifferent world possible.

Index

Note: *Italic* page numbers refer to figures and page numbers followed by "n" denote endnotes.

Adorno, T. 154, 158
aesthetic tradition/aesthetics 4, 14, 18, 19, 20, 23, 27, 28, 29, 31, 158, 182, 183, 186
affects of shame and guilt 12, 14, 47, 48, 86, 198
affects, revolutionary theory of 47, 67n5
Alexander, J.C. 168
All the Time in the World (Doctorow) 3
altruistic behavior 190, 194n4
Americanization of the Holocaust 7, 156–158, 174n9
anachronism 129
Andrew's Brain (Doctorow) 3
anti-Semitism 168–169
Anzaldúa, G. 20, 22
Appelfeld, A. 161
Arendt, H. 53, 150
Arnold, M. 17
Atwood, M. 180
Auerhahn, N.C. 80
Augustine 28, 149, 150
Austen, J. 17
autodiegetic story 73, 89, 97, 145, 148, 167, 170

Baldwin, J. 179, 184
Bal, M. 88
Barrett, M. 21
Barthes, R. 186
Barth, J. 27, 194
Beauvoir, S. de 16
Bellow, S. 160
Beloved (Morrison) 180
Benjaminian constellation 110

Bennett, J. 192
"berserking" concept 114
Bertens, H. 181, 184
Bevilacqua, W. 56
Bewes, T. 47, 134
Biddle, J. 51
Big as Life (Doctorow) 2
Bildungsroman 72
Billy Bathgate (Doctorow) 3
binarism 52–54, 183
black feminist criticism 19–20
Black Women Novelists: The Development of a Tradition (Christian) 20
Bloom, S. 50, 52
Blum, A. 83
The Book of Daniel (Doctorow) 2–3, 5, 6; adult focalization 78, 92; anachronous feel 78; autodiegetic narrator/narration 73, 89–90, 97; *Bildungsroman* 72; characters' autonomy and strength 94; childhood trauma 99; chronology 77, 78; circulation and commodification 85; coherent novel 89; complex PTSD 86; conservatism of McCarthyism 72; conventional linear sequence 77; conviction and execution of Isaacsons 72; countercultural radicalism 94; creation of silences and gaps 82–83; critical recognition 72; decontextualized memory fragments 80; disrupted attachments 90–91; "distance suffering" 96; empathic listener 86–87; erasure of female subjectivity 92; espionage 72;

ethical hesitancy 95, 97, 98; execution by electrocution 73–74; experimental narrative techniques 182; explicit/implicit narratee 87, 102n6; false document 84–85; fantasy of communication 83; feelings of shame and guilt 85–86; female domestic roles 94; feminist revision 88; free indirect style 78; gender roles 93–94; gender violence 94–97; healing 85–89, 97; helplessness and disempowerment 76; historiographic intersections 74, 102n4; history dissertation 72, 102n1; homodiegetic and heterodiegetic narration 73; interpolated narration 78; intertextuality 100–101; Künstlerroman 72; life coping skills 76; metafiction 81–82; multiple readings 89; narrative technique 77–78; National Book Award for fiction 72; new life at the Shelter 82–83; Old and New Left 72, 94, 98, 102n2; omniscient narration 93; oppression 94–97; overpowering narratives 80; overwhelming authority 90–91; polyphony 93; postmodernism 85; post-traumatic "acting out" 98–99; post-traumatic stress disorder 73–79; powerlessness 98; psychological distress 74; psychological trauma 73–79, 101; psychosomatic reaction 74–75; radical politics 76–77; random shifts of voice 78–79; reader identification patterns 88; Red Scare 72; repetition narrative 79; sadistic drive 96–99; "schizophrenic" behavior of the electron 77; scriptotherapy 86; sex martyr 95; sexual violence 94–95; shame/guilt and silence 83, 102n5; subjectivity 89–93; Susan's silencing 91–92; "talking cure" 86; transference episodes 80; traumatic experience/memory 88–89; traumatic experiences of childhood 81; traumatic life experiences 75–76; traumatic memories 73, 79–85; traumatic micro-aggressions 75; traumatic reenactment 95–96; unnatural precision details 80–81; unreliability 83–84; ventriloquism 93; victimization 81; violence into spectacle 96; working through trauma 100, 101
Booth, W. 24, 189
Borges, J.L. 28
Borzaga, M. 118
Broderick, M. 12
Brown, L.S. 8
Buelens, G. 12
Burrows, V. 48, 98
Busby, M. 184
Butler, J. 22
bystanders 5, 11, 52–54, 66, 179, 182, 192, 198, 200

canonization of novel 41
capitalism 121, 169, 200
Carr, H. 17
Caruth, C. 8, 9, 43, 50, 74, 80, 83
Cather, W. 17
childhood trauma 6, 8, 75, 81, 86, 91, 99, 108
"Children's Crusade" 115, 137n9
Christian, B. 20
chronicle-like narration 118–119, 133, 134, 183, 194
Cicero 155
City of God (Doctorow) 3, 5, 7; Americanization of the Holocaust 156–158, 169–170, 174n9; anti-Semitism 168–169; autodiegetic story 145; biographical fallacy 159; and *The City of God* (Augustine) 149–150; colonialism 150; commercial profit 158; cosmic checks and balances 146; dialogism 165–167; 'doublevoiced discourse' 149; ethics and injustice 145, 171–172; explicit allusion 153; explicit tension 148–149; female submission and dominance 163, 170–171; femininity 163–165; fictional truth 153–154; focalization 147, 166; gender models 162–165; historical truth 153–154, 156; Holocaust consciousness 157, 174n10; Holocaust fiction 152–156; Holocaust representation 145–152, 168; imaginative truth 154; intertextuality 149–150; irony 146, 155; lives and beliefs 172; main plot 144, 173n1; mental evocation 146; metafiction 148–149; metalepsis 150–151; metaphysical quest for

meaning 144; mode of writing about Holocaust 152; *Muselmänner* 147; museum inventory appendix 155, 173n8; narrative levels *151*; "normalization and routinization" 170, 175n20; North-American Jews 156–157; postmemory 159–161, 174n15; posttraumatic culture 158–159; 'power of dissimilarity' 155; reception 144; retribution 161; self-conscious discussion 145–152; self-reflexivity 148, 173n3; survivor guilt 147; Synagogue for Evolutionary Judaism 146; trauma novels 158, 174n12; traumatic realism 151–152; universalization and trivialization of Holocaust 157, 170, 174n11; unspeakable horror of death camps 146–148, 155, 172; ventriloquism 165–167, 175n19; women rabbi 163–164, 175n18

The City of God (Augustine) 149–150
Cixous, H. 22
classical trauma theory 5, 6, 9–12, 42, 54, 111, 158
Clayton, J. 159
collective historical traumas 198
compulsion to repeat 44
Connell, R. 55, 56, 123, 128
conservatism of McCarthyism 72
constellation of singular traumas 111
contemporary trauma fiction 13–14
Cooper, S. 72
Cornier-Michael, M. 7, 30, 31, 181
Craps, S. 118
Critique of Postcolonial Reason (Spivak) 133
Culp, M. 90
cumulative traumatic experiences 111

Davis, T. 188
"Days of Remembrance" 157
death drive 42, 44–46, 109
death of the self 48–49
decontextualized memory fragments 80
deconstruction 4, 8, 9, 10, 16, 21, 23, 181, 182
DeRosa, A. 92
Derrida's philosophy of deconstruction 8, 11
dichotomy 22, 31, 60, 111, 118, 134, 182
Dillon, B. 92, 100

discrimination 6, 15, 110–112, 115, 119, 120, 122, 123, 126, 134–136, 164, 179, 185, 198–200
dissociation 50, 52, 79, 96
"distance suffering" 96
Doctorow, E.L.: *All the Time in the World* 3; *Andrew's Brain* 3; *Big as Life* 2; *Billy Bathgate* 3; book-length critical analyses 3–4; *The Book of Daniel* 2–3, 5, 6; *City of God* 3, 5, 7; corpus of analysis 4–5; *Drinks before Dinner* 3; early age 1; "epic poet of America's past" 2; ethical and postmodernist allegiances 7; "False Documents" (1977) 3; fiction 1, 2; *Homer and Langley* 3; life 2; literary career 2–3; *Lives of the Poets* 3; *Loon Lake* 3; *The March* 3; narrative empathy 7; *oeuvre* 3–4; prices and honors 3; Pulitzer Prize (1990) 3; *Ragtime* 3, 5, 6; recognition 1; *Sweet Land Stories* 3; versatility 1; *The Waterworks* 3; *Welcome to Hard Times* 2, 5–6; works 1–3; *World's Fair* 3; *see also* literary analysis of ethics; literary analysis of feminism; literary analysis of trauma; postmodernism
Drinks before Dinner (Doctorow) 3
Dutton, D. 188

Eagleton, M. 16, 17, 19
Edkins, J. 124
Eichmann trial (1961) 152
Einstein, A. 169
Ellmann, M. 16–18
"empathic unsettlement" 101, 134, 189, 192, 193
Escudero, M. 47
espionage 72
ethical criticism 23, 187
ethical hesitancy 95, 97, 98, 133, 134
ethical impulses 5, 181, 183, 184
ethical turn 23, 180, 184, 187, 189
ethics and politics of literature: aesthetic tradition 186; altruistic behavior 190, 194n4; *The Book of Daniel* 182; chronicle-like narration 182–183; *City of God* 183; cognitive science and evolutionary psychology 188; consciousness 185–186; contemporary Western societies 193; "empathic

204 *Index*

unsettlement" 189; ethical criticism 187; ethical turn 180; experimental narrative techniques 182–183; gender and trauma 179; grand narrative of history 181; "imperialism of the same" 191; "impulse" 181; literary genres 181; masculinity and femininity 181–182; meaning and justice 184–185; metanarratives 183; narrative empathy 189–193; neohumanist tradition 186; new narrative form 180–184; Other into the Self 190, 192, 194n5; philosophy and criticism 179; "poetics of engagement" 180, 187; political dimension 187; "postmodern humanism" 184; postmodernism 180–182; "postmodernist realism" 184; postmodernist subversive strategies 182–183; "power of invitation" 188; radical postmodernist fiction 180; *Ragtime* 182–183; reader response 189–193, 194n3; "the passion of calling" 184, 194; universalism 190–191; *Welcome to Hard Times* 181–182
ethnicity 31, 110, 130, 136, 183, 188
"ex-centrics" 31, 110, 111, 118
exceptionalism, American 41, 181
execution by electrocution 73–74
explicit/implicit narratee 87, 102n6
extreme individualism 121

false document 84–85
"False Documents" 3, 26, 84, 149
Fanon, F. 149, 150
Farrell, K. 114, 115, 158
Feder, A. 108
Felman, S. 8, 9, 21, 81, 83
Felski, R. 16, 30, 186, 189
The Female Imagination (Spacks) 19
female otherness 6; *see also The Book of Daniel*
feminist critique 17–18
feminism 15, 16, 18, 21, 22, 25, 30, 31, 55, 63, 66, 198
Fetterley, J. 16
Figes, E. 16
Flaherty, S. 106
focalization 22, 78, 81, 92, 107, 119, 120, 122, 126, 133, 147, 165, 166
Foley, B. 154, 185
Ford, H. 107, 121

Forman, M. 106
Forrey, R. 96
Foucault, M. 186
"Foundation for Revolution" 97
fragmentation 13, 14, 32, 47, 72, 77, 79, 80, 84, 85, 86, 182, 183
Freudian spiral of repetition compulsion 46
Freud, S. 17, 107, 120; trivialization of affect system 47
Friedl, H. 27
The Future of Trauma Theory 12

gendered socialization 15
gender identity 55, 63, 198
Genette, G. 78
Gentry, M.B. 62, 93
Gibson, A. 24
Gilbert, S. 16, 19, 84
Gilligan, J. 48, 49, 98
Goldman, E. 107, 125, 127–131
Gracen, J. 165
"grand narratives" 26, 181
Granofsky, R. 13, 31, 32, 88
gray zone 11, 53
Green, G. 157
Greer, G. 16
Gregory, M. 188, 189
Gross, D. 44
Gubar, S. 16, 19
gynocriticism 19, 186

The Handmaid's Tale (Atwood) 180
Haraway, D. 22
Harpham, G. 77
Hart, O. van der 81, 88
Hartman, G. 8–10, 83
Hekman, S. 30
helplessness 8, 43–44, 76, 92, 98, 101, 111, 115, 130, 135
hegemonic masculinity 56–57, 60
Henke, S. 52, 86
Herman, J. 9, 80, 86, 88
Hillman, J. 185
Hirsch, M. 7, 159
historical fiction 2, 3, 5, 6, 41, 72, 106–107
historical trauma 9, 10, 11, 52, 169, 198
historiographic intersections 74, 79, 102n4
historiographic metafiction 29
Hite, M. 30
Hitler, A. 146, 148

Hogeland, L.M. 15
Holocaust and trauma 9–10; see also *City of God* (Doctorow)
Holocaust fiction 7
'Holocaust novel' 152; see also *City of God* (Doctorow)
Homer and Langley (Doctorow) 3
hooks, bell 16, 20
Horatio 155
Houdini, H. 107
Hume, D. 190
Hume, K. 96, 99
Humm, M. 15, 20
Hutcheon, L. 28, 31, 110, 119

Ickstadt, H. 184
"images of women" approach 17, 18
"imperialism of the same" 191
insidious trauma 6, 14, 110–111, 115, 117, 118, 119, 122, 131, 133, 135
instinct for recovery 109
intellectual distance 193
intertextuality 4, 14, 28–29, 100–101, 149–150, 182, 183
Irigaray, L. 22
irony 107, 114, 119–120, 122, 126, 137n11, 146, 155, 183, 198

Jacobus, M. 21
Jones, P. 125, 130
Joyce, J. 17

Kakutani, M. 144
Kaplan, A. 189
Kaplan, C. 21
Kauffman, J. 47, 52
Keen, S. 190, 193
Kinzie, J.D. 115
Kirn, W. 144
Kolk, B. van der 9, 80, 81, 88
Kovno Ghetto Diary 149
Kristeva, J. 22
Künstlerroman 72

LaCapra, D. 10, 11, 52, 54, 98, 158, 169, 170, 189
Lang, B. 153, 156
Langer, L. 85, 147, 154
"language of freedom" 26
latent trauma 9, 33n6
Laub, D. 9, 80, 81, 86
Lawrence, D.H. 17
Lawrence Textile Strike (1912) 115, 136n8

Lemelson, R. 110
lesbian feminist criticism 19, 20, 33n11
Levinas, E. 24, 48, 173, 191
Levine, P. 154
Levi, P. 11, 53
life coping skills 76, 92, 109, 131
literary analysis of ethics: ethical criticism 23–24; "ethical turn" 23; 'ethics of alterity' 24; generational posttraumatic stress response 24–25; Other in literature 23, 24; Self 24
literary analysis of feminism: black feminist criticism 19–20; "female subculture" 18–19; feminist criticism 15–16; feminist critique 17–18; gendered socialization 15; gynocriticism 19; heterosexism 20; "images of women" approach 17, 18; lesbian feminist criticism 19, 20, 33n11; male-authored texts 18; Marxist/socialist feminist critics 21; patriarchal masculinity 18; patriarchy 16–17; phallocentrism 17, 21; poststructuralism 21; *The Resisting Reader: A Feminist Approach to American Fiction* 18; second-wave feminism 15; *Sexual Politics* 17, 33n9; sexual politics of language and style 15; *Thinking about Women* 17; totalizing studies of oppressed women 16–17; witty and biting style 17
literary analysis of trauma: classical cultural trauma theory 10; contemporary trauma narratives 13–14; Derrida's philosophy of deconstruction 8; Freud's legacy for trauma 9, 33n5; genealogy of trauma 7–8, 32n1; historical trauma 10, 11; Holocaust and trauma 9–10; latent trauma 9, 33n6; *The Longest Shadow: In the Aftermath of the Holocaust* 10; memorialization 12, 14; post-traumatic acting out 11; post-traumatic stress disorder 8, 33n2; psychological trauma 13; shame and guilt of trauma 12, 14; socio-historical phenomena 11–12; structural trauma 10, 11; stylistic techniques 13–14; *Testimony: Crises of Witnessing*

in *Literature, Psychoanalysis, and History* 9–10; thematic and formal tools 14; *Trauma and Survival in Contemporary Fiction* 13; *Trauma Fiction* 14; trauma novel 12–13; trauma theory 8–9, 33n3; *Unclaimed Experience* 9; vicarious victimization 11; working through trauma 11; *Writing History, Writing Trauma* 10
Literary Women (Moers) 19
A Literature of Their Own: British Women Writers from Charlotte Brontë to Doris Lessing (Showalter) 19
Lives of the Poets (Doctorow) 3
The Longest Shadow: In the Aftermath of the Holocaust 10
Loon Lake (Doctorow) 3
Lorde, A. 16, 20
Luckhurst, R. 8, 9, 14

McDowell, D. 16
McNally, R. 83
McNally, T. 106
The Madwoman in the Attic: The Woman Writer and the Nineteenth-Century Literary Imagination (Gilbert and Gubar) 19
Mailer, N. 17
manliness 55–57, 128
The March (Doctorow) 3
Margalit, A. 99
Martínez-Falquina, S. 23
Marxist/socialist feminist critics 21
masculine "parade" of virility 56
masculinity 5, 18, 55–57, 60, 65, 66, 68n10, 123, 126, 128, 181
Measham, T. 112
melancholia 117–118
memory 6, 7, 9–14, 24, 43, 50, 79, 80, 83, 84, 88, 145, 156, 157, 159, 161, 168, 172
Mendelson-Maoz, A. 24
mental evocation 146
metafiction 81–82, 148–149
metafictional self-reflexivity 29
metalepsis 150–151
metanarratives 26–28, 182, 183
metapsychology 116
Midrash Jazz Quartet 144
Miller Budick, E. 153
Miller, H. 17
Millett, K. 16–18

Mitchell, J. 21
"Modest Proposal" 119
Moers, E. 19
Moi, T. 17, 21–22
Morgan, J.P. 107, 121
Morgenstern, N. 80, 84, 96
Morris, C. 122
Morrison, T. 180
Muselmänner 147

narrative empathy 7, 180, 189–193
neohumanist tradition 186
Nesbit, E. 107
New Introductory Lectures on Psychoanalysis 109
New Left 72, 94, 98, 102n2
'new Western' 41, 65, 67n1
North-American society 5, 30, 101, 114, 126, 133–136, 199
nostalgia 4, 121, 137n13
Novick, P. 7, 156, 157, 160, 170, 185
Nussbaum, M. 24, 189, 190, 194

Oates, J.C. 72
objectification 22, 123–126, 131, 135, 198
Old Left 72, 102n2
Olsen, T. 21
oppression 5, 6, 14–17, 19–22, 25, 30, 54, 57–60, 66, 89, 94–97, 110–112, 115, 118, 120– 126, 129–133, 135, 136, 150, 170, 179, 183, 184, 192, 198, 199
The Origins of Totalitarianism (Arendt) 150
Other in literature 23
Other into the Self 24, 190, 192, 194n5
Other to the Same 199
Ozick, C. 160

Papaleo, J. 1
Parks, J. 72, 93
parody 27, 28, 181, 183
"the passion of calling" 184, 194
patriarchal system 15–18, 22, 60, 61, 63–66, 111, 123–128, 130, 133–136, 179, 183, 199
perpetrator 5, 6, 8, 11, 14, 52–54, 66, 99, 101, 131–133, 135, 136, 156, 157, 179, 182, 192, 198, 200
"petites histories" 26
phallocentrism 17, 21
Plagens, P. 144

Plain, G. 15, 16, 22
pleasure principle 44
"poetics of engagement" 30, 180, 187
Poovey, M. 21
"postmodern humanism" 184
postmodernism 85, 180–182;
  decentering of metanarratives
  26–27; feminism and 30; formal
  and thematic affinities 26;
  "historiographic metafiction" 29;
  history, reality and fiction 27–28;
  intertextuality 28–29; "literature
  of exhaustion" 27; metafictional
  self-reflexivity 29; parody usage
  28; poststructuralist theory and
  feminism 30–31, 34n13; "regime
  language" and "language of
  freedom" 26; self-reflexive mode
  of writing 27–28; thematic and
  stylistic features 25; and trauma
  theory 31–32, 34n14; truthful
  textual representation 29–30;
  Welcome to Hard Times, *The Book
  of Daniel* and *City of God* 26
"postmodernist realism" 184
postmodern novel 3, 28, 31–32
poststructuralism 20, 21, 23, 25,
  26, 30
post-traumatic "acting out" 11, 42,
  79, 98–99, 117
post-traumatic stress disorder (PTSD)
  8, 33n2, 73, 86, 131
'post-Western' 41, 67n1
"power of invitation" 188
power struggle 22, 127–128, 198
Priesand, S. 164
progressive masculinity 57
Psychoanalysis and Feminism
  (Mitchell) 21
psychological aftereffects 6, 42, 198
psychological trauma 5, 6, 8, 9, 13,
  23, 33n2, 54, 64, 73, 96, 101,
  115, 179

radical politics 76–77
Ragtime (Doctorow) 1, 3, 5, 6;
  anachronism 129; awards and
  rewards 106; "berserking" concept
  114; characters 107; chronicle-
  like narration 118–119, 133,
  182–183; cope with traumatic
  experiences 108; coping with
  insidious traumatization 116–117;
  cumulative traumatic experiences
  111; depathologization 112;
  domestic self-fulfillment 126;
  ethical hesitancy 134; event-
  based model of trauma 111;
  "ex-centrics" 110, 111, 118;
  extreme individualism 121; female
  bonding 131, 137n15; female
  compliance 124–125; femininities
  126–128; feminist ideology
  128–130; *femme fatale* 112–113;
  film and music 106; filmic quality
  120, 137n12; focalization shifts
  120; free direct style 120; gender
  oppression 123–125; helplessness
  110–111; heterodiegetic narration
  119–120, 133–134; historical
  fiction 106–107; human defense
  mechanism 116; implicit ideology
  118; innovative interpretation
  130; "insidious trauma" 110–111;
  instinct for recovery 109; irony
  119–120, 137n11; marked
  racist bias 114; masculinities
  126–128; melancholia 117–118;
  metanarratives 183; miscegenation
  and multiculturalism 121–122;
  "missing person" 124; "Modest
  Proposal" 119; monographs
  106; "moral degeneracy" 124;
  narratological features 118–119;
  North-American myth 121,
  135–136; nostalgia 121, 137n13;
  objectification 125–126; pattern
  of repetition and variation 110;
  power of creativity 117; power
  struggle 127–128; psychological
  aftermath 111; publication 106;
  racist injustices 114; recovery from
  chronic trauma symptoms 108;
  resilience 108–115, 131; reviews
  and critiques 106, 136n2; satire
  120–121, 132; self-healing bias
  109, 112; self-reliance and survival
  109, 113; sexual and physical
  abuse 113; sexual politics 126–128;
  sexual radicalism 129; social and
  economic injustice, racism and
  oppression 118, 119, 123, 135–136;
  sublimation 115–118, 137n10;
  submissiveness 114; superficial
  narrative style 118; three-fold
  model of gender structure 123;
  transformation/metamorphosis
  109; trauma as transformative force

113–115; trauma category 118; traumatic immobilization 115; two epochs 134–135; ventriloquism 133–134; victim-perpetrator characters 131–133; working-class immigrant 123–124
Rasmussen, E. 94, 99
reader response 7, 186, 189–193, 194n4
Red Scare 72
Reed, T.V. 184
referentiality 152, 162, 181, 184
"regime language" 26
Remembering Trauma (McNally) 83
repetition technique 13, 14, 79, 110, 182
Reporting the Universe 159, 167
resilience 6, 12, 14, 107–116, 118, 122, 130, 131, 135, 136, 179
The Resisting Reader: A Feminist Approach to American Fiction (Fetterley) 18
Rich, A. 16
Rodgers, B. 106
Root, M. 24, 110, 111, 184
Rosenfeld, A. 157
Rosen, N. 160
Rothberg, M. 85, 151, 152, 162, 188
Roth, M. 10, 33n7
Roth, P. 160
Rousseau, C. 112
Rutter, M. 109

satire 120–121, 132, 187, 198
Schulz, D. 27
Schwarz, D. 23, 24, 189
scriptotherapy 52, 86, 101, 108
Sedgwick, E.K. 22
Seeskin, K. 160
Segal, D. 2
Self 24, 187, 190, 191, 192
self-blame 50–51
self-healing bias 109, 112
self-preservation 44
self-reflexivity 11, 29, 148, 173n3, 182, 183
Seligman, M. 165
Sellers, S. 15, 22
Seltzer, M. 158
sexual politics 15, 17, 33n9, 126–128
Sexual Politics (Millett) 17, 33n9
Sexual/Textual Politics (Moi) 21
Shalev, A. 131
Shay, J. 114
shell shock 8

Showalter, E. 16–19
Shulman, A.K. 129
Sicher, E. 152, 154, 156, 157, 172
Silove, D. 131
Singer, L. 31
Slaughterhouse-Five, or The Children's Crusade: A Duty-Dance with Death (Vonnegut) 180
Smith, A. 190
Smith, B. 16, 20
Socialist Labor Movement 129, 137n14
socio-historical forces 94, 199
Spacks, P.M. 19
Spencer, L. 118
Spiegelman, A. 160
Spielberg, S. 157
Spivak, G. 22, 133
Starr, K. 41
Steiner, G. 160
structural trauma 10, 11
stylistic techniques 13–14, 25, 27
subjectivity 18, 21, 22, 27, 30, 31, 84, 89–93, 96, 97, 134, 154, 182, 183, 186
sublimation 6, 115–118, 135, 137n10
subordination 30, 60, 63, 68, 94, 123, 128, 129, 138, 170, 183, 198, 200
survivor guilt 147
Sweet Land Stories (Doctorow) 3
Swift, J. 119
Synagogue for Evolutionary Judaism 146

Tal, K. 85, 154
"talking cure" 86
Testimony: Crises of Witnessing in Literature, Psychoanalysis, and History 9–10
Thinking about Women (Ellmann) 17
Thomas, C. 18
Tokarczyk, M. 76, 98
"Tomkins-Ekman paradigm" 47, 67n5
Tomkins, S. 47
totalizing narrative traditions 26
Tractatus Logico-Philosophicus (Wittgenstein) 149
transference episodes 80
trauma novel 12–13, 31, 32, 73, 89, 158, 174n12
Trauma and Survival in Contemporary Fiction (Vickroy) 13
trauma and violence 5; *see also individual topics*
Trauma Fiction (Whitehead) 14

The Trauma Novel: Contemporary Symbolic Depictions of Collective Disaster 13
"traumatic realism" 151–152
traumatic reenactment 43, 95
Traverso, A. 12

Unclaimed Experience (Caruth) 9
unspeakable horror of death camps 146–148, 155

Vaillant, G. 116
ventriloquism 62–63, 68n14, 93, 133–134, 165–167
Vickroy, L. 13, 32, 76–79, 83, 88, 98
victimization 6, 11, 14, 66, 81, 88, 95, 115, 119, 122, 123, 124, 130, 132, 133, 135, 136, 159, 170
victim-perpetrator 52–54, 131–133, 135, 192
violence: into spectacle 96; trauma and 5; *see also individual topics*
Vonnegut, K. 180

Walker, A. 20
Walker Bergström, C. 183, 187
The Waterworks (Doctorow) 3
Waugh, P. 29–30
Welcome to Hard Times (Doctorow) 2, 5–6; affects, revolutionary theory of 47, 67n5; artificial performance of femininity 61–62, 68n12; binarism 52–54; body memories 43; canonization of novel 41; capitalism 58–59, 68n11; characters 42; Christian faith 45–46; compulsion to repeat 44; death drive 44–46; death of the self 48–49; defective masculinity 56; dissociation, theorization of 50; duality of psychic structure of shame 51; effects of shame 48; *Eros* and *Thanatos* 44; ethical grounding 59–63, 67; extreme humiliation 48–49; Freudian 'return of the repressed' 50; Freudian spiral of repetition compulsion 46; Freud's latter model of trauma 44; Freud's trivialization of affect system 47; Frontier settlement 41, 42; gender oppression and violence 57–59; grand narrative of history 181; guilt and responsibility 53; guilt *vs.* shame 47; hegemonic masculinity 56–57, 60; hegemonic model of gender domination 61; helplessness 43–44; historical fiction 41; historical trauma 52; "ladylike" manners 60–61; literary genres 181; male protagonist 54; manliness 55–56; masculine "parade" of virility 56; masculinity 55, 57, 68n10; masculinity and femininity 181–182; moral superiority 48, 67n6; new Western 41, 67n1; plausible 'feel' for experience 52; polyphonic text 63; post-traumatic 'acting out' 42–43; post-traumatic stress 42–43, 53, 64; progressive masculinity 57; psychic trauma 42, 67n3; repressed memories 50; repression and dissociation 52; retribution 45–46; revisionist swing 65; scriptotherapy 52; self-blame, traumatic 50–51; self-preservation 44; sexual harassment 58–59; shame and guilt 46–52; story telling 66; subversion of gender 55–57, 64; suffering and pain 42; symbolic representative of evil 58; town destruction 46; traditional gender configurations 54; trauma categories 53, 66; traumatic grief shame 47–48; traumatic reenactment, Winnicot's theorization of 43; traumatic victimization 66; understanding of events and nature of evil 62–63; ventriloquism 62–63, 68n14; victim-bystander-perpetrator 52–54; violent heroism 56, 57; working through trauma 52
Whitehead, A. 14, 32, 43, 77, 79, 82
Wilde, L. 171
Williams, J. 25, 41
Williams, W. 41
Wittgenstein, L. 149, 150
Wolff, J. 31
Wollstonecraft, M. 16
Womack, K. 188
womanliness 61, 68n12
Woolf, V. 16
working through trauma 11, 46, 52, 89, 100, 101
World's Fair (Doctorow) 3
The Wretched of the Earth (Fanon) 149

Zautra, A.J. 108, 131
Zimmerman, B. 16, 20

Printed in the United States
By Bookmasters